Collaborative
Information
Technologies

Mehdi Khosrow-Pour, D.B.A.
Information Resources Management Association, USA

IRM Press
Publisher of innovative scholarly and professional
information technology titles in the cyberage

Hershey • London • Melbourne • Singapore • Beijing

Senior Editor: Mehdi Khosrow-Pour
Managing Editor: Jan Travers
Assistant Managing Editor: Amanda Appicello
Copy Editor: Amanda Appicello
Cover Design: Tedi Wingard
Printed at: Integrated Book Technology

Published in the United States of America by
        IRM Press
        1331 E. Chocolate Avenue
        Hershey PA 17033-1117
        Tel: 717-533-8845
        Fax: 717-533-8661
        E-mail: cust@idea-group.com
        Web site: http://www.irm-press.com

and in the United Kingdom by
        IRM Press
        3 Henrietta Street
        Covent Garden
        London WC2E 8LU
        Tel: 44 20 7240 0856
        Fax: 44 20 7379 3313
        Web site: http://www.eurospan.co.uk

Library of Congress Cataloguing-in-Publication Data

Collaborative information technologies / [edited by] Mehdi Khosrow-Pour
      p. cm.
   Includes bibliographical references and index.
     ISBN 1-931777-14-4 (paper)
      1. Information technology. 2. Organizational learning. I. Khosrowpour, Mehdi, 1951-

HD30.2 .C625 2002
658'.05--dc21   2002017214

eISBN: 1-931777-25-X

British Cataloguing-in-Publication Data
A Cataloguing-in-Publication record for this book is available from the British Library.

Other New Releases from IRM Press

Collaborative Information Technologies

Table of Contents

Foreword

During the past two decades, advances in computer technologies combined with telecommunication technologies have had tremendous impact on every facet of life. These technologies have offered many new opportunities to organizations of all types and sizes. No longer is computing considered the main use of computer technologies; instead, today, the primary use is in the area of communications and information retrieval and sharing. In recent years, through the use of Web-enabled technologies, businesses have managed to identify new ways of doing business and reaching customers and suppliers through the use of E-commerce; educational institutions have developed new ways of delivering education programs through distance learning programs; government entities have learned how to conduct their business and information sharing through E-government concepts; and libraries have begun disseminating vast library information resources electronically to all remote sites.

In the area of educational technologies, many colleges and universities worldwide now can offer academic programs and courses regardless of distance and location. Through the use of information technologies, the communication gap between providers and receivers of education has been closing and narrowing. Many of the traditional students who could not previously attend campus-based educational programs now can attend educational programs that are either offered through various Web-based programs or offered through different distance learning technologies. In addition, these technologies have allowed students to be able to collaborate with each other more effectively and easily. Today, Web-enabled technologies allow everyone regardless of age, gender, and location around the world to have access to a vast number of Web-based sources of information knowledge. No longer is information or knowledge the domain of only a few entities with limited access due to their location limitation and restrictions. The idea of virtual libraries that until a few years ago was not even imagined now is a reality. Information technology now is the most effective facilitator of information and knowledge dissemination around the world, and as a result, the accumulation of knowledge related to all topics is multiplying by the second rather than the traditional pace of every year or two.

These technologies have been beneficial not only to academic programs but also to organizations and their training and knowledge management efforts. Through the use of collaborative learning technologies, organizations of all types and sizes now can collaborate in different organizational learning and developments. In reality, all organizations are knowledge–based entities that require constant processing, utilization and updating of their knowledge regarding different products, services, functions, and procedures. Information technologies of the modern years have allowed organizations to develop much more effective techniques and methodologies in managing organizational knowledge and information. Obviously, the collaborative technologies of recent years have been very instrumental toward organizational knowledge management and learning processes. Furthermore, these technologies have been utilized effectively in support of learning new and innovative ways of dealing with modern organizational reengineering and downsizing, paving the way toward more leaner and efficient organizations.

Like many other new technologies, these technologies are not free of controversies and challenges. Many of the technology related challenges are not technically oriented, but instead they are related to the non-technical components—most in the area of human aspects. Perhaps, we can argue that most challenges impacting the overall utilization and management of information technologies are "people related challenges." These challenges range from training related issues to overall innovation and adoption of emerging modern technologies in organizations. Modern organizational theorists should understand the true organization and management of these technologies and devise ways for contemporary organizations to cope more effectively with the issues of information technology management. No longer can effective organizations afford to place the majority of their focus on hardware and software technologies and ignore the "people" side of these technologies. It is time to place the major focus on the human side of technology and to recognize the true man-machine relationships.

The influence and impact of information technologies on organizations during the past two decades have far exceeded the majority of organizational scholars' and managers' imagination and foresight. No longer should information technology be viewed as technologies in support of organizational functions and day-to-day functions and operations, but, instead, successful organizations have been utilizing information technologies of modern years as major strategic tools. Information technology can reshape the overall focus and mission of the organizations in ways that was never imagined and envisioned. The biggest challenge today facing organization leaders is to understand the strategic values of information technology and allow themselves to view the ways that technology can bring their organization cost savings methods, facilitate customer service, and identify new markets and growth areas. Information technology can be a very powerful strategic tool if it is correctly positioned and utilized within the overall organization structure.

Mehdi Khosrow-Pour, D.B.A.
Executive Director
Information Resources Management Association
November 6, 2001

Preface

As computer use becomes more widespread, its applications become broader. Computers are used today as information sharing entities and mediums for all kinds of communication. Ever more frequently, computers are being used as a source of collaboration among workers, students and teachers, and organizations. Collaborative technologies offer simpler ways of managing virtual organizations and supporting distance learning initiatives. In order to get the most from these technologies, managers, teachers and researchers must have access to the latest research and practice concerning the development and use of collaborative technologies. The chapters in this book represent a wide array of applications and developments of collaborative technologies and the authors, all renowned experts in their respective fields, represent a diverse organizational and cultural background and provide the most current insights into this emerging field.

Chapter 1 entitled, "Extending Collaboration Support Systems: Making Sense in Remote Innovation" by Thekla Rura-Polley and Ellen Baker of the University of Technology (Australia) examines the role of collaboration and collective learning in regional and industry-wide innovation and how innovation through electronic collaboration can be enhanced by comprehensive computer support tools. The chapter describes a Web-based computer system called LiveNet that incorporates sensemaking aids to facilitate remote innovation.

Chapter 2 entitled, "Conceptual Linkages: An Analysis of the Organizational Learning, Collaborative Technology and Intellectual Capital Literature" by Robert Neilson of the National Defense University (USA) establishes a conceptual link between three distinct bodies of literature dealing with learning organizations, collaborative technologies and intellectual capital. The author offers the results of a content analysis of the literature, explores the theoretical bases of organizational learning and technology use and focuses on an integrated critical review of the three literature bodies.

Chapter 3 entitled, "Process Improvement and Knowledge Communication" by Ned Kock of Temple University (USA) discusses the need for knowledge sharing, organizational learning and knowledge transfer. This chapter specifically looks at evidence to suggest that the number of knowledge-bearing communication exchanges in improvement processes is much higher than that observed in routine processes. The chapter also shows that the proportion of knowledge content in communication exchanges is much higher as well.

Chapter 4 entitled, "The Effects of Collaborative Technologies" by Ned Kock of Temple University (USA) presents and discusses evidence pointing to an increase of process improvement group efficiency due to computer support. The evidence indicates efficiency gains are reflected in reduced group cost, lifetime and reliance on managers and also points to increases in perceived group outcome quality and organizational learning effectiveness. The results presented in this chapter provide a sound endorsement for the use of collaborative technologies in process improvement.

Chapter 5 entitled, "The Collaborative Use of Information Technology: End-User Participation and System Success" by William Doll of the University of Toledo and Xiaodong Deng of Oakland University (USA) uses a sample of 163 collaborative and 239 non-collaborative applications to answer three research questions: is user participation more effective in collaborative applications?; what specific decision issues enhance user satisfaction and productivity?; and can permitting end-users to participate as much as they want on some issues be ineffective or dysfunctional? The chapter reports on the results of the study designed to answer these important questions.

Chapter 6 entitled, "Promoting Collaboration among Trainers in the National Weather Service" by Victoria Johnson and Sherwood Wang of the Cooperative Program for Operational Meteorology, Education and Training discusses the use of science operations officers (SOO) by the National Weather Service to train local meteorologists in the latest technologies in their field. The authors discuss how technology has improved collaboration in these training efforts and the lessons learned in this massive undertaking of modernizing the National Weather Service.

Chapter 7 entitled, "A KM-Enabled Architecture for Collaborative Systems" by Lina Zhou and Dongsong Zhang of the University of Arizona (USA) proposes a knowledge management (KM)-enabled architecture for collaborative systems. The authors discuss current research issues related to knowledge management in the new architecture and show that, by applying the architecture to a virtual global business company, the proposed architecture would be able to support and integrate collaborative systems and knowledge management effectively.

Chapter 8 entitled, "Computer-Mediated Inter-Organizational Knowledge-Sharing: Insights from a Virtual Team Innovating Using a Collaborative Tool" by Ann Majchrzak, Nelson King, and Sulin Ba of the University of Southern California, Ronald Rice of Rutgers University and Arvind Malhotra of the University of North Carolina at Chapel Hill (USA) generates three propositions about the likely behavior of a team using a collaboration tool and reusing the knowledge put in the knowledge repository and then conducts a research study of these three propositions. The reports of this study are reported in the chapter. Finally, the authors discuss the theoretical and practical implications of their findings.

Chapter 9 entitled, "Alignment of Collaboration Technology Adoption and Organizational Change: Findings from Five Case Studies" by Bjørn Munkvold of Agder University College (Norway) presents an analysis of the alignment process of the adoption of collaboration technology and related organizational changes through a multiple case study in five organizations. The authors place special emphasis on the sequential relationship between technology adoption and organizational change. The case studies discussed illustrate how elements of learning and maturation in the implementation process can help in overcoming barriers to adoption.

Chapter 10 entitled, "Information Retrieval Using Collaborating Multi-User Agents" by Elaine Ferneley of Salford University (United Kingdom) presents a model that supports collaborative information retrieval from a range of information sources. The system discussed, known as CASMIR, has been implemented as a set of cooperating Java agents communicating in KQML. The chapter discusses the results of an early evaluation of CASMIR using the North West Film Archive's catalog and queries.

Chapter 11 entitled, "A Framework for the Implementation of a Collaborative Flexible Learning Environment for Academic Institutions" by R. K-Y Li, S.T. Cheng and R. J. Willis of Monash University (Australia) explains the collaborative learning approach and explores barriers to collaborative flexible learning. The authors then propose a framework to guide the development of a team-based flexible learning environment and show how this environment can be built using existing technology.

Chapter 12 entitled, "Information Technology, Core Competencies and Sustained Competitive Advantage" by Terry A. Byrd of Auburn University (USA) presents and describes a model that illustrates the possible connection between competitive advantage and IT. Furthermore, the chapter shows how one major component of the overall IT resources, the information systems infrastructure might yield sustained competitive advantage for an organization. By showing that information systems infrastructure flexibility acts as an enabler of the core competencies, the author demonstrates the relationship to sustained competitive advantage.

Chapter 13 entitled, "Fitting EMS to Organizations" by Carlos Costa of ISCTE (Portugal) and Manuela Aparício of Lusocredito-Sociedade de Estudos e Contabilidade, lda. reports on the development of a new electronic meeting system (EMS). The authors developed and implemented a prototype into a corporate environment. The preliminary results show that this approach creates a better fit to organizational needs than traditional electronic meeting systems.

Chapter 14 entitled, "Ad Hoc Virtual Teams: A Multi-disciplinary Framework and a Research Agenda" by Guy Paré and Line Dubé of École des Hautes Études Commerciales de Montreal (Canada) develops a comprehensive framework for ad hoc virtual teams' success. Ad hoc virtual teams are teams that come together for a finite time to tackle a specific project. The authors discuss the myriad of conditions and factors which lead to the success of a virtual team.

Chapter 15 entitled, "Overcoming Barriers in the Planning of a Virtual Library: Recognizing Organizational and Cultural Change Agents" by Ardis Hanson of the University of South Florida (USA) addresses the interaction among the University of South Florida Libraries, consisting of five separate entities, located at two region campuses and one main campus, in defining and realizing institutional commitment to its virtual library plan. Specifically, the chapter looks at various assignments made and the necessity of organizational change, and attempts to integrate the literature with action.

Chapter 16 entitled, "The Wicked Relationship between Organizations and Information Technology" by Gill Mallalieu, Clare Harvey and Colin Hardy of the University of Sunderland (United Kingdom) describes how the relationship between an organization's business processes and its legacy IT systems is considered a "wicked problem" (Churchman, 1967) within the framework of the RAMSES (Risk Assessment Model: Evaluation Strategy for Existing Systems) project. The authors then offer a detailed method within the framework of the grounded theory to understand this relationship and solve the "wicked problem."

Chapter 17 entitled, "Inspecting Spam: Unsolicited Communications on the Internet" by Ellen Foxman and William Schiano of Bentley College (USA) begins with a brief history of advertising on the Internet and then defines spam within a typology of undesirable Internet communications. The authors examine conflicting definitions of spam in light of their suggested remedies. The chapter concludes with recommendations on controlling spam for individuals, managers and policy makers.

Chapter 18 entitled, "Application of Information Management with Meeting Automation Tool" by Andrey Naumenko and Alain Wegmann of the Swiss Federal Institute of Technology (Switzerland) describes technologically supported solutions that assist people within a workgroup to deal with information related to their common projects. The solution proposed supports different scenarios of group organizations including geographically separated workgroups. The authors suggest that workgroup meetings are a key concept within the project framework and explain their value in the everyday workgroup.

Chapter 19 entitled, "A Distributed Cognition Analysis of Mobile CSCW" by Mikael Wiberg and Åke Grönlund of Umeå University (Sweden) uses a distributed cognition perspective to analyze mobile computer supported cooperative work (CSCW) among service technicians at a telecom operator. The chapter focuses on three aspects: the physical conditions for the interaction, the knowledge necessary for the management of the interaction, and the technology that can support the interaction.

From gaining and maintaining organizational process improvement and competitive advantage to utilizing electronic meeting applications and dealing with spam, the chapters in this book represent the most timely theoretical discussion and practical applications of collaborative technologies. Business people will benefit from the discussion of improving virtual teams and developing effective collaborative applications. Academics will be able to improve their teaching with a better understanding of the theoretical concepts discussed herein. Librarians, and other organizational members will have a greater understanding of how collaborative technologies can be most efficiently and effectively utilized within their respective organizations. This book is a must have for all those interested in improving their organization through more effective communication and collaboration with the benefits of technologies.

IRM Press
January 2002

Chapter 1

Extending Collaboration Support Systems: Making Sense in Remote Innovation

Thekla Rura-Polley and Ellen Baker
University of Technology, Sydney

This chapter first examines the role of collaboration and collective learning in regional and industry-wide innovation and how remote innovation–that is, innovation organized through electronic collaboration–could be enhanced by comprehensive computer support tools that include sensemaking aids. We look at the importance of sensemaking in collaborations and report on a study in which we analyzed sensemaking processes among students collaborating remotely. We describe a web-based computer system called *LiveNet*, that incorporates sensemaking aids to facilitate remote innovation. It brings together members within one workspace, provides them with the ability to locate needed information quickly, and supports this process with an agent-based structure that can assist members to achieve their goals. In addition, *LiveNet* supports the development of a common language and facilitates knowledge sharing, processes deemed important in the innovation and collective learning literatures. In the final section, we describe how this system can be used in remote innovation.

INTRODUCTION

Collaboration is recognized as an important organizational practice by many academics (Gray, 1989; Huxham, 1996; Pasquero, 1991; Roberts & Bradley, 1991; Wood & Gray, 1991). In particular, inter-organizational collaboration is becoming an increasingly common business practice as organizations focus on their

Previously Published in *Managing the Human Side of Information Technology: Challenges and Solutions* edited by Edward Szewczak and Coral Snodgrass, Copyright © 2002, Idea Group Publishing.

core competencies and outsource peripheral activities in their attempts to innovate, develop emerging markets, respond to global competition or implement new technologies. Accordingly, a wide variety of new organizational forms such as networks, strategic alliances, cooperatives and joint ventures have emerged, that allow different organizations to work together (Palmer & Dunford, 1997).

The innovation literature often refers to collaboration as an important factor for enhancing innovativeness in organizations as well as in industries. For instance, Dougherty and Hardy (1996, p. 1122) suggested that mature organizations that want to develop a capacity for sustained innovation must "provide collaborative structures and processes to solve problems creatively and connect innovations with existing businesses." Similarly, Smith, Ahmed and Takanashi (1999) reported that open collaboration between different organizations represents a main driver for technological innovation in the late 20th century, while Wycoff and Snead (1999, p. 55) claimed that innovation itself was "a collaborative skill that involves actively scouting the future, generating new ideas, choosing the best ones, rapidly and effectively implementing them, and then learning the lessons from successes and failures to begin again."

As far as regional or industry-wide innovation is concerned, researchers also increasingly point to the importance of collaboration and networks. For example, Keeble, Lawson, Moore and Wilkinson (1999) as well as Asheim (1996) developed the concept of collective learning to refer to the development of the capacity of a regional innovative milieu amongst member firms. Successful collective learning is characterized by establishing a common language and by sharing technological or engineering knowledge as well as organizational knowledge across organizational boundaries (Lorenz, 1996). Establishing a common language helps to build trust between collaborating partners. Because of unanticipated events and uncertainties that often arise after formal contracts have been arranged, trust helps the partners move forward. Sharing technological or engineering knowledge often involves the detailed product design, testing and production of the innovation. Organizational knowledge may include the division of responsibilities or the choice of procedures to ensure consistent, collective decision making. In addition to these three elements, Camagni (1991) and others (e.g., Simmie, 1997) have pointed to the importance of common culture, as well as psychological and social background as facilitators of collective learning. In an empirical study of the biotechnology industry, Powell, Koput and Smith-Doerr (1996) found that collaboration within networks was an important mechanism to gain access to knowledge that was widely distributed and not necessarily produced within the boundaries of any one member of the network. Thus, there is ample evidence suggesting that collaborating with other organizations can enhance innovation. Most of this research, however, has focused on face-to-face or locally bounded rather than geographically-dispersed, remote collaboration.

Even though collaboration has received increasing attention by academics only during the last decade, as an organizing form it has been part of many industries for a long time, e.g., film production since at least the 1950s (Birkmaier, 1994; Faulkner & Anderson, 1987; Miller & Shamsie, 1996). Remote collaboration as an organizing form, however, is a phenomenon of the 1990s. Remote collaboration is an advanced form of collaboration that entails collaboration through the use of electronic networks (Mizer, 1994). While several studies have investigated remote collaboration in general, and the management of remote collaboration in particular (e.g., Baker, Geirland, Fisher, & Chandler, 1999; Palmer, Dunford, Rura-Polley, & Baker, 2001), little systematic study of managing innovation in remote collaborations exists so far.

This chapter looks at two main issues confronting the management of innovation in remote collaborations, or, as we will call it, the management of remote innovation. First, remote innovation – by definition – is managed through electronic networks and systems, but little comprehensive computer-support is available so far. A variety of group support systems exists (Huseman & Miles, 1988), but these often are not sufficiently comprehensive to support the number of processes involved in a collaboration. They may support the decision-making process or the sharing of documents, but not the development of a joint vantage point (cf. Hardy, Phillips, & Lawrence, 1997; Hardy & Phillips 1998).

Second, existing group support tools for electronic collaboration mostly address group problem solving and miss the crucial element of sensemaking (Weick & Meader 1993). This may be because, as Tenkasi (1999), among others (Lyytinen, 1987; Boland, Tenkasi, & Te'eni, 1994), argues, the prevailing technologies draw upon models from decision theory rather than upon interpretive approaches to organizations and organizational actors. Thus, they support knowledge sharing in collaborations through collating information on certain parameters, similar to collating personal preferences in electronic decision-support systems. They rely on rational actors and objectivity of information and knowledge. They support neither the situatedness nor subjectivity of knowledge nor the framing of the knowledge arenas, all of which have to be explicit before knowledge can be created and shared in remote innovation teams.

Some authors propose that reliance on decision theory has hindered the development of information technology that is capable of supporting sensemaking processes in organizations (Boland et al., 1994; Feldman & March, 1981). Also, most researchers into group support systems have favored problem definition rather than problem framing. Their research has focused on "answers rather than questions, outcomes rather than inputs, and structure rather than process" (Weick & Meader, 1993, p. 231). This leads to problems, because "in real-world practice, problems do not present themselves to the practitioners as givens. They must be constructed from the materials of problematic situations which are puzzling, troubling, and uncertain" (Weick, 1995, p. 9). In other words, problems are shaped by, and in turn shape, sensemaking, a set of activities that occurs prior to the decision-making stage.

As mentioned earlier, for Lorenz (1996) developing a shared language was as crucial for regional innovativeness as was sharing technical and organizational knowledge, while Camagni (1991) pointed to the importance of synergy effects based on common cultural, psychological and political backgrounds in successful collaborative innovation. Essentially, both authors are referring to sensemaking aids. A common language or culture helps people make sense of what somebody else means when making a request, commenting on an idea or voicing an objection. Thus, a computer system that is intended to facilitate remote innovation has to go beyond existing group support systems by incorporating devices that help with sensemaking. The next section looks at sensemaking in remote collaboration in general, before applying these insights within a web-based computer system that can be used to manage remote innovation.

SENSEMAKING IN REMOTE COLLABORATION

Generally, when individuals seek to understand phenomena that do not appear sensible, they rationalize these phenomena by using prior experiences, contextual information, or other available means. In other words, when individuals make phenomena, events, or information sensible, they engage in sensemaking (Weick, 1995). Sensemaking is a crucial organizational capacity. As Brown (1999) has observed, managers increasingly engage in making sense rather than products for their stakeholders. They interpret the market, the forces shaping the competitive landscape, and the risks and opportunities presented to their company. Thus, one essential task of managers concerns creating knowledge out of disparate data and complex information, providing guidelines for action, and understanding problems in detail so that they can be solved (Weick, 1985).

Failures in sensemaking can have disastrous consequences, as Weick's (1993) analysis of the 1949 Mann Gulch disaster showed. Thirteen fire fighters died in the process of trying to contain a fire. When the team leader, Dodge, ordered his team members to drop their tools and lie down in an area where he had lit an escape fire, no one did, because taking such extraordinary action did not make sense to them. Instead, they ran for the ridge and only two of them survived. If they had followed Dodge's directive, all would have survived.

The problem alluded to here is that individuals differ in their sensemaking. Individuals have different experiences on which they rely when making sense of phenomena and events. Thus, engaging in shared sensemaking and attaining shared meaning can be quite difficult in an organization (Weick, 1995). This difficulty is exacerbated in collaborations that are intentionally set up to bring together people with differing experiences and view points. As Hewitt and Hall (1973, p. 370) point out, "participants who differ in social class, ethnicity, religion, or other important dimensions may find common ground only with difficulty." Therefore, communication, let alone sensemaking, within such collaborations is often complicated, since effective communication relies on common language and shared meanings. In fact, Weick (1995) cited lack of shared sensemaking as a frequent cause of collaboration failures.

When it comes to sensemaking in collaborations for innovation, it is important to keep in mind that such collaborations involve not only different individuals with different prior experiences and contextual information, but also individuals who represent different functions, expertise and modes of rationality. Different functions within business often have their own languages. For instance, the language of accounting differs substantially from the language of engineering or marketing (Clegg, 1989). Moreover, each function uses its own terminology and methods of communication that may not correspond with that used by another function. Bechky (1999) showed that design engineers used different terms than assembly workers, and when the two teams used a common term, the term actually referred to different objects. The technicians, located organizationally between the design engineers and the assembly workers, brokered knowledge transfer between the teams in order to create new products successfully. These technicians made sense of, and for, the other occupations.

In face-to-face collaborations such differences in definitions of terms and resulting miscommunication will become evident very quickly in the confused looks of the participants and through other contextual cues. In electronic collaborations such cues are missing. Therefore, Weick and Meader (1993, p. 232) thought it essential for a remote collaboration "to construct moderately consensual definitions that cohere long enough for people to infer some idea of what they have, what they want, why they can't get it, and why it may not be worth getting in the first place." Moreover, electronic representations are often flawed, because the data "contain only what can be collected and processed through machines. That excludes sensory information, feelings, intuitions, and context" – all of which are important for sensemaking

(Weick, 1985, p. 51). Thus, facilitating sensemaking in remote collaborations may be a crucial process for successful innovation.

The Theory of Sensemaking

This section describes the theoretical perspectives on sensemaking that inform our thinking about a remote innovation system. The first perspective is based on Weick's (1993; 1995) approach. He (1995, p. 17) understands sensemaking as "a process that is grounded in identity construction, retrospective, enactive of sensible environments, social, ongoing, focused on and by extracted cues, and driven by plausibility rather than accuracy." He uses these characteristics "to investigate what sensemaking is, how it works and when it can fail" (Weick, 1995, p. 18). Weick (1995) views sensemaking as both an individual and a social activity by acknowledging the impact of others on the sensemaker. Through interaction with others, sensemakers can compare multiple sources of data, ponder the results and place the confusing event or information into context (Weick & Meader, 1993).

When it comes to sensemaking in organizations, shared terminology, definitions and language are important, but one should not forget that meaning is also constructed and conveyed through rites, symbols, artifacts and ceremony. As Weick (1995, p. 3) points out, organizations do not only have their own language, but also symbols "that have important effects on sensemaking." After all, sensemaking also includes "the standards and rules for perceiving, interpreting, believing, and acting that are typically used in a given cultural setting" (Sackman, 1991, p. 33). Explicit standards and rules represent underlying values of an organization. Weick's (1995, p. 28) suggestion that people need "values, priorities, and clarity about preferences to help them be clear about which projects matter" when they experience equivocality, makes sense intuitively.

Our second perspective on sensemaking comes from Boland and Tenkasi's (1995) work on perspective making and taking. They (1995, p. 356) define perspective making as a "process whereby a community of knowing develops and strengthens its own knowledge domain and practice." Perspective taking is a process where organizational knowledge emerges out of exchange, evaluation and integration of knowledge (Duncan & Weiss, 1979). It involves a range of inferential and judgmental processes, which opens the process to systematic errors and biases (Boland & Tenkasi, 1995). The usage of language and narrative is particularly important in perspective making and taking. For example, Dougherty (1992) writes that perspective taking processes in cross-functional product development teams failed because members interpreted and understood linkages between technology and marketing qualitatively differently. Different departments had different internally consistent and coherent thought worlds. Members of a cross-functional team worked from their departmental thought worlds and assumed they knew the entire story; however, each story told within the team differed substantially from one another. Successful perspective taking involves "an increased capacity for communities of knowing to take each other into account within their own language games, and to construct new language games for their interaction" (Boland & Tenkasi, 1995, p. 359).

The third perspective on sensemaking comes from Bolman and Deal's (1997) work on frames of reference and reframing. They list four frames that managers might use when making sense of organizations: the structural frame, the human resource frame, the political frame, and the symbolic frame. Individuals interpret events in different ways depending on the frames that they adopt (Morgan, 1993). In collaboration, it is important that individuals are aware of their own preferred frame as well as being capable of reframing an event. According to Bolman and Deal (1997, p. 5), "effectiveness deteriorates when managers and leaders cannot reframe." Reframing, or deliberately viewing events from different perspectives, broadens cognitive perceptions of organizational events or problems, and helps to identify appropriate courses of action (Bolman & Deal, 1997). Being capable of reframing an event is especially important in cross-functional collaborations where participants may generally prefer the frame of reference most closely related to their own professional expertise. For instance, an engineer may prefer to look at events within a structural frame while a general manager may frame everything in political terms. Reframing an event may help members to overcome such professional blind spots.

In the following section, we report some research on sensemaking processes in electronic discussions among students before describing the development of an electronic support technology for facilitating sensemaking in remote collaborations. We will report on general sensemaking processes and terminology as well as on frames of reference used by the students.

THE PRACTICE OF SENSEMAKING IN REMOTE COLLABORATION

The setting for this exploratory study was an advanced research methods class in Management. There were 15 participants whose ages ranged from 21 to 55; some of the participants actually worked as academic staff in other faculties and universities. Their backgrounds included engineering, accounting, psychology, operations management, sociology, communications studies, as well as management. Thus, the participants resembled a typical cross-functional team. The majority of the students were male (11) and came from English-speaking backgrounds (13). Some of the objectives of the class included the development and critical assessment of theories and models at different levels of analysis; generating and justifying propositions and research questions; making intelligent choices of research settings and methods; and writing a succinct and feasible proposal or publishable article.

The class met weekly for one three-hour face-to-face seminar. The seminars contained discussions of publications as well as ongoing research work of the participants. A large proportion of the class work focused on collaborative learning. For instance, participants provided detailed feedback on one another's exercises and proposals. They also participated in electronic discussions on a special Internet site. On this Internet site, electronic discussion forums were organized under six specific themes, such as *Coffee Chat, Exercise Extravaganza, Reviewing Roundrobin, Theorizing Team, Methods Meeting, Paper Pulp*, and *Ask Thekla*. Students were given some guidelines about appropriate topics within each discussion list to make access to and retrieval of information easier. For example, in the *Exercise Extravaganza* forum, students were encouraged to share their weekly exercises, discuss them, get feedback from others, and help one another to progress in their learning. The *Theorizing Team* represented a section where students could discuss their own theories and theorizing endeavors. All in all, 27 messages were clocked on *Coffee Chat*, six on *Exercise Extravaganza*, seven on *Reviewing Roundrobin*, 68 on *Theorizing Team*, 15 on *Methods Meeting*, 21 on *Paper Pulp,* and 18 on *Ask Thekla.*

Some students contributed 17 or 19 times, while others did not contribute at all. The contributions ranged from six words to 920 words, and on average contained 247 words. The standard deviation was 222. The length of these contributions go far beyond what we have seen in other electronic discussions among students in other management classes at this school, or at other universities. In fact, the longest contribution had to be excluded from part of our analysis, because it crashed the system every time we tried to analyze it. Students' submissions to these discussions were saved on file for analysis in this study. Sixty-seven messages from one discussion forum, the *Theorizing Team*, were chosen for analysis.

Data Analysis

The data analysis consisted of two parts. In the first part, two of the researchers carried out an informal analysis of the discussions to try to increase our understanding of sensemaking processes. All the transcripts of the *Theorizing Team* discussions were read. We immersed ourselves in these texts in order to investigate the specific sensemaking processes that were manifest in the discussions. We looked for examples of attempts at sensemaking by the students and indications as to what these discussants found helpful in their attempts at sensemaking in this situation.

The second part of the analysis was more formal. It involved the construction and application of a dictionary to be used for computer-aided processing of electronic discussions, and was guided by the experience of Kabanoff, Waldersee and Cohen (1995), who developed a computer-aided content analysis system for categorizing organizational values from text documents. In contrast to Kabanoff et al., our analysis did not focus on organizational values, but was based on Bolman and Deal's (1997) typology of organizational analysis and their four frames of reference: the structural, human resources, political and symbolic frames. Identification of key words in their book led to a database that listed the four frames of reference and a dictionary of words that are typically associated with each of those frames. We supplemented these terms with words from lists that Palmer (1999) developed in his study of metaphor usage among managers. In addition, two researchers scanned a number of introductory management texts for the types of keywords used for organizational phenomena related to each of the four frames and added those to the dictionaries.

We extended those dictionaries by manually analyzing a small proportion of the total text database, *Methods Meeting* and *Exercise Extravaganza* discussions, searching for words that intuitively seemed to reflect one of the four frames and included terms so identified in the dictionaries. We specifically looked for words that might not be provided in an academic discourse or within academic descriptions of the frames but would be typical of the discussion style among practitioners. Examples for the structural frame included "template" and "automate"; for the human resource frame, "burnout" and "helpful"; for the political frame, "hammered" and "revolution"; and lastly, for the symbolic frame, "decode" and "connotations."

The above words and phrases were then modified so that they would be suitable for computer-aided processing. The main change was the elimination of terms that had more than one meaning. These words may be easily processed by humans who would take the context into account but at this stage would provide erroneous categorizing if carried out by computer. Another modification involved the addition of all variations of a term, for example: motivate, motivated, motivates, motivation. We then used this dictionary to analyze the 67 submissions to the *Theorizing Team* discussion forum. The total word count for each discussion item and the number of hits for each frame of reference were recorded.

Results

In their remote sensemaking, participants utilized four different vehicles. They made sense by referring to shared readings, their own and one another's disciplinary background, common popular culture, and normal day-to-day experiences to which others could readily relate. For example, one message referred to a popular children's show on TV.

> Your comments of what framework we look at things through reminds me of Play School (I have x2 kids so I have been widely exposed to the show). You know, when they say "what window will we look through today?.....aagh that's right, the arched window" and depending on what window you look through determines what you'll see. (Of course we shouldn't neglect the temporal nature of their investigations!) Kid's books are also a great source of understanding (I read to both of my children each night). There's one book that makes the proposition "suppose you had no nose." By researching the phenomena the author is able to make some statements of causal inference and theorize as to the effects of the cause of no nose, and finally examine the implications of such to children. The framework adopted is one of a functionalist. The theories are really quite generalizable to other parts of the anatomy. (Funny how the kids don't seem to enjoy my interpretations!?) By the way, my favorite's Monica - how about you?

Over time, a common popular culture frame emerged, which became the main sensemaking vehicle in the class. In the second half of the semester, references to *Star Wars and the Phantom Menace* dominated the discussions. Students even took on nicknames from the movie. Positivist researchers were classified as the "Dark Side" and their most outspoken proponent was referred to and started to sign his messages as "Darth Vader." Non-positivist, postmodern, and cultural-symbolist researchers referred to themselves as the "Light Side," their most senior proponent–a doctoral student–became "Obi-Wan," the junior–an Honors student–became "Luke." Students who were undecided about the paradigm in which to do their research did not participate much in this debate and even had to be careful where to sit during the weekly face-to-face seminar, where "Dark" and "Light" Side were clearly marked. However, using the term "Light Side" backfired, when the "Dark Side" claimed that "Light Side" stood for "light-weight" argument.

We also found that students engaged in three different sensemaking processes. The first sensemaking process involved making sense of the class itself and the tasks required from them. The second sensemaking process involved making sense of each other, and the third sensemaking process involved making sense of the collaboration process. An example of the first sensemaking process is the following statement on the discussion list:

> I am just sending some of my thoughts, on the notion of theorizing with which I have and still am having great difficulty. Grappling with the distinction between typologies and theories has been of great concern

especially considering that my area of interest is International Human Resource Management (IHRM). This area is inundated with typologies and frameworks such as one outlined by Samuel Bacharach in his paper "Organizational Theories: some criteria for evaluation." That is, the example he gives of the search for a goodness of fit between empirically derived categorizations of business strategy and human resource strategy (Schuler and Jackson: 1987). This is what a lot of the literature in HRM/IHRM is based on. Originally, I thought that these typologies were part of a theory. However, the past two weeks in particular have enlightened my thinking on this. I understand now how this falls in the realm of description, not theory. I too have been following this type of theorizing– the descriptive type. It is precisely the "why" and "how" questions that I am having trouble with and then contextualizing them within theories that are both internally and externally consistent to IHRM. The articles in this course are certainly moving me toward this end. However, if anyone has come across a very simplified, almost prescriptive (?) article outlining theorizing according to some basic steps I would much appreciate it. Or if anyone has any storylike or novel way of conceptualizing the practice of theorizing, I would really like to know about it as I am sure others are also having at least some difficulty with "theorizing."

Another student's reply was:

I too have been enlightened by the information provided over the past few weeks to such an extent that I am now confused. I am not familiar with any literature that provides a step-by-step process on theorizing, however there is an article by Easterby, Smith, Thorpe and Lowe entitled "What is Management Research" that gives a pretty good idea of the fit between practitioner and academic research–that is, it is what is done with the knowledge that defines the research outcome. Within this article they use some typologies by Clarke to support of their argument. I thought that this may be useful for you since it seems to me that you may be experiencing a dissonance between the practitioner and academic literature rather than difficulty with the actual theorizing process. As far as theorizing for your research, as I mentioned, I too am having difficulty. After doing the stop and thinks, readings and talking with ... I was still no closer. So I did two things. Firstly, I went back to basics. For many years I have been a person who has said "I have a theory" about many topics. For example, I have a theory, based on an observation, that the fog on the F3 freeway is always worse on the weekend. There may be several reasons for this, e.g.,: because there is less traffic to dispurse the fog at road level on the weekends; the amount of fog is actually the same on weekends and weekdays - it is actually a passageway that is created by cars during the week; there is no difference—it is less cars that create an illusion of more fog because of a greater field of vision that enables you to focus on the fog, etc. However to be sure I need to check out a few things - do some tests. Funnily enough all this fitted in some way into the stuff we've been learning.

Another student entered the discussion:

So far I have found myself just writing, much the same like ... Brainstorming and questioning their arguments in a non-structured way. Getting the ideas and coming up with a research question is one thing but theorizing and coming up with a conceptual framework, looking for constructs and then thinking about possible variables, with the limited expertise and experience in this area is something I am barely coming to grips with in the framework of the readings for this class. The current stage I am at is that I have the literature on quality in management accounting and generally readings in TQM. I have some readings in quality in the collaborative setting and have developed questions on quality strategy as to the differences between both forms of literature. The question is how does one progress from merely asking basic and encompassing questions to developing constructs and variables that fall within the parameters material given in the reading. Are there articles on the how to of conceptualizing and the relationship with constructs and variables or should I just keep reading more articles in the literature and copy them?? From brainstorming to........

The discussions on making sense of the class and the exercises also affected how they made sense of readings in other classes. One student requested that "this course should come with a warning about the effects on reading research. I read a piece this morning and found myself stopping all the way through to repeat the constructs and their relationships. It took forever to read."

The earlier description of the Star Wars metaphors and nicknames is a good example of the second sensemaking process, how the students made sense of each other, especially of one another's functional background and research epistemology.

An example of the third sensemaking process, i.e., making sense of their collaboration processes, is the following. Here, one student tried to make sense of the previous week's electronic discussion by linking it to management literatures and came to the following conclusion:

It could be argued that the recent debate surrounding the topic "Re: social Science and Organizational Theories" (Refer "Top Class"\ "Theorizing" herein) was indeed an example of intragroup conflict. This is a valid assertion if the definition by Boulding (1963) is accepted. Boulding suggests that conflict can be considered as "perceived incompatabilities or perceptions" and that " the parties hold discrepant views." It is interesting to note, therefore, how the conflict developed from a task-related conflict into a type of interpersonal conflict. It could also be suggested that the "benefits" of this conflict diminished as the transformation took place. This demonstrates a consistency with organizational behavior theories suggesting that conflict can be interpersonal or task related and indeed destructive or beneficial depending on the circumstances and context of the group. As Jehn (1995, p.256) asserts in relation to intragroup conflict within an organization, "whether conflict is beneficial depends upon the type of conflict, the structure of the group and group norms." Wow guys! A natural experiment unfolded right before my eyes and I think that I was able to explain it from an organization behavior perspective!!! I think that this theorizing stuff has some potential ! - don't you???? Now I wonder what the social psychologists would make of it ....mmmmmm.

At some other point, a different student summarized parts of the discussion that had gone on, and thereby made sense of, and constructed meaning for the other participants.

I'm really enjoying the debate on this topic. Obviously I see it as one of the fundamental issues that need to be resolved (if that's possible) and I do believe the discussion has gone some way to resolving it for me. I won't weigh in on the various philosophical arguments except to say that there seem to be valid points in all of them. Then again, ...'s cool so she must be right ;-). My thoughts on the issue to emerge from the debate are: * we need to be at least aware of the various theories and attempt to relate some of them to our work; * the best way to get a handle on these theories is to consider the "categories" or "classifications" that they are grouped in (thanks ... and ...); * an extensive reading exercise of each theory or category of theory can be avoided by reading overview books (thanks ...) or review articles (thanks ...); * we shouldn't let the use of theories stifle our creativity or get in the way of reality (thanks ..., ... and ...). I really enjoyed ...'s listing. There are some beauties there!

His statement was rewarded with the following comment: "Thanks for your comment and summary. Have you thought of joining the diplomatic service. :)."

To a large extent, the early discussions on making sense of the class and the tasks centered on terminology and developing a shared terminology. Our analysis also indicated that the initial period of team interaction contained the more overt attempts at defining terms and explicitly talking about sensemaking. Thus, the initial start-up phase in a team may be a particularly useful period for intervention and support for sensemaking. We also noticed that it was not just the definitions but even which terms needed to be defined by the team that were a subject for argument. For example, the term "ontology" was highly relevant for some of the team who considered it crucial to their work on theorizing their own research, but considered "waffling" and "irrelevant" to theorizing by other members.

Formal analysis of the frames of reference underlying each statement led to the following indicative trends. Fifty-five messages contained one or more reference to the Human Resource Frame (average 3.6 hits per message), while 45 messages contained one or more reference to the Structural Frame (average 2.8 hits). The Power Frame was referenced in 41 messages (average 2.8 hits), while the Cultural Frame was referenced in 37 messages (average 1.7 hits). It became clear that most messages contained references to more than one frame. Our analysis also showed that no one frame emerged as the dominant frame of reference in this class; students continued to use all four frames of reference in their discussion. The moving average for the Power Frame, though, showed the clearest upward trend, while the moving average for Structure declined (see Figure 1).

Figure 1: Number of hits for each frame of reference over time

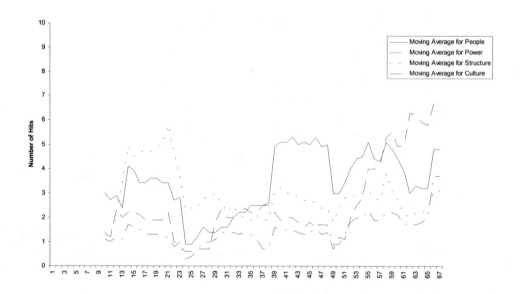

Discussion

In this study, the students' discussions dealt with terminology and language, and their technical and organizational knowledge, and they drew upon their common experiences to clarify their communication. Thus our findings support current conceptions of collective learning. As mentioned earlier, collective learning refers to the capacity of a regional innovative milieu to facilitate innovative behavior amongst member firms (Keeble et al., 1999) and successful collective learning is characterized by developing a common language and by sharing technical and organizational knowledge (Lorenz, 1996). In addition, common cultural, psychological and social backgrounds are facilitators of successful collaborative innovation (Camagni, 1991).

Providing support mechanisms for each of these activities can facilitate cooperation and joint solutions to common problems. However, innovative firms cannot rely only on intra-firm knowledge sharing, or even on collective learning within regional clusters of firms. Research indicates that national and global innovation networks, linking the firms with selected partners outside of their geographical location, are also important (Camagni, 1991; Keeble et al., 1999). The challenge then becomes how to provide this support within a remote collaboration system. In the next section, we describe a computer system that incorporates these ideas and can be used for remote innovation.

THE PRACTICE OF SENSEMAKING IN *LIVENET*

We have developed modules for a web-based system, *LiveNet* (Hawryszkiewycz, 1998), to enhance sensemaking and, subsequently, innovation in remote collaborations. The *LiveNet* system is based on networked electronic workspaces. It is an integrated system that provides access to the team's own documents and discussions, to documents within the parent organization(s), and to agent-based tools to assist team members to carry out their tasks effectively. Users themselves create the workspaces and configure them to suit their needs. As a team continues working together, it can tailor its workspaces to suit its changing tasks and needs. There is also access within the system to sensemaking aids. A demonstration of *LiveNet* can be accessed at http://livenet.it.uts.edu.au/. In the following paragraphs we briefly describe how remote collaborators can use *LiveNet* to engage in collective learning and innovation.

As mentioned, past research identified several key elements of collective learning, such as establishing a shared language, sharing technical, engineering and organizational knowledge, and having a common cultural background. Within *LiveNet*, development of a common language is supported by a number of separate modules. One module that supports the development of shared terminology involves a database of key terms and definitions, as well as a means for discussing the database contents. This database is created through a discussion where users can ask for clarification and discuss connotations and meanings within the specific context of their team's tasks. Users are cautioned about the occurrence of similar terminology in different disciplines and suggest that collaborators set up a separate discussion in which definitions can be agreed upon and questions can be more comfortably raised about what specific words mean.

Another module assists the members to recognize different frames of reference being used within the team and encourages them to develop more flexible ways of thinking about the team's problems. This module allows participants to uncover their own latent frames of reference, as well as those of others. At any time a workspace user may request an analysis of the frames of reference to be carried out on a given portion of the electronic discussions or documents, and the analysis is conducted immediately. Thus the module provides instantaneous electronic feedback on the frames of reference being used within a particular discussion or by a specific participant. This module utilizes Bolman and Deal's (1997) work on frames of reference and reframing, in particular a dictionary of words typical of each frame of reference, as described in the earlier section on the students' remote collaborations.

Within *LiveNet*, sharing knowledge specific to the project is facilitated by threaded discussions that can draw out tacit knowledge, by easy access to individual and team-produced documents, and by links to outside expertise as well as background information from organizational databases. Initial actions in most knowledge processes involve accessing explicitly stored background and sharing experiences, typically narratives that provide understanding and meaning (Boland & Tenkasi, 1995). Such experiences and insights are shared during electronic discussions, and can be captured in discussion databases, providing a form of externalizing tacit knowledge. They then feed into the explicit output documents of the team.

Sharing of organizational knowledge is supported through customizing a team's workspace in terms of participants' roles, rules about access to information, rules about the obligations that apply to the different roles, and norms regarding project management. The team can also specify milestones for measuring its project's progress and set up agents to automatically notify members when a milestone has been reached or when inputs are required from members. Thus, much organizational knowledge can be built into the workspace's procedures by the team. Combining stored knowledge with agent systems provides improvements to collaboration processes. Two kinds of agencies have been found useful – technical agency and process agency. The technical agency primarily assists users in gathering both the information and the people needed to accomplish the workspace goal. Events within workspaces may be directed to agents that can perform a number of tasks. Process agency may be expressed by agents that facilitate workflows (Hawryszkiewycz & Debenham, 1998) through basing plans on the status of workspaces and the organizational state when events are occurring, and creating new workspaces. When combined, the technical agents provide users with a workspace that contains access to information and actions needed by the knowledge worker. The process agency then directs any outcomes from a workspace to other related workspaces.

A final factor important to facilitating collaborative innovation is the reinforcement of common cultural, psychological and social backgrounds (Camagni, 1991). In contrast to regional innovation networks, assumptions of common values or backgrounds may not be valid in remote collaboration. Thus, within *LiveNet*, we try to help members recognize differences in backgrounds, as well as to assist a team to establish its own team culture by clearly identified common workspace and membership. This helps the team develop a sense of shared identity and its members are more motivated to contribute to the achievement of the team's goals. As noted earlier, in the study of remote collaboration among students, their shared identity became increasingly framed within Star Wars metaphors, and they increasingly used Star Wars figures and images to make sense of the class events.

Remote Innovation Through *Livenet*

We now provide an example to illustrate how a remote collaboration system such as *LiveNet* could be applied to remote innovation. In Figure 2, we depict how an innovation process might be organized remotely within an organization; however, the team members could as easily come from different organizations and engage in remote innovation.

The major modeling terms of *LiveNet* are based on ideas from soft systems methodologies. They are combined as shown in Figure 2 and include activities, actors, and objects. Activities, shown as cloud-like shapes, are organizationally recognized tasks in that they produce some outputs, which are then used in other activities. Objects or outcomes are represented by rectangular boxes and actors by their names. A line from an activity to an object means that the activity may change the object. An arrow from one activity to another activity means that these two activities may affect each other and can be linked. A dashed arrow between two objects means that these objects are part of each other. Links between actors and activities mean that people who undertake these roles participate in the activity. Dashed lines between activities mean that these activities are part of a workspace network.

In this example, one team's task may be to generate innovation ideas. To facilitate this remotely, a workspace called *Idea Generation* could be set up. This team may include a large number of staff from various organizations and different levels within those organizations. It could even involve clients and customers. All members may be allowed to participate in the discussions and to make suggestions. A second workspace could be set up to review these ideas. Membership in the *Initial Screening* workspace may be limited to a select team of financial, marketing, design, production and innovation experts. Alternatively, the *Initial Screening* workspace could be read-accessible to all employees, but only write-accessible to a select team. The two teams may work in parallel or in sequence, depending on the preferences of the managers and teams involved.

When discussing ideas and screening them with respect to their potential in the marketplace, it will be important for the experts representing various functional roles to understand each other and to make sense of one another's comments and ideas. Thus, the modules that support developing a common language and making underlying frames of reference explicit may be essential elements of this cross-functional workspace.

Figure 2: Organizing remote innovation

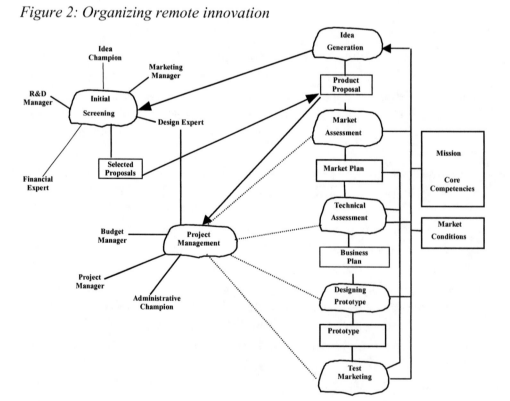

Without describing other activities and workspaces in detail, it may suffice to say that essentially each innovation activity could occur in a separate workspace with changing membership while still providing overall coherence through the linked tree structure of the network between the workspaces. Some people may only be a member in one workspace, while others are involved in several workspaces. The responsible senior manager may have access to the various teams' outputs, but not the discussions, if that is the agreed-upon governance structure of the workspace network.

Each workspace has access to the sensemaking modules described in the previous section. Each workspace team may have its own discussions about terms in order to develop a common language. Alternatively, the terminology database could be shared within the entire workspace network. Each workspace has access to the module that makes underlying frames of reference explicit. The sharing of knowledge can be restricted within a workspace or shared across several workspaces. Workspace members make these decisions themselves and can revisit their decisions as their team evolves.

To achieve exploration as well as exploitation of innovation ideas in the remote collaboration system, it is important that the workspace network supports both rationally planned as well as opportunely emerging processes (cf. March, 1995; Weick, 1996). Thus, *LiveNet* incorporates some preset discussions such as setting goals, setting milestones, sharing news, and discussing surprises, but also allows members to set up their own discussions.

The activity represented graphically in Figure 2 may produce some output that may be used in other activities. The way that these activities are carried out is usually collaborative in nature and often cannot be strictly predefined. The activities are dependent on each other but not necessarily sequential. The emphasis is not on sequencing but on the activities, their participants and the outputs that they produce. The sequencing relationships between activities should not be viewed as workflows, but simply as events in one activity that could initiate actions in another. In *LiveNet*, some of the coordination across workspaces can be automated through a variety of work process support tools, such as built-in project tracking support, built-in discussion tracking notification, wizards for creating a new workspace, and automated event-triggered actions within and across work spaces and teams.

CONCLUSION

In this chapter we have explored how innovation can be supported electronically in remote collaborations. Four major aspects of effective remote innovation include: (1) providing tools for establishing a common language; (2) providing a workspace for sharing technological and engineering knowledge specific to a project among members; (3) allowing sharing of organizational knowledge and developing joint organizational procedures through supporting flexible team formation and evolving structures and governance forms; and (4) facilitating the development of a common culture and identity among members. A prototype system, *LiveNet*, was described, that brings together members from different organizations within one workspace, provides them with the ability to locate needed information quickly, and supports this process with an agent-based structure that can assist members to achieve their goals. Members can re-define their tasks dynamically as they evolve, and *LiveNet* supports the building of relationships amongst the members within a workspace network. Modules within *LiveNet* assist the development of shared terminology as well as making underlying frames of reference explicit. Appropriate agents can facilitate coordination and sensemaking processes and thereby improve communication in remote innovations.

ACKNOWLEDGMENT

We are grateful to the Australian Research Council, the University of Technology, Sydney and the Organizational Researchers on Collaboration and Alliances group at UTS for financial support. We thank the 1999 students of Advanced Research Methods for permission to analyze their discussions, and numerous colleagues, in particular Prof. I. Hawryszkiewycz, for their support and feedback. Earlier versions of this chapter were presented at the 1999 Academy of Management Annual Meetings and the ACR/ANZAM Workshop on Interorganizational Collaboration, University of Melbourne, 1999.

REFERENCES

Asheim, B. (1996). Industrial districts as "learning regions": A condition for prosperity? *European Planning Studies*, 4, 379-400.

Baker, E., Geirland, J., Fisher, T., & Chandler, A. (1999). Media production: Towards creative collaboration using communication networks. *Computer-Supported Cooperative Work*, 8, 303-332.

Bechky, B. (1999). Creating shared meaning across occupational communities: An ethnographic study of a production floor. Paper presented at the *Academy of Management Meetings*, Chicago, IL.

Birkmaier, C. (1994). Through the looking glass: Re-engineering the video production process. *Videography*, 19(3), 60-70.

Boland, R. J., & Tenkasi, R. V. (1995). Perspective making and perspective taking in communities of knowing. *Organization Science*, 6, 350-372.

Boland, R. J., Tenkasi, R. V., & Te'eni, D. (1994). Designing information technology to support distributed cognition. *Organization Science*, 5, 456-475.

Bolman, L. G., & Deal, T. E. (1997). *Reframing Organizations: Artistry, Choice and Leadership* (2nd Ed.). San Francisco, CA: Jossey-Bass.

Brown, J. S. (1999). Sustaining the ecology of knowledge. *Leader to Leader*, Spring, 12, 31-36.

Camagni, R. (1991). Local milieu, uncertainty and innovation networks: Towards a new dynamic theory of economic space. In Camagni, R. (Ed.) *Innovation Networks: Spatial Perspectives*, 121-142. London: Belhaven.

Clegg, S. R. (1989). *Frameworks of Power*. Newbury Park, CA: Sage Publications.

Dougherty, D. (1992). Interpretive barriers to successful product innovation in large firms. *Organization Science*, 3, 179-202.

Dougherty, D., & Hardy, C. (1996). Sustained product innovation in large, mature organizations: Overcoming innovation-to-organization problems. *Academy of Management Journal*, 39, 1120-1153.

Duncan, R., & Weiss, A. (1979). Organizational learning: Implications for organizational design. In Cummings, L. and Staw, B. M. (Eds), *Research in Organizational Behavior*, 1. Greenwich, CT: JAI.

Faulkner, R. R., & Anderson, A. B. (1987). Short term projects and emergent careers: Evidence from Hollywood. *American Journal of Sociology*, 92: 878-909.

Feldman, M. S., & March, J. G. (1981). Information in organizations as signal and symbol. *Administrative Science Quarterly*, 26, 171-186.

Gray, B. (1989). *Collaborating: Finding Common Ground for Multiparty Problems*. San Francisco: Jossey-Bass.

Hardy, C., & Phillips, N. (1998). Strategies of engagement: Lessons from the critical examination of collaboration and conflict in an interorganizational domain. *Organization Science*, 9, 217-230.

Hardy, C., Phillips, N., & Lawrence, T. (1997). Swimming with sharks: Tensions in the Canadian HIV/AIDS domain. Paper presented at the *EGOS Colloquium*, Budapest, Hungary.

Hawryszkiewycz, I. T. (1998). Extending workspaces for knowledge sharing. In Traunmuller, R. and Csuhaj-Varju, E. (Eds.), *Proceedings of the XV. IFIP World Computer Congress, IFIP98*, 77-88. Vienna-Budapest.

Hawryszkiewycz, I. T., & Debenham, J. (1998). A workflow system based on agents. In Quirchmayr, G., Schweighofer, E. and Bench-Capon, T. (Eds). *9th*

International Conference on Database and Expert Systems, DEXA98, 135-144. Vienna, Berlin: Springer-Verlag.

Hewitt, J. P., & Hall, P. M. (1973). Social problems, problematic situations, and quasi-theories. *American Sociological Review, 38,* 367-374.

Huseman, R. C., & Miles, E. W. (1988). Organizational communication in the information age. *Journal of Management, 14,* 181-204.

Huxham, C. (1996). Advantage or inertia? Making collaboration work. In Paton, R., Clark, G., Jones, G., Lewis, J. and Quinlan, P. (Eds.), *The New Management Reader.* London, New York: Routledge (in association with The Open University).

Kabanoff, B., Waldersee, R., & Cohen, M. (1995). Espoused values and organizational change themes. *Academy of Management Journal, 38,* 1075-1104.

Keeble, D., Lawson, C., Moore, B., & Wilkinson, F. (1999). Collective learning processes, networking and "institutional thickness" in the Cambridge region. *Regional Studies, 33*(4), 319-332.

Lorenz, E. (1996). *Collective Learning Processes and the Regional Labor Market.* Unpublished research note, European Network on Networks, Collective learning and RTD in regionally-clustered high technology SMEs.

Lyytinen, K. (1987). Two views of information modeling. *Information Management, 12,* 9-19.

March, J. G. (1995). Exploration and exploitation in organizational learning. In Cohen, M. D. and Sproull, L. S. (Eds). *Organizational Learning,* 101-123. Thousand Oaks, CA: Sage Publications.

Miller, D., & Shamsie, J. (1996). The resource-based view of the firm in two environments: The Hollywood film studios from 1936 to 1965. *Academy of Management Journal, 39,* 519-543.

Mizer, R. A. (1994). From post-production to the cinema of the future. *SMPTE Journal,* December, 801-804.

Morgan, G. (1993). *Imaginization: The Art of Creative Management.* Newbury Park, CA: Sage Publications.

Palmer, I. (1999). Framing managers' experiences of collaboration: A metaphor-based analysis. Under review at *Journal of Management Inquiry.*

Palmer, I., & Dunford, R. (1997). Organizing for hyper-competition: New organisational forms for a new age? *New Zealand Strategic Management,* 2(4), 38-45.

Palmer, I., Dunford, R., Rura-Polley, T., & Baker, E. (2001). Changing forms of organizing: Dualities in using remote collaboration technologies in film production. *Journal of Organizational Change Management, 14*(2), 190-212.

Pasquero, J. (1991). Supraorganizational collaboration: The Canadian environmental experiment. *Journal of Applied Behavioural Science, 27*(2), 38-64.

Powell, W. W., Koput, K. W., & Smith-Doerr, L. (1996). Interorganization collaboration and the locus of innovation: Networks of learning in biotechnology. *Administrative Science Quarterly, 41*, 116-145.

Roberts, N. C., & Bradley, R. T. (1991). Stakeholder collaboration and innovation: A study of public policy initiation at the state level. *Journal of Applied Behavioural Science, 27*(2), 209-227.

Sackman, S. A. (1991). *Cultural Knowledge in Organizations.* Newbury Park, CA: Sage Publications.

Simmie, J. (Ed.). (1997). *Innovation, Networks and Learning Regions?* London: Jessica Kingsley.

Smith, R. K., Ahmed, M. U., & Takanashi, A. (1999). International collaboration for technological change in the 21st century. *International Journal of Technology Management, 18*(3-4), 285-292.

Tenkasi, R. V. (1999). Information technology and organizational change in turbulent environments. Symposium presented at the *Academy of Management Annual Meeting,* Chicago, IL.

Weick, K. E. (1985). Cosmos vs. chaos: Sense and nonsense in electronic contexts. *Organizational Dynamics, 14*(2), 51-64.

Weick, K. E. (1993). The collapse of sensemaking in organizations: The Mann Gulch disaster. *Administrative Science Quarterly, 38*, 628-652.

Weick, K. E. (1995). *Sensemaking in Organizations.* Thousand Oaks: Sage Publications.

Weick, K. E., & Meader, D. K. (1993). Sensemaking and group support systems. In Jessup, L. M. and Valacich, J. S. (Eds.), *Group Support Systems,* 230-252. New York: Macmillan.

Weick, K. E., & Westley, F. (1996). Organizational learning: Affirming an oxymoron. In Clegg, S. R., Hardy, C. and Nord, W. R. (Eds). *Handbook of Organization Studies,* 440-458. Thousand Oaks, CA: Sage Publications.

Wood, D. J., & Gray, B. (1991). Towards a comprehensive theory of collaboration. *Journal of Applied Behavioral Science, 27*(2), 139-162.

Wycoff, J., & Snead, L. (1999). Stimulating innovation with collaboration rooms. *Journal for Quality and Participation, 22*(2), 55-57.

Chapter 2

Conceptual Linkages: An Analysis of the Organizational Learning, Collaborative Technology and Intellectual Capital Literature

Robert Neilson
National Defense University

The purpose of this chapter is threefold. First, it seeks to establish a conceptual link between three distinct bodies of literature dealing with:

(1) learning organizations,
(2) collaborative technologies also referred to as groupware, and
(3) intellectual capital.

Huber (1991) notes in his critique of the organizational learning literature that much opportunity exists for any further investigation that seeks to link these seemingly disparate bodies of literature that cover knowledge acquisition (intellectual capital), information distribution (groupware), information interpretation, and organizational memory. Second, the analysis reviews the theoretical underpinnings of aforementioned bodies of literature to ascertain the scope and breadth of the theory base behind organizational learning. Third, candidate areas for further research are explored.

The following macro- and micro-level questions raised by authors and researchers who study organizational learning and groupware technologies serve as a point of departure.

Previously Published in *Collaborative Technologies and Organizational Learning* edited by Robert Neilson, Copyright © 1997, Idea Group Publishing.

1. In an information age economy is organizational learning increasingly dependent on information technology to transfer information and knowledge (Huber 1984; Drucker, 1994)?
2. Do information age organizations need to develop and transfer intellectual material to survive (Badaracco, 1991; Peters, 1992; Drucker, 1994)?
3. Can organizations survive without continual learning (Garvin, 1993)?
4. Do collaborative technologies such as Lotus Notes (Notes) foster collaboration (Kling, 1991, 1993)?
5. How can organizations accelerate the process of converting individual learning into organizational learning (Kim, 1993)?

These structuring questions serve as focal points for a critical review of the literature. Particular attention is focused on how individual learning, knowledge, and insight is transferred to the organizational level. Within the intellectual capital literature, the focus is on capturing and transferring intellectual material. To accomplish the goals of this analysis, this section is broken into three parts. Part 1 contains the results of a content analysis of the literature.[7] Part 2 explores the theoretical bases underpinning organizational learning and technology use. Part 3 focuses on an integrated critical review of the three literature bodies. This section is organized to respond to the aforementioned questions posed in the introduction to this chapter. Also, conceptual linkages, common themes, and gaps in the literature are discussed.

PART 1—CONTENT ANALYSIS

To explore the aforementioned questions and to ascertain if conceptual links exist between the aforementioned bodies of literature, a review of the qualitative and empirical research is necessary. A content analysis was conducted to accomplish this task. A fundamental assumption underlying an analysis of the literature and the content analysis is that organizational learning is increasingly dependent on information exchange and sharing and technology use (Kling, 1991; Hendrick, 1994; Stewart, 1994; Schein, 1993; Drucker, 1994). The object of the content analysis is to ascertain if commonalities exist within the context of the articles, books and studies that comprise these respective bodies of literature. The literature is full of normative prescriptions and anecdotal references to linkages between these three bodies of literature. With the exception of Brynjolfsson's (1993) review of the related information technology and productivity literature, there is scant systematic analysis of the nexus between these literature bodies (Huber, 1990).

Why conduct a content analysis? First, content analysis is a methodology that can handle large volumes of written material, is unobtrusive, and can be validated by other researchers (U.S. GAO, 1989, p. 25). It is also systematic in nature, and its task of devising reliable and useful categories is rigorous (U.S. GAO, 1989, p. 25). Second, a content analysis can help identify conceptual linkages in seemingly disparate bodies of literature by identifying specific context units as units of analysis. Third, content analyses can systematically identify gaps in the literature. Fourth, content analysis provides a more rigorous and systematic link between the literature search and the formulation of hypotheses for further study. Prior to conducting the content analysis, it was anticipated that if commonalities exist within the groupware and intellectual capital literature, the majority of the documents would fall into a HI or MED category, representing a high or medium level of emphasis authors place on technology use, information exchange and organizational learning.[8] Context units serve as units of analysis to see if commonalities exist. For purposes of this study, the term "commonalities" must be limited to the inherent emphasis—HI, MED, and LO—authors place on the terms contained in the context units. Exploration of more finite relationships is subject to development of subsequent propositions.

RESULTS OF CONTENT ANALYSIS

The results of the content analysis are presented in two formats: (1) a series of summary tables and (2) a three-by-three matrix. The summary tables show the results of the content analysis within the confines of the respective literature bodies. The three-by-three matrix provides an integrated visual representation of the nexus of the groupware and intellectual capital literature.

The following summary tables (Tables 1-3) show the overall level of emphasis authors place on groupware and collaborative technologies, information capital, and organizational learning within the context of their respective articles and books. The term "information exchange," a more inclusive term, is used as a context unit to represent the intellectual capital literature. Correspondingly, "technology use" represents the groupware and collaborative technology literature, and the context unit "organizational learning" is self-identifying. A more complete explanation and justification of the context units are contained in Appendix A and the Findings section.

The number in the table cells is the total number of references classified as HI, MED, or LO, followed by a total of the HI and MED columns and a percentage representing the HI and MED percent of total. For example, in Table 1, a total of 13 authors highly (HI) emphasized the importance of information exchange in organizations; 2 authors moderately (MED) emphasized information exchange, and so on.

One would expect that authors categorized as intellectual capital writers would emphasize information and knowledge exchange in organizations as a primary focus. All authors either highly (HI) or moderately (MED) emphasized information exchange. There was a fairly equal relative emphasis paid to the use of technology and organizational learning. Sixty percent of the authors either highly (HI) or moderately (MED) emphasized technology use, while 67% felt that collaboration, cooperation, or sharing information as indicators of organizational learning are important.

Again, one would expect groupware authors would emphasize technology use. Twenty-one of the 23 highly (HI) referenced authors emphasized technology use in their writings, not a surprising finding. Of interest is that they also recognized that information exchange and collaboration through the sharing, networking, or transfer of information is also of relative importance. The groupware authors, as a whole, seem to give greater relative emphasis to information exchange and organizational learning as compared to writers on the subject of intellectual capital.

Organizational learning writers gave almost equal relative emphasis to organizational learning (87%) as to information exchange (93%). Surprisingly, 60 percent of the authors paid little (LO) attention to technology use in their discussions of organizational learning.

Another way of displaying the results of the content analysis is in a three-by-three matrix. The purpose of the matrix is to ascertain if one can observe clusters of data indicating a possible nexus of the groupware and intellectual capital literature.[9] The matrix presented in Figure 1, displays the groupware and intellectual capital literature in one of nine cells of a three-by-three matrix.

The groupware and collaborative literature is represented by circles and the intellectual capital literature by triangles. The numbers contained in the circles and triangles correspond to the relevant articles and books contained in the content analysis. The vertical axis is labeled "information exchange." It represents the overall relative emphasis, ranging from HI to LO, authors and researchers place on the use of *information*[10] as a critical dimension of organizational growth and survival. *Technology* use as a critical dimension of organizational growth and survival is represented on the horizontal axis.[11] Why select these dimensions as the underlying basis for the content analysis? Garvin (1993), Shrivastava (1983), Schein (1993), Argyris (1992), Kim (1993), Pinchot (1994) and others in the organizational learning field maintain that information in the form of data, knowledge, or wisdom must be transferred, by whatever means, to individuals or organizations if learning is

Table 1: Summary of Content Analysis of the Intellectual Capital Literature

Context Units	Overall Level of Emphasis				
	(a) HI	b) MED	(c) LO	(a+b) HI+MED	% HI-MED
Information Exchange	13	2	0	15	100
Technology Use	5	4	6	9	60
Organizational Learning	5	5	5	10	67
n=15					

Table 2: Summary of Content Analysis of the Groupware Literature

Context Units	Overall Level of Emphasis				
	(a) HI	b) MED	(c) LO	(a+b) HI+MED	% HI-MED
Information Exchange	10	10	3	20	87
Technology Use	21	2	0	23	100
Organizational Learning	10	9	4	19	83
n=23					

to occur. In simple terms, information is primary grist for learning. Correspondingly, the means of information transference is also a critical dimension (Huber, 1991). It is captured in the term "technology." The term "technology" was chosen because it, too, is an underlying premise of authors who write about groupware and collaborative technologies as key components in information age organizations (Lou, 1994; Kling, 1993; Orlikowski, 1992; Orlikowski and Gash, 1994; Engelbart, 1992). Use of technology to transfer information is a critical component of many knowledge-based organizations, especially in the public sector where information is the only product or service of many agencies and departments (Osborne & Gaebler, 1992).

Table 3: Summary of Content Analysis of the Organizational Learning Literature

Context Units	Overall Level of Emphasis				
	(a) HI	b) MED	(c) LO	(a+b) HI+MED	% HI-MED
Information Exchange	7	7	1	14	93
Technology Use	3	3	9	6	40
Organizational Learning	9	4	2	13	87
n=15					

Figure 1: Nexus of the Groupware and Intellectual Capital Literature*

Technology Use

	HI	MED	LOW
	I	**II**	**III**
HI	③⑥⑧⑪⑯⑰ ⑱⑲⑳ ▲11 ▲12 ▲13 ▲14	⑮ ▲2 ▲3 ▲5 ▲9	▲1 ▲4 ▲6 ▲10 ▲15
	IV	**V**	**VI**
MED	①②④⑤⑦⑩ ⑫⑬㉒ ▲7	⑨	▲8
	VII	**VIII**	**IX**
LOW	⑭㉑㉓		

● - Groupware literature n = 23
▲ - Intellectual capital literature n = 15

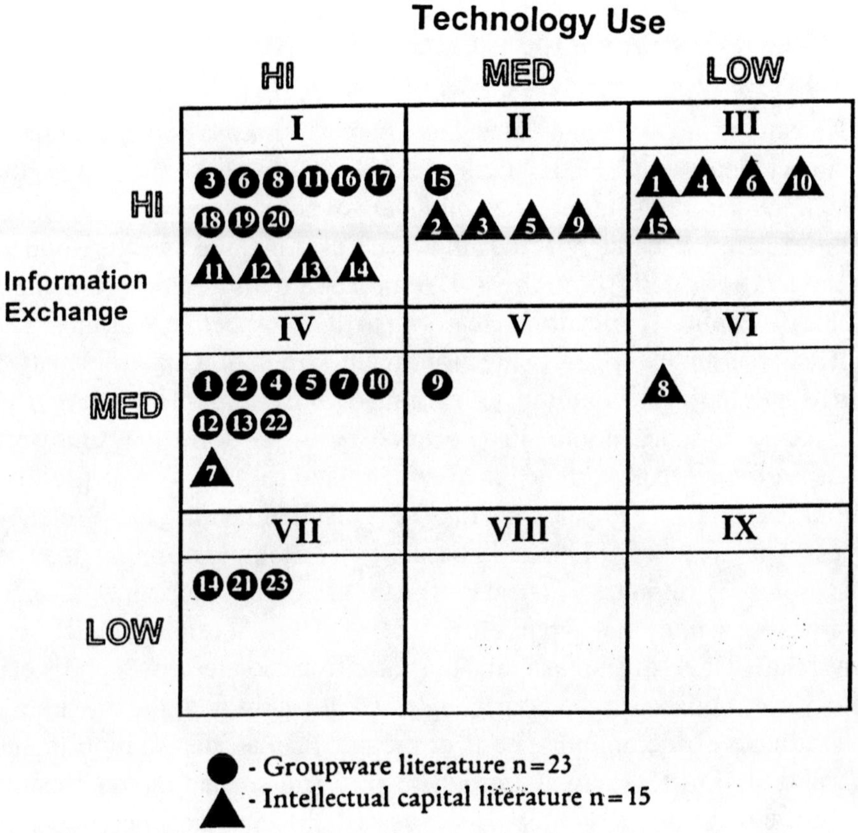

Arraying the results of the content analysis in a matrix provides a visual picture of what commonalities, within the limitations of the context units, exist in the groupware and intellectual capital literature. Again, the context units serve as units of analyses to see if commonalities exist. Of the 38 groupware and intellectual capital articles and books arrayed in the matrix, 29 or 76 percent of the documents reviewed were classified as MED-HI on both the technology use and information exchange dimensions. From a visual perspective, one can observe clusters in cells I, II, and IV indicating that the bulk of the groupware and intellectual capital authors place a medium to high level of emphasis on both of these dimensions. Besides the outliers in cells

III and VIII that ranked highly (HI) on only one dimension, it is significant to note only 2 of the references appeared in cells V, VI, VIII, or IX indicating a moderate (MED) or low (LO) level of emphasis.

FINDINGS: ANSWERING THE "SO WHAT?" QUESTION

The content analysis indicates that there is at least some degree of interconnectedness between the literature bodies. With the exception of the organizational learning authors' seeming lack of emphasis on technology to share information, a majority of the authors across the three literature bodies either moderately (MED) or highly (HI) emphasized information exchange, technology use, and organizational learning in their respective writings. The content analysis lends support to the aforementioned notion that information exchange and sharing is important to learning organizations. However, there is little support for the notion that technology in the form of groupware products is of relative importance to organizational learning. These preliminary findings could possibly be a result of several phenomena: (1) the relative "newness" of groupware and collaborative technologies applications in organizations; (2) the paucity of research on the effects of groupware products on organizations; and (3) a gap in the literature. Viewed through a different lens, the relative level of emphasis and purported interconnectedness between these literature bodies is, metaphorically speaking, similar to the movement of an Alexander Calder mobile. Parts of the mobile may start in motion, but it may take time for the remaining oddly sized and shaped interconnected objects to start moving. Perhaps, because of the relative "newness" of groupware technologies, the groupware part of the mobile may not have "started moving" in the eyes of the organizational learning theorists.

In sum, this content analysis provides: (1) a source of quantifiable data that can be corroborated with qualitative data gleaned from additional case study investigation; (2) a starting point for a critical analysis of the literature; and (3) a basis to go beyond the all-too-often-cited normative prescriptions and anecdotal descriptions prevalent in these literature bodies.

PART 2—THEORETICAL BASES

Many of the articles contained no theoretical bases and, therefore, were not included in this section. This subsection is limited to the organizational learning literature. A succinct synthesis of the theoretical bases underpinning organizational learning concludes Part 2.

Introduction To Theoretical Bases

There is no one complete theory of organizational learning. Also, there is little agreement among researchers on the specific theoretical issues underlying organizational learning. Current discussion of the theoretical bases underlying organizational learning and technology use ranges widely. Theories examined in this section of the literature review include: double loop learning theory (Argyris, 1977, 1992, 1994), expectancy theory (Snead & Harrell, 1994; Orlikowski & Gash, 1994), push-pull theory (Zmud, 1984), systems theory (Huber, 1984), contingency theory (Gutek, 1990; Huber, 1984), coordination theory (Malone & Crowston, 1994), rational, power and politics (Levine & Rossmore, 1993), punctuated equilibrium theory (Gersick, 1988, 1991; Mason, 1993; Romanelli & Tushman, 1994), optimal curve theory (Dorroh, Gulledge & Womer, 1994), feedback theory (Stata, 1989), and experience curve theory (Stata, 1989).

Double Loop Learning Theory

Argyris (1972, 1992, 1994) classifies much of organizational life as a learning challenge. Organizational learning is a process of detecting and correcting errors (Argyris, 1977). Error is any feature of knowledge that inhibits learning. Argyris further classifies the type of learning that organizations undertake in response to error detection. Single loop learning involves simple correction of errors when existing policies enable organizations to continue to meet objectives. Double loop learning extends notions of simple error detection and correction to challenge organizational members to assess the fundamental basis for actions, decisions or policies. Argyris uses the example of a thermostat to explain single and double loop learning. Single loop learning occurs when a thermostat turns on a heating system to satisfy a predetermined heat setting—simple error and correction. Double loop learning involves examining the underlying basis behind the entire heating system. Using the example of the thermostat, a more fundamental double loop approach to the heating deficiency situation would involve asking questions such as: Should we replace our furnace with a heat pump, so we can get heating and cooling with one system? Double loop learning goes beyond notions of simple error detection and correction and prompts decision makers to ask fundamental questions about decisions, actions, or policies beyond simple facts.

Argyris' (1977, 1992, 1994) discussion focuses attention at the macro level of organizational learning theory. It is a global approach to understanding how organizations learn. Missing from Argyris' discussion is understanding of how individuals and organizational leaders know when to employ single and double learning theories. His Model I, theories of action, and Model II, theories in use, attempt to give practitioners some guideposts on what organizational learning strategies to employ; but they suffer from an overly complex knowledge base. To bridge the gap between organizational learning theory and practice, practitioners need simple "rules of thumb" to ascertain whether they need to simply correct errors or fundamentally change organizational practices. Argyris' works establish academic and research bases for organizational learning theory development. Those works do little to provide guideposts to practitioners to ascertain whether their organizations have "learning disabilities."

Organizational Learning Typology

Capitalizing on research by Cyert and March (1963) and Argyris (1977), Shrivastava's typology of organizational learning systems sets a stage for new thinking about the theoretical roots of organizational learning. Shrivastava's (1983) typology was a first step in developing accurate descriptions of learning situations in organizations. He classifies organizational learning as: (1) adaption, (2) assumption sharing, (3) developing knowledge of action-outcome relationships, and (4) institutionalized experience (p. 9). Subsequent research capitalized on Shrivastava's typology. For example, Shrivastava's and Argyris and Schon's notions of organizational learning as assumption sharing and adaptive learning are reflected in Senge's (1990) and Stata's (1989) concept of shared insights and mental models. Garvin (1993) incorporates the concept of developing knowledge of action-outcome relationships into his definition of organizational learning by adding to his definition an action orientation in the form of creating, acquiring and transferring knowledge.

Push-Pull Theory

Push-pull theory, as used by Zmud (1984) to explain process innovation in knowledge work, focuses on technology use in organizations.[12] One of the major issues in this case study is to ascertain what role technology plays in transferring learning from individual to organizational levels. Zmud also examines three separate literatures (organizational science, engineering management, and management science) to ascertain if push-pull theory explains the success or failure of technology interventions to effect change and learning. Zmud puts forth a series of hypotheses to generate insight into notions that: "'Need-pull' innovations have been found to be characterized by higher probabilities of commercial success than have 'technology-pull inno-vations'" (1984, p. 728). Although not all of the hypotheses were supported in his research, Zmud's empirical work lends support to this study in the following areas: (1) a multi-disciplinary approach provides greater insight into the role of technology in effecting change and learning (Snead & Harrell, 1994); (2) preparing organizations for the introduction of technology can be characterized as a learning challenge; and (3) top management's attitude towards technology introduction is similar to top management's commitment to learning.

Coordination Theory

Malone and Crowston's (1994) interdisciplinary study of coordination lends support to the theoretical underpinning and conceptual linkages be-tween cooperative work tools (groupware) and managing shared resources (organizational learning). Coordination theory refers to theories about how coordination can occur in diverse kinds of systems (Malone & Crowston, 1994). Further refined, coordination theory is a process of managing dependencies among activities. Managing dependencies associated with sharing intellectual material through use of groupware products is applicable to the study of organizational learning in determining potential behavioral incentives to foster the sharing of individual learning with others. Snead and Harrell's (1994) discussion of expectancy theory in the context of a manager's intention to use a decision support system adds an additional psychological dimension linking an individual's intention to subsequent behavior. Relating expectancy theory to the study of expected gains of groupware use to foster organizational learning may prove fertile theoretical ground for exploration.

Punctuated Equilibrium

Punctuated equilibrium theory maintains that there is an alternation between long periods of stable organizational behavior permitting only incremental adaptions and brief periods of revolutionary upheaval where transformational change is possible (Gersick, 1991). If one ascribes to the belief that learning is a change in behavior, then one must focus on change processes (Argyris, 1977). Introducing Lotus Notes into an organization is a change. Notes has the potential to fundamentally alter social structures, formal and informal power relationships, and group subcultures. Change characterized as punctuated equilibrium may help explain the potential organizational upheavals and the influence of Notes on learning patterns at the individual and organizational levels (Mason, 1993). Romanelli and Tushman

(1994), in a study of the U.S. minicomputer producers, found that rapid and discontinuous change over all organizational activities produced fundamental transformations, while small changes in structures, strategies, and power relationships did not engender fundamental change. The significance of this finding may have implications for Notes implementation strategies. If Notes is implemented in an organization simply as a technological investment over time, it may be viewed as an incremental adaptation. If Notes is implemented rapidly coupled with overarching business strategy that affects all sectors of an organization, it may be viewed as an organizational transformation agent, thereby increasing the potential for collaboration and fundamental change in individual and organizational learning behavior.

Technological Frames

Building on the socio-cognitive literature, Orlikowski and Gash (1994) introduce a new approach to building emergent theory about information technology use in organizations. They suggest that "technological frames" are central to understanding technology use in organizations. Technological frames are sets of assumptions, expectations, and knowledge of technology which shape subsequent actions towards it (Orlikowski & Gash, 1994, p. 125). Different groups, users, managers, and technologists may have different views on the expectations of technology's use. Orlikowski and Gash suggest that where technological frames of key groups are significantly different, difficulty and conflict may result around its use and desired effects (1994).

Expectancy Theory

Orlikowski and Gash's concept of technological frames is anchored in expectancy theory (Snead & Harrell 1994). Matching various groups' expectations to the introduction of groupware technology may have a profound effect on their eventual satisfaction with the technology. Orlikowski and Gash's concept of technological frames coupled with Snead and Harrell's (1994) application of expectancy theory provide bases for hypothesis development regarding the relationship between groupware as a knowledge transfer mechanism from individuals to the organizational level.

Optimal Control and Systems Theory

Learning is often perceived as an end-product of production processes. Grounded in optimal control theory, Dorroh, Gulledge, and Womer (1994) assert that investments in knowledge generation early in programs is more valuable than the same investment late in programs. Coupled with Stata's

(1989) rejection of experience curve theory, investments in knowledge generation and learning early in processes at the individual and organizational levels may enhance overall individual and organizational learning.[13] Stata (1989), Senge (1990) and Thach and Woodman (1994) ground their discussions of organizational learning in systems theory, also known as systems thinking. As applied to the study of organizational learning, systems approaches encourage managers to analyze inputs and outputs from a holistic perspective including processes, organizational and reward structures, relationships between people, and boundaries, as well as technical issues. The holistic systems approach is a clear departure from reductionist philosophy which involves breaking down phenomena into their smallest parts. In the case of organizational learning, a reductionist approach may result in a misrepresentation or oversimplification of the complexities of human interaction in learning processes (Levine & Rossmore, 1993). Holistic systems thinkers add a new lens to the organizational learning theory debate by attempting to define the boundaries and interrelationships between the pieces of a complex jigsaw puzzle rather than focus on the size and shape of specific pieces. Irrespective of theoretical bases used, Dorroh, Gulledge, and Womer (1994), Stata (1989) and Senge (1990) advocate that the time to invest in knowledge generation is at the beginning of developmental processes; and they reject notions of on-the-job training. The significance of this finding has a direct bearing on this research in developing hypotheses regarding the timing of groupware training to foster the transfer of intellectual material to organizational levels.

Causal Agency Theory

Markus and Robey (1988) discuss causal structures found in theories about the relationship between information technology and organizational change. Specifically, they focus on causal agency theory as it applies to information technology's purported role in effecting organizational change.[14] What they find in their survey of the theoretical bases includes:

1. Mixed levels of analysis to explore interplay between individuals, technology, and organizations are a preferred method of analysis. Too often research methods are selected to meet the parameters of a predetermined theoretical approach.

2. Ethnographic research methods, i.e., case studies, are better suited to emergent theory generation versus survey research (Markus & Robey, 1988, p. 596).

Markus and Robey's (1988) contribution to organizational learning research is twofold. First, they emphasize the difficulty of determining causality in social science research, especially where multiple units of are involved. By the very nature of the subject matter, organizational learning researchers must also deal with multiple units of analyses—individuals and organizations. Second, Markus and Robey (1988) lend support to the case study method of analysis. Case studies provide greater understanding about the macro relationship between variables from a holistic perspective as opposed to focusing on issues of causality between selected variables representing a microcosm of the phenomena under study. Hence, the "big picture" is lost which may serve to obfuscate the further understanding.

Synthesis of Theoretical Bases

Synthesizing the discussion of the theoretical bases yields the following insights: (1) organizational learning is multi-disciplinary in character employing varying theoretical frames of analysis; (2) no one theory explains organizational learning and the effects of technology on organizational learning; (3) reliance on one theoretical frame (expectancy, coordination, systems, causal agency, or others) is too limiting; (4) the theoretical bases behind organizational learning are an eclectic grouping that add robustness to the study of organizational learning, yet frustrates the researchers' search for singularity in theoretical understanding; and (5) action science in the form of ethnographic research or case studies is probably a preferred method of inquiry to produce knowledge which contributes to practice prescriptions about organizational learning.

PART 3—CRITICAL ANALYSIS OF THE LITERATURE

The introduction to this chapter begins by posing five questions about the nature of organizational learning and technology use. The sequence in which these questions are posed is significant. Question 1 starts with a macro perspective on organizational learning and technology use as it relates to the overall economy. Question 5 finishes with a micro perspective focusing on learning at the organizational level—the focus of this study. This section is organized to respond to these questions with a specific goal of gaining insight into: (1) use of interventions over time to accelerate processes of converting individual learning and knowledge into organizational learning and (2) indicators of organizational learning. The five questions are:

1. In an information age economy are organizations increasingly dependent on information technology to transfer information and knowledge (Huber, 1984; Drucker, 1994)?
2. Do information age organizations need to develop and transfer intellectual material to survive (Badaracco, 1991; Peters, 1994; Drucker, 1994)?
3. Can organizations survive without continual learning (Garvin, 1993)?
4. Do collaborative technologies foster collaboration (Kling, 1991, 1993)?
5. How can organizations accelerate the process of converting individual learning into organizational learning (Kim, 1993)?

Discussion in response to each question pulls from each of the three literature bodies to further identify commonalities and differences in the response to these questions. Insight gained from a critical review provides a foundation for framing key questions or propositions for further research.

1. In an information age economy are organizations increasingly dependent on information technology to transfer information and knowledge (Huber, 1984; Drucker, 1994)?

The next wave of economic growth is going to come from knowledge-based businesses. The U.S. Department of Commerce (1994) estimates that organizations that collect, analyze, disseminate, or add value to information represent 15% of the Gross National Product (GNP). The information industry, as defined by the U.S. Department of Commerce, is growing at a rate of between 12-25% per year.[15] Based on an average growth rate of 18% per annum, information-based service providers, value-added producers of information products and services, computer equipment manufacturers, software developers, and telecommunications firms will account for 20-24% of the GNP by the year 2000. U.S. industry now spends more on computers and communications equipment than on all other capital equipment combined (Huey, 1994). The General Services Administration (1989) estimates that 85% of all government work is information-based. Additionally, in an era of decreasing federal budgets, expenditures for information technology and information resources management has remained relatively constant ranging from 3-7% of federal agencies' budgets. The introductory statement to this paragraph, coupled with the aforementioned statistics, paint a picture of a third wave economy based on knowledge and information (Toffler, 1980, 1990).

If the economy and government are increasingly knowledge-based and if knowledge-based organizations are increasingly reliant on information technology to transfer information and knowledge, it follows that accelerating knowledge transfer from individual to individual, from individuals to groups, from individuals to organizations, and eventually to customers or citizens is beneficial.[16] Examining what economists, business consultants, organizational developers, and contemporary writers say about organizational knowledge as an engine of economic growth may provide insight into whether organizations are dependent on IT as a means to transfer information and knowledge.

Knowledge acquisition has its roots in economic theory. Economists Schultz (1971), Machlup (1984) and Becker (1993) are credited with advancing the theory of human capital from classical economic theory based on analytic reasoning to a modern stage based in empirical research. Much is now known about the effects of knowledge acquisition on earnings, employment, unemployment, training, and occupations (Becker, 1993). Human capital is now recognized as an integral part of economic theory (Schultz, 1971; Machlup, 1984; Becker, 1993). What is unknown is how human capital is used at the organizational level.

For purposes of this study, the concept of human capital anchors notions of knowledge acquisition in macro economic theory. It is also recognized as a key component of economic growth and productivity. Economists recognize that human capital is critical to information age organizations. What they fail to address is how to capture, amass, store, and leverage the accumulated stock of knowledge in organizations to create additional physical or intellectual assets. Recognizing a phenomenon exists is important. Doing something with it is the next crucial step in bridging the theory-practice dichotomy.

Crawford (1991) and Hudson (1993) advance the concept of human capital as a macroeconomic theory to the microeconomic level. Both authors offer management prescriptions that rest on the premise that increased organizational competence is the result of more intellectual capital. Hudson defines intellectual capital as a combination of genetic inheritance, education, experience, and attitude about life and business (Hudson, 1993, p. 16). Hudson's definition goes beyond notions of intellectual capital as an individual phenomenon to ground his discussion of intellectual capital as an organizational phenomenon influence by organizational systems and culture. Klein and Prusak (1994) define intellectual capital "operationally as intellectual material that has been formalized, captured, and leveraged to produce a higher level asset" (p. 2). By providing a working definition that goes beyond

Hudson's emphasis on genetic inheritance, Klein and Prusak set the stage for further research in managing intellectual capital effectively (1994). They have pushed the process of bridging the theory-practice dichotomy in response to their recognition that organizations are increasingly competing on the basis of intellectual resources (Klein & Prusak, 1994, p. 1).

Benjamin and Levinson (1993), Huey (1994), Kirkpatrick (1993), Stewart (1994), and Zuboff (1988) emphasize that "informating" (Zuboff, 1988) organizations to permit IT-enabled change is a common characteristic of information age organizations. Verifone, an international credit verification firm, relies on IT to manage its business operations. The only reason they have a home office is because of Security and Exchange Commission (SEC) requirements. Verifone is a virtual corporation relying solely on an IT backbone to run its day-to-day business. "Thomas," an on-line, publicly run, information access and retrieval system for Congressional testimony via Internet, is another example of how IT has "informated" the fiber and fabric of public and private organizations.

McKinnon and Bruns (1992) takes a counter view citing research that finds that even though there is an overabundance of information proliferating through information systems, we still are not certain what information managers use to make decisions. Much of the literature cited here concentrates on access and retrieval of information and knowledge enabled by IT— a common characteristic of information age public and private organizations. Conspicuously missing is a discussion of collaboration as a regenerative source of ideas and intellectual capital. Ideas generated through iterative collaborative processes are the source of innovation that will advance organizations to learn, change, and excel (McGregor, 1960; Menon, 1993; Stewart, 1994). Grand strategies or simply accelerating transmission of increasing amounts of information contribute little added value to information-based products or knowledge.

Crawford (1991) provides a schema for examining the characteristics of knowledge. Table 4 encapsulates Crawford's listing of macroeconomic properties of knowledge. The neighboring column expands the implications of these characteristics from the macro level to the micro level providing insight for further research and discussion. Missing from Crawford's (1991) list is the notion that information and knowledge have value. Information and knowledge are not free (Machlup, 1980). Therefore, "valuable" should be added to Crawford's list of knowledge characteristics (Monk, 1989; Porat, 1977).

In sum, knowledge, although hard to measure, is increasingly recognized as a factor of production along with the traditional factors of land, labor, and capital. As a critical factor of production, it must be managed as an organizational asset. Additionally, the literature supports the supposition that information age organizations are increasingly dependent on IT for the transfer of knowledge and information (Badaracco, 1991; Drucker, 1994; Hamel & Prahalad, 1994; Quinn, 1992; Pinchot & Pinchot, 1994; Schrage, 1990). Simply transferring information at accelerated speeds, however, does not automatically augment or add value to knowledge-based products (Schrage, 1990).

2. Do information age organizations need to develop and transfer intellectual material to survive (Badaracco, 1991; Peters, 1992; Drucker, 1994)?

It is becoming widely recognized that organizations increasingly compete on the basis of their intellectual resources. Just as firms leverage financial, human, and physical capital to create value and wealth, "intellectual capital" likewise has come to represent an essential asset. . . . (Klein & Prusak, 1994).

Question 2 moves the discussion from the importance of information, knowledge, and technology at the macroeconomic level to the organizational or micro level. A fundamental assumption underlying this question is that intellectual material in the form of information, knowledge, ideas, experience, patents, and other intellectual property is a valued organizational asset (Marchand & Horton, 1986; Morin, 1994; OMB Circular A-130). Like good wine, intellectual material is best enjoyed if shared with colleagues. Unlike wine, which once consumed is gone, intellectual material is expandable, self-generating, and transportable for consumption and regeneration by others.[17]
James Bryant Quinn (1992) moves the discussion of intellectual material beyond notions based in economics and calls for a new paradigm about the way managers, leaders, and policymakers think about intellectual material in the form of knowledge-based activities. The focus of his case study research is on managing intellect (Quinn, 1992, p. 3). New metrics are needed and "no one yet has a complete fix on precisely what the new metrics are. . . ." (Quinn, 1992, p. 439). Like the private sector, the public sector needs new measures of organizational intellect. Why measure organizational intellect? According to Quinn (1993), three-fourths of an organization's value derives

from knowledge.[18]   The federal government is also a knowledge-based industry (GSA, 1989). Federal agencies collect, analyze, provide, and use information as primary source material.

To illustrate commonalities between the public and private sectors' fundamental reliance on knowledge and intellect, a list of Quinn's research results are displayed in the left column in Table 5. Arrayed next to Quinn's research results are public sector corollaries developed by the author of this study.

A comparison of both columns reveals striking similarities in the nature of knowledge work in both sectors. Both sectors are: (1) increasingly knowledge-based, (2) reevaluating core missions, (3) focusing on developing intellectual capital, (4) increasingly boundaryless, and (5) eliminating non-value added activities and processes. Quinn (1992) lends additional support that organizations are increasingly knowledged-based but is silent on the issue of knowledge transfer as a matter of organizational survival.

Klein and Prusak (1994) and Schrage (1990) address the issue of intellectual material transfer as an element of organizational survival. The term "transfer" implies moving. Moving intellectual material does little to add value to information-based products or services. Klein and Prusak, and Schrage ground their respective normative prescriptions on the idea that organizations must go beyond simple information transfer processes to survive and prosper. Adding value at each step in value chains is the goal. Leveraging, transforming, embellishing, sharing, and collaborating are terms that add value or an outcome orientation to simple notions of information transfer. These terms embrace and operationalize value chain concepts.

Without outright reference to it, the National Performance Review embraces the concept of value chains under the term "re-engineering." The object is to eliminate non-value added activities or people in processes as information moves along value chains. Business process re-engineering programs have been the rage of both the public and private sectors (Hammer & Champy, 1993). Re-engineering, as a management tool, has captured the attention of public and private officials alike. Results, however, have been mixed (Champy, 1995). Recent research by Champy, a pioneer in the re-engineering movement, reveals that simply changing or eliminating non-value-added processes does not guarantee success. Re-engineering does not account for the human side of management (McGregor, 1960). Organizational culture, reward systems, leadership, empowerment, and motivational interventions are integral parts of change efforts. Radical change is impossible unless managers know how to organize, inspire, deploy, enable, measure, and reward value-adding work (Champy, 1995). Champy's findings have public sector implications.

NPR initiatives may be in trouble if there is an over-reliance on structural interventions, e.g., re-engineering, at the expense of human interventions. This discussion of the reengineering movement illustrates the principle that over-reliance on structural interventions, e.g., transferring information and knowledge at accelerated speeds through automated networks, does not guarantee that organizations will learn, change, or do something new. The terms "leveraging," "transforming," "embellishing," "sharing," and "collaborating," explicitly and implicitly indicate that human intervention has entered into value chains. To add another dimension to the re-engineering discussion, one can reframe re-engineering efforts as a learning issue. Sole reliance on structural interventions is similar to single loop learning—finding and correcting errors. Examining root causes and assessing fundamental bases for actions, decisions, or policies by incorporating structural and human interventions can also be characterized as double loop learning (Argyris, 1977, 1992, 1994).

In addition, one can make a parallel argument about the issue of transferring intellectual material as a matter of organizational survival. As Champy (1995), Galegher & Kraut (1990), Locke (1992), and Pinchot &

Table 4: Characteristics of Knowledge in an Information-Based Economy: Implications for Further Research

Knowledge Characteristics	Implication for Research
Expandable and self-generating	Notions of spontaneous knowledge application development may be facilitated by using Lotus Notes
Substitutable	Knowledge can replace land, labor, and capital (traditional elements of economics) as a factor of production.
Transportable	Use of IT provides a backbone for information exchange establishing a knowledge base for collaboration.
Shareable	Collaboration and the use of collaboration technologies permit expanded sharing of knowledge and information beyond face-to-face communications.
Perishable	Sustainable advantage of knowledge and information is short lived. Information and knowledge must therefore be shared quickly and broadly or it may diminish in value.

Pinchot (1994) have discovered, transferring intellectual material between individuals, groups, and within and among organizations does not ensure success. Simply transferring intellectual material is a techno-utopist approach.[19] As expectancy theory indicates, an intervention's chance of success is greater if expectations of groups, users, managers, and technologists are congruent.   Congruence implies human intervention to reach consensus. Sharing, leveraging, and collaborating through human intervention expands the notion of transfer to a higher level value-added activity.

3. Can organizations survive without continual learning (Garvin, 1993)?

The framing of this question specifically orients the reader to focus on the relationship between learning and organizational survival. Saint-Onge (1992) makes a key distinction between an organization of learners and organizational learning.   An organization of learners is a collection of individuals who take ownership for their own development and learning on a self-directed basis. A learning organization has the capability of capturing learning in its different paths and incorporating that learning into the organizational knowledge base to generate new knowledge (Saint-Onge, 1992, p. 41). McGill and Slocum (1993) differentiate between four kinds of organizational learning: (1) the knowing organization, (2) the understanding organization, (3) the thinking organization, and (4) the learning organization.[20] Schein (1993) grounds his discussion of organizational learning in the concept of dialogue. Schein's contribution focuses on the importance of dialogue and organizational culture as central elements in organizational transformation and survival. Dialogue at the executive level is not enough for a learning organization to occur (Schein, 1993). Schein foresees the importance of "communication technology" as a means for dealing with clashes between subcultures in organizations (p. 40).   He is making an implicit justification for groupware use as a means to foster dialogue across organizational boundaries and levels. Garvin (1993) characterizes organizational learning as a continual search for new ideas. Learning organizations must be skilled at: (1) systematic problem-solving, (2) experimentation with new approaches, (3) learning from experiences, past history, and best practices, and (4) transferring knowledge quickly and efficiently throughout the organization (Garvin, 1993, p. 81).

The key point of discussion is that exploring the relationship between organizational survival and learning is a complex issue—no longer characterized in traditional learning terminology. Learning as a generic term no longer conveys the scope, depth, and breadth of learning activities needed for organizational survival. A more sophisticated vocabulary describing kinds of learning is needed to engender greater understanding of the linkage between learning and organizational survival. A common theme running through the works of the authors cited here is that the type of learning needed for organizational survival must extend beyond simple error detection and correction efforts. Irrespective of discipline, authors cited in this section advocate asking fundamental questions about organizational decisions, actions, and policies beyond simple facts as the type of learning needed for survival. In other words, Argyris' (1977) double loop learning theory provides a solid theoretical foundation for much of the discussion about organizational learning. Mason (1993) further characterizes the type of learning needed for organizational survival as strategic learning:

> ...Strategic learning is the process by which an organization makes sense of its environment in ways that broaden the range of objectives it can pursue or the range of resources and actions available to it for pursuing these objectives (p. 843).

Organizational survival in an information-based economy is increasingly characterized as a learning issue (Kim, 1993; Kofman & Senge, 1993; McGill & Slocum, 1993; Sullivan, 1991). As organizations become increasingly knowledge-intensive, learning, training, and development is no longer a luxury; it is how organizations discover the future and ensure survival.

4. Do collaborative technologies foster collaboration (Kling, 1991, 1993)?

Collaboration is the process of shared creation involving two or more individuals interacting to create shared understanding where none had existed or could have on its own (Schrage, 1990, p. 40). To collaborate is to work in a joint intellectual effort. Partitioning problem solving to produce a synergy such that the performance of the whole system exceeds that of any individual contributor is the essence of collaboration (Bird & Kasper, 1993). Collaborative technologies are automated tools that provide a means for collaboration. Expanding these concepts of collaboration and the successful use of collaborative technologies is based on a series of assumptions, including:[21]

1. For complex problems requiring many skills and operations, groups outperform their best member because problem-solving skills and knowl-

edge are beyond those of any one member (Bird & Kasper, 1993; Russo & Shumaker 1989).

2. Working in task oriented teams and sharing knowledge are critical elements of success (Katzenbach & Smith, 1993; Manzi, 1994).

3. Work group technology creates new opportunities for teams, organizations, and supra organizations that span boundaries (Rothstein, 1994).

4. Effective communication is a prerequisite for coordination and collaboration (Lou, 1994).

5. Work group computing plays a pivotal role in leveraging knowledge and expertise in a rapidly changing environment (Klein & Prusak, 1994; Manzi, 1994).

But how does one measure collaboration and collaborative technology's role in fostering collaboration? Measuring collaboration does not lend itself to traditional metrics. Much of the preliminary research on collaboration focuses on the technological aspects of collaborative technologies at the expense of the organizational, human, or business aspects (Coleman, 1994; Dennis et al., 1988; Gessner, McNeilly & Leskee, 1994; Kling, 1991; Mason, 1993; Orlikowski, 1992; Radosevich, 1994; Rothstein, 1994). Traditional information systems development methodologies emphasize that there is a greater chance of successful information system implementation if one uses IT applications as a means to solve identified business problems (Brynjolfsson, 1993).

Preliminary research results indicate that Lotus Notes implementation may not have lived up to expectations, because it was viewed as an automated "means" looking for a problem (Grudin, 1994; Held, Hurley & Piesner, 1994; Keselica, 1994; King, 1994; Orlikowski, 1992). The aim of Notes is to enable collaboration between people, regardless of their physical location or time zone (Lotus Notes, 1993). It "democratizes" information access rendering traditional structures meaningless. In Taylor-like organizations, Notes implementation wreaks havoc with command and control Weberian hierarchies. In information heterarchies, Notes provides a means for any-time and any-place access to information. Notes success is dependent on: (1) management commitment to implementation, (2) an IT infrastructure that permits information sharing across locations, and (3) users committed to work in ways much of which focus on group work (Johansen et al., 1991; Katzenbach & Smith, 1993; Lotus Notes, 1993). Notes may work well in Theory Y organizations, but fail miserably in Theory X organizations (Lou, 1994; McGregor, 1960).

Orlinkowski's (1992) exploratory case study of a Fortune 500 company's experience with Notes investigates whether and how collaborative technologies change the nature of work and the pattern of social interaction in an office environment, including intended and unintended consequences. Her findings include:

> ...When confronted with a new technology, individuals try to understand it in terms of their existing technological frames, often augmenting these frames to accommodate special aspects of the technology. How they change their technological frames is influenced by: (1) the kind and amount of information about the product communicated to them, and (2) the nature and the form of training.

Orlinkowski's contribution to the study of collaborative technology implementation focuses on her recognition of: (1) cognitive elements including mental models or frames people use to evaluate Notes, and (2) structural elements including reward systems, work practices, policies, and organizational norms.

In an empirically-based study of user satisfaction with Notes, Lou (1994) finds that Notes use is contextual; and users' reaction to Notes implementation may depend on how Notes is implemented and used in particular organizational contexts. Future studies, according to Lou (1994), should address individual and organizational aspects of Notes implementation, including: (1) factors that have been proposed to explain individuals' adoption, use, and assessment of Notes, (2) strategies to implement Notes, and (3) organizational structure and culture elements that influence how Notes is implemented and used.

Orlinkowski (1992) also calls for additional research on strategies to implement Notes. One strategy would be to deploy Notes anticipating that through experimentation and use over time, creative ideas, innovations, and applications would flourish. A second strategy would be to prototype Notes in a representative group within the organization with the intent of solving a specific business problem requiring collaboration. The first strategy represents a techno-utopian approach, while the second approach represents a traditional systems implementation approach. A third strategy would be to deploy the technology accompanied by a series of interventions or requirements to use Notes. The third strategy is a hybrid of the first two. It combines the techno-utopist orientation of the first approach coupled with interventions that require Notes use to address specific organizational requirements. To

Table 5: Public and Private Sector Reliance on Knowledge and Intellect: A Comparison

Quinn's Private Sector Research Results	Public Sector Corollaries
1. Intellectual activities now occupy critical spots in most companies' value chains regardless of whether the company is in the services or manufacturing sector.	1. Intellectual activities in the form of knowledge-based work now occupy critical spots in federal agency's value chains regardless of agency mission.
2. If one is not the best in the world at a critical activity, the company is sacrificing competitive advantage by performing that activity internally or with existing techniques.	2. If an activity is not supporting the agency's mission and the agency is expending resources to conduct that activity, contract out that function if not prohibited by law.
3. Each company should focus its strategic investments and management action on those core competencies, usually intellectual activities, where it can achieve "best in the world" status and long term advantage.	3. Each agency should focus its strategic investments (R&D, human capital, IT infrastructure) on its core competencies, usually intellectual activities, to better serve internal and external customers (citizens).
4. The scale, specialized activities, and efficiencies of outside service entities have so changed industry boundaries that vertical integration is no longer desirable	4. Boundaries between federal agencies are blurring requiring more intra and interagency coordination and collaboration.
5. All the foregoing necessitate a reevaluation of agency roles and missions; a reinventing of government	5. All the foregoing thoughts necessitate a redefinition of what constitutes a truly focused company.
6. Strategically approached, this approach does not "hollow out" a corporation. It decreases internal bureaucracies, flattens organizations, heightens strategic focus and improves competitive responsiveness.	6. Strategically approached, this approach does not "hollow out" government. It decreases internal bureaucracies, flattens organizations, heightens agency focus and improves service delivery.

date, there is a paucity of qualitative or quantitative research that explore these implementation strategies.

Bird and Kasper's (1993) research in collaborative systems focuses on identifying problem characteristics that are amenable to collaborative problem solving. They conclude that "collaboration is most effective in discrete problem-solving domains where the problem is decomposable into dynamic parallel subgroups and requires multiple domains of expertise" (Bird &

Kasper, 1993, pp. 278-279). Bird and Kasper's (1993) findings provide: (1) grist for further research, and (2) a typology of problem characteristics that may help explain why specific Notes applications have not met expectations.

Additional studies address traditional business indicators of success. Gaffin (1994a, 1994b) and Radosevich (1994a, 1994b) look at Notes through a return on investment (ROI) lens. Overall, they find a 179% ROI with an average payback period of 2.4 years. Radosevich (1994b) qualifies the ROI findings indicating that payback was attributed to completing projects and solving problems—single loop learning. Lotus Notes, however, is falling short on promises to act as a collaborative tool—acting as double loop learning agent. Perhaps, ROI should be recast to reflect information-age thinking and redefined as "return on intellect" (Software for a New Age, 1994). Return on intellect acts as an indicator of knowledge-based work in an increasingly information-intensive interdependent work environment. Return on investment does little to capture the notion that organizations will succeed or fail based on a continuous supply of new ideas.

Much of the research on Lotus Notes as a collaborative tool has focused on technological aspects of implementation. Besides traditional business measures, there is little definitive research on Notes as a collaborative tool. Collaboration is difficult to measure. New metrics are needed. Research on strategies to implement Notes are also few in number. The extant research has been exploratory in nature and has not addressed the promise of Notes as an engine for collaboration. Unintended consequences of Notes implementation are a concern to implementors and researchers alike, providing opportunities for additional exploratory research as a precursor to more directed research.

5. How can organizations accelerate the process of converting individual learning into organizational learning (Kim, 1993)?

The central issue in organizational learning is how individual learning is transferred to the organizational level (Kim, 1993). Only with a clear understanding of the transfer process can one manage learning processes consistent with organizational goals, issues, and values (p. 37).

The intellectual material transfer process is at the heart of organizational learning. Kim (1993) reviews March and Olsen's and Daft and Weick's models of organizational learning and concludes that these theorists do not identify an explicit transfer process from individual learning to the organizational level. Garvin (1993) also addresses the transfer process as one of his five key activities of learning organizations, but does not explain how the transfer process works. Specifically, Garvin (1993, p. 87) admonishes that "knowledge must be spread quickly and efficiently throughout the organization. Ideas carry maximum impact when they are broadly shared rather than held in a few hands." Kim (1993) and Garvin (1993) anchor their discussions of the transfer process in what Senge (1990) calls shared mental models. Kim makes a case for facilitating the transfer of individual learning to organizational levels through the use of "learning laboratories, microworlds, and simulations" (p. 48).

Conspicuously missing from Kim (1993) and Garvin's (1993) discussion of the transfer process is the role collaborative technologies can play to facilitate the knowledge-transfer process. Transferring knowledge through shared mental models assumes all parties are collocated. It implies face-to-face communications. In an increasingly knowledge-intensive, geographically-dispersed, and an electronically network-dependent society, it is unlikely that individuals will have the luxury of face-to-face communications. Hence, knowledge transfer processes are more likely to occur electronically.

Capitalizing on Kim (1993) and Garvin's (1993) efforts, this research takes the next logical step in the investigation process by exploring knowledge transfer mechanisms. Simply stated, there is very little known about how individual learning is transferred to the organizational level. Normative prescriptions on this subject abound, but there is no substantive empirical research on this subject.

SUMMARY

The absence of definitive studies ensures future adventurers exploring the wilds of collaborative technologies will repeat costly mistakes. In the absence of grounded research, intuition-governed and trial-and-error approaches are proving expensive and failure-prone (Grudin, 1994). With collaborative technologies proliferating fueling expectations for enhancing organizational effectiveness, the implementation of such technologies is more difficult—yielding unintended consequences (Lou, 1994). In light of increased pressure to increase productivity in organizations, studying collaborative technologies may yield valuable insight regarding how and if these technologies effect organizational dynamics and productivity.

Chapter 3

Process Improvement and Knowledge Communication

Ned Kock
Temple University

ORGANIZATIONAL KNOWLEDGE AND COMPETITIVENESS

Knowledge, whether stored in the brain or in computer databases, is necessary for the processing of information. Information processing, in turn, has been identified as the main reason why organizations exist[1] (Galbraith, 1973). That is, purposeful organization of people, capital, and other resources is necessary so information processing can be done efficiently and effectively. Information processing, in turn, is seen as a fundamental step in the generation and delivery of products and services by organizations to their customers.

Given the prominent role that information processing seems to play in organizational processes, and the assumption that information processing relies heavily on knowledge, the frequent claims that the collective knowledge held by organizations is the single most important factor defining their competitiveness do not seem unreasonable. The amount of relevant shared knowledge among individuals in process teams has been linked to the efficiency and effectiveness of such teams (Boland and Tenkasi, 1995; Nelson and Cooprider, 1996; Nosek and McNeese, 1997). Shared team knowledge has been equated to higher flexibility of organizational processes, as it can reduce the need for bureaucratic and automated procedures to mechanize and standardize procedures (Davidow and Malone, 1992). That is, more shared knowledge among team members may reduce the need for workflow control and automation.

Previously Published in *Process Improvement and Organizational Learning: The Role of Collaboration Technologies* edited by Ned Kock, Copyright © 1999, Idea Group Publishing.

But, what is organizational knowledge, and how is it related to team knowledge? Knowledge exists in organizations in a dispersed way, and is predominantly held by the individuals who perform process activities. A new concept that tries to expand the locus of knowledge, from the individual towards the group, is the concept of *team* knowledge (Katzenbach and Smith, 1993). Team knowledge is defined as the collective knowledge possessed by groups of individuals involved in the execution of organizational processes, regardless of process scope. Such processes can be as diverse as the processes of *home loan approval* and *hamburger preparation*.

An even higher level concept has been created to refer to the collective knowledge of an organization, namely *organizational* knowledge or "knowledge of the firm" (Kogut and Zander, 1992), which can be defined as the combined knowledge of the various process teams that make up an organization. Part of this collective knowledge can also be stored in data storage devices, often as components of computer-based systems (Strassman, 1996).

THE NEED FOR KNOWLEDGE SHARING

Due to its associative nature, the continuous build up and intensive use of knowledge is a necessity in a complex society. Here, the term "complexity" implies a large number of associations or interdependencies, whether we look at society from an environmental, artifact-oriented, sociological, psychological, or any other relevant perspective (Stacey, 1995; Gleick, 1993; Lewin, 1993).

Knowledge creation feeds complexity and vice-versa (Probst and Buchel, 1997), in what could be seen as an open-ended spiral. For example, new discoveries about a terminal disease and its genetic roots can trigger the development of new technologies and drugs for treatment and prevention of the disease. This in turn can lead to the development of new equipment, and, on a different scale, new drug manufacturing companies. New governmental market regulations may follow. New militant groups fighting for their rights may emerge as those who have the genes that cause the disease organize themselves against possible discrimination by insurance companies. New research fields, theories, and academic disciplines may be spawn.

As knowledge becomes more voluminous and complex, so does the need for knowledge specialization by individuals. Through formal and informal education as well as practice, experts in fields as diverse as accounting and medicine absorb and use specialized knowledge that is not held by large sections of the population in general. The market rewards knowledge specialization and expertise through higher paying jobs and social status.

Obstacles, particularly in the form of time constraints, prevent individuals from becoming experts in several different knowledge specialties at the same time. For example, earlier studies by Simon and Chase (1973) suggest that a chess player cannot reach the grandmaster level in fewer than nine or ten years, regardless of how hard she tries and how intelligent she is.

A large and highly educated mass of people spanning many countries ensures that knowledge is created at a very fast rate so as to push individuals into focusing their cognitive efforts onto narrow fields of expertise.

As knowledge becomes more specialized, so does the need for information and knowledge sharing, which can be achieved through oral and written communication among those who possess different pieces of specialized knowledge. This need is motivated by the fact that even though knowledge has grown very specialized (or precisely because of it), most processes in society require the engagement of several individuals, each of them contributing their own expert knowledge. In organizations as well as in society in general, knowledge to carry out processes is not found in concentrated form. As Hayek (1996, p. 7) points out in his seminal article *The Use of Knowledge in Society*:

> The peculiar character of the problem of a rational economic order is determined precisely by the fact that the knowledge of the circumstances which we must use never exists in concentrated or integrated form but solely as the dispersed bits of incomplete and frequently contradictory knowledge which separate individuals possess.

An analysis of the shop floor of two automobile manufacturers provides a good illustration of the distributed nature of knowledge. Volkswagen and Ford's plants in Sao Paulo manufactured several car models. Although Volkswagen and Ford usually designed each of the models assembled in their plants, most of the parts that went into the models came from their suppliers, which could easily amount to several hundreds for each automobile manufacturer. Breaks, engine parts, or even something as simple as an exhaust pipe or a seat belt, were individually obtained from different suppliers and assembled into a car by the auto-makers.

Among the reasons why outsourcing the manufacturing of car parts was more economical for Volkswagen and Ford than making those parts in-house, was that the cost of keeping and managing the specialized knowledge that went into economically and effectively building each car part was too high.

Outsourcing pushes the responsibility of keeping and managing part-specific knowledge to the supplier. But, although the knowledge that goes into manufacturing each car part is largely possessed by the supplier, Volkswagen and Ford's engineers need to hold part of it in order to design their cars. For example, they need to know whether an airbag, which is manufactured elsewhere, will inflate properly if they reduce the size of the airbag's compartment. That is, sharing knowledge becomes a necessity if the automobile manufacturers and their suppliers are to build low cost cars that meet car buyers' expectations. And such expectations are likely to be increasingly inflated in a highly competitive marketplace such as that of the 1990s and beyond.

ORGANIZATIONAL LEARNING AND KNOWLEDGE TRANSFER

The example of the automobile manufacturers in the previous section highlights the need for knowledge sharing between different organizations; the manufacturers themselves and their suppliers, in the case. One management movement has consistently argued for the development of knowledge creation and sharing capabilities within *and* between organizations as a fundamental step towards achieving heightened competitiveness. This management movement is the *learning organizations* movement (Garratt, 1994; Kofman and Senge, 1993; Senge et al., 1994).

In order to foster knowledge creation and sharing, it is argued that learning organizations should establish an organizational culture that is conducive to these. A climate of risk-taking and experimentation has been found to be an important factor in establishing such organizational culture (Senge, 1990). Such climate can be achieved through the adoption of new management practices and paradigms that stimulate creativity and proactive behavior (Nevis et al., 1995), as well as social interaction (Roskelly, 1994).

In spite of attempts to create organizational cultures conducive to learning, the transferring of acquired knowledge from one part of an organization to another remains a complex and problematic issue (CHE, 1995). This is particularly unfortunate, as transfer of acquired knowledge across different organizational areas has been itself presented as one of the most important components of organizational learning (Redding and Catalanello, 1994) and competitiveness (Boland and Tenkasi, 1995).

TYPES OF EXCHANGES IN ORGANIZATIONAL PROCESSES

Given the relatively high significance placed on inter-functional knowledge communication as a component of organizational learning, the search

Table 1: Organizational processes studied

Process description	Organization
Product design	Westaflex
Parts manufacturing	Westaflex
Order delivery	Westaflex
Raw material purchase	Westaflex
University course preparation	Waikato University
University course teaching	Waikato University
Communication of a pest/disease outbreak	MAF Quality Management
Quality management consulting	MAF Quality Management
Quality inspection of parts/materials	Westaflex
Plant machinery maintenance	Westaflex
Equipment adaptation for new product	Westaflex
Software support for users	MAF Quality Management
Internal newspaper editing	MAF Quality Management
IT users support	MAF Quality Management
Staff training and development	MAF Quality Management

Figure 1: Distribution of exchanges according to their type

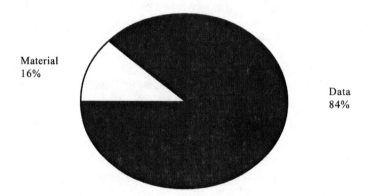

for ways to improve this communication is warranted. In order to do so, it is important to understand knowledge communication from a product exchange perspective. Such perspective takes into consideration the exchanges of tangible (e.g. parts, materials) and intangible (e.g. information, knowledge) elements between organizational functions (or roles).

Inter-functional exchanges in processes can be seen as being of two main types, namely material and data exchanges. As mentioned before, there have been repeated claims, particularly since the 1970s, that we are now living in an information (or symbolic) society (Toffler, 1970; 1991). To these, were added claims that we are in the midst of an information explosion where more and more people are working in the "information sector" (Hirschheim, 1985), and that organizations have become "information organizations" (Drucker, 1989).

As a result of these claims, I have been long since curious as to the extent to which information-bearing exchanges (i.e. exchanges of data) outweigh material exchanges in organizations. This curiosity led, in 1996, to a study of 15 business processes in three organizations. A description of each process is provided in Table 1 along with the name of the organization where each process was located.

One of the organizations from which process-related data were obtained was Westaflex, an international car parts manufacturer based in southern Brazil. The other two organizations were based in New Zealand. One was Waikato University, whose main campus was based in the city of Hamilton, and the other was MAF Quality Management, a semi-autonomous branch of the New Zealand Ministry of Agriculture and Fisheries with offices spread throughout the country.

The study of the processes involved the identification of data and material exchanges between the organizational functions that performed activities in each process. Overall, 123 exchanges were identified. One hundred and three of these exchanges were found to be data exchanges, which amounts to approximately 84 percent. Only 20 of these exchanges were found to be material exchanges, approximately 16 percent. The distribution of these exchanges according to type (i.e. data or material) is illustrated in Figure 1.

The number of data exchanges was over five times that of material exchanges. Although the sample of business processes analyzed was small (i.e. 15), the large contrast between the quantity of data and material exchanges and the fact that the sample was obtained from three different organizations suggests that such contrast may be found in other organizations. Moreover, nearly half of the processes studied came from Westaflex, a manufacturing organization. Thus, one can reasonably expect the proportion of data exchanges to be even higher in organizations outside the manufacturing sector.

PROCESS IMPROVEMENT AND KNOWLEDGE COMMUNICATION

The idea that data can be seen as carriers of information and knowledge was proposed. I also pointed out that information is predominantly descrip-

Table 2: Improvement processes studied

Process description	Organization
University course improvement	Waikato University
Undergraduate academic support improvement	Waikato University
Student computer support improvement	Waikato University
Student assignment handling improvement	Waikato University
International graduate student support improvement	Waikato University
International student adaptation support improvement	Waikato University
Software support improvement	MAF Quality Management
Newsletter editing improvement	MAF Quality Management
Pest/disease outbreak communication improvement	MAF Quality Management
Quality management consulting improvement	MAF Quality Management
IT users support improvement	MAF Quality Management
Staff training and development improvement	MAF Quality Management

tive, whereas knowledge is predominantly associative. Information allows us to describe the world through assertive statements about it, such as, "Today it is going to rain!" Knowledge allows us to associate different assertions that can occur at the same time or at different points in time, such as in "If today it is going to rain, then the road is going to be wet."

Process improvement has been at the heart of what is often referred as organizational learning, particularly regarding the concept of double-loop learning proposed by Argyris (1977; 1992). However, hard evidence that empirically suggests that process improvement is in some way causally linked with organizational learning has been very scarce, practically nonexistent.

If we look at the set of processes described in the previous section, we can see that they can provide *the basis* for showing that process improvement can lead to organizational learning. For this to happen, however, a control group of *improvement* processes is needed. The reason is simple, the 15 processes studied are all routine core and support processes in the organizations they were taken from. None of them is an *improvement* process.

Improvement processes are usually *group* (or team) processes, whereby business processes are analyzed and redesigned for improvement. An example of an improvement process is MetaProi, which stands for Meta-Process for Process Improvement. MetaProi is called a *meta*-process because it is itself a process and yet it is used for improving other processes[2].

Since none of the processes described in the previous section is an improvement process, a comparison between these processes and a new set of improvement processes could shed some light onto the different nature of *improvement* and *routine* processes regarding knowledge and information communication. It would

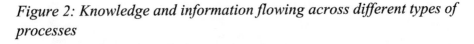

Figure 2: Knowledge and information flowing across different types of processes

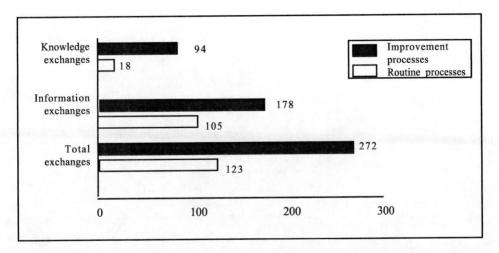

have been even better if the new set of improvement processes could be obtained from the same three organizations mentioned in the previous section, so organizational "culture" and other organization-specific factors could be eliminated as possible sources of bias in the analysis.

Data could not be obtained from improvement processes at Westaflex, but I was able to collect data from the other two organizations. Twelve improvement processes (or meta-processes) conducted at MAF Quality Management and Waikato University by process improvement groups were analyzed, and then compared to the 15 routine core and support processes described in the previous section. A description of these processes is provided in Table 2. Groups conducted process improvement activities according to MetaProi's guidelines (see Appendix A).

Different communication channels have been used during the discussions. Group communication took place predominantly through an e-mail conferencing system (developed by me using Novell Groupwise[3] macros), face-to-face meetings, and phone conversations. The e-mail conferencing system allowed members to send e-mail messages to a central mailbox, which then automatically distributed the messages to all the other members of the group (e.g. as in Internet e-mail lists, a.k.a. *Listservs*). Typically, group members were physically dispersed, either in different offices of the same building or campus, or across different cities or campuses. Most group members were drawn from the same process team, that is, they were involved in the execution of the same (typically interdepartmental) process.

I analyzed discrete and written exchanges of data (e.g. forms, reports, e-mail

Figure 3: Normalized knowledge content per exchange across process types

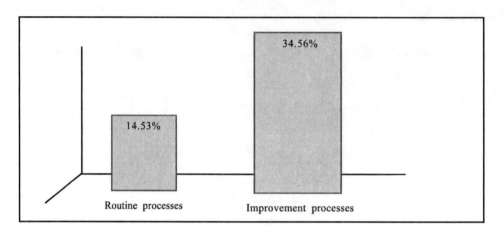

messages, memos, faxes etc.) in both groups of processes (i.e. routine and improvement processes). In doing so, I was particularly concerned with identifying information and knowledge occurrences in each of these exchanges. I did so consistently with the operational definitions of knowledge and information, discussed in Chapter 3. A given data exchange was seen as carrying information if it had at least one purely descriptive statement. Such statements were identified by the presence of isolated *object-verb-attribute* sequences, without any associative (either causal or correlational) reference. Examples of these are "John is in Singapore this week," "Our cycle time has increased 20 percent in comparison with the same quarter last year," and "Our sales figures always go down at this time of the year.".

A given data exchange was seen as carrying knowledge if it had at least one associative statement that could be expressed as an *if-then* statement. Associative statements are those which associate different pieces of information in a causal or correlational way. These associations can be more or less general (or specific). General associations express knowledge in a relatively generic way. For example, consider the following statement: "I think that increased instances of litigation have been caused by our lack of understanding of our customers' needs." This statement carries knowledge that is relatively generic, because it associates two *classes* of phenomena "increased instances of litigation" with a "lack of understanding of customer needs". Specific associations express knowledge in a relatively specific context. Consider the statement: "The reluctance of our chief operations officer was the main reason why our re-engineering project failed." This is a much more specific statement insofar as it associates two specific *instances* of phenomena, namely "the reluctance of a specific organization function" and "the failure of a specific re-engineering project."

The absolute counts of knowledge and information exchanges across different process types (i.e. routine and improvement processes) are shown in Figure 2. There are a few important points to be made based on these aggregate numbers.

- There were considerably fewer data exchanges that carried knowledge in comparison to those that carried only information.
- Almost all data exchanges carried information. Only two data exchanges in improvement processes did not carry any information (these exchanges did not carry any knowledge either). This makes sense, as at least "something" (i.e. some knowledge of information) is meant to be transferred in data exchanges anyhow, otherwise they would never happen in the first place.
- The number of knowledge-bearing exchanges in improvement processes (94) was much higher than in routine processes (18), in spite of the fact that more routine processes than improvement process were analyzed. Remember that 15 routine processes were compared with only 12 improvement processes.

Even though the number of knowledge-bearing exchanges in improvement processes was higher than that found in routine processes, a careful analysis has to account (an control) for the fact that there were more data exchanges in improvement processes than in routine processes. That is, process improvement group members exchanged more data than members of teams performing routine processes.

If there were more data exchanges in improvement processes, then it is reasonable to expect that there would be more knowledge exchanges, even if the ratio between knowledge-bearing exchanges and total exchanges is the same for improvement and routine processes. In this sense, the comparison of the figures—ninety-four obtained for the improvement processes and 18 obtained for the routine processes— may not be a totally fair one. Nevertheless, this comparison indicates that process improvement leads to an increase, in absolute terms, in knowledge exchanges in organizations.

What is needed to complete a careful analysis is to find out what the percentage of knowledge-bearing exchanges is when all exchanges are considered. This normalized figure gives an idea of how much knowledge there is *per data exchange* in improvement as well as routine processes.

Figure 3 shows the normalized knowledge content per data exchange for improvement and routine processes, which was obtained by dividing the number of knowledge-bearing exchanges by the total number of exchanges for each process type. The percentages shown, 34 and 14 percent, suggest a much higher knowledge content in data exchanges taking place in improvement processes than in those observed in routine processes.

In the face of the analysis of knowledge and information exchanges discussed above, one may argue that no conclusions can be made about knowledge and information *communication* patterns. The reason is because I cannot be sure that the knowledge and information extracted from the data exchanges would *actually be transferred* between the originator of each data exchange and its recipient. In other words, the fact that knowledge and information are apparently being exchanged (according to my analysis) does not mean that they are being actually *communicated*. My answer to this is based on one important, and in my view sound, assumption, which is that decreases in *communication fidelity* should occur uniformly across the sample of exchanges analyzed.

What I mean by *communication fidelity*, is the ratio between what is exchanged and what is really communicated. Communication fidelity can be reduced by many factors, such as:

- Different types of "noise," that is, extraneous elements that distort the meaning of what is meant to be communicated;
- Lack of a shared understanding of the language used for communication; or
- Lack of interest in the topic about which information or knowledge is being communicated.

My point is that if communication fidelity is reduced, it is reasonable to expect that such reduction will take place in more or less the same way throughout the routine and improvement processes studied. Since my conclusions are based on the comparison of figures obtained for each of these types of processes, they should be uniformly affected by a possible reduction in communication fidelity. Such reduction could be seen as a multiplicative factor f that would be equally applied to improvement and routine process variables. Whenever relative considerations are made, f would automatically be cancelled out. For example, if f was .5, the percentages in Figure 3 would have been *26.11 percent* for improvement processes, and *8.57 percent* for routine processes. That would not alter the fact that the relative knowledge content of data exchanges in improvement processes is much higher than that found in routine processes, which is one of the main findings of my analysis.

One of the main conclusions that can be inferred from the results presented here is that process improvement fosters knowledge communication. And, since knowledge communication is an important component of organizational learning, then it follows that process improvement fosters organization learning.

SUMMARY AND CONCLUDING REMARKS

Knowledge is predominantly stored in organizations by means of individuals working in process teams. Given the increasing volume of existing knowledge in all areas, knowledge holders are pushed into specialization, that is, they focus on a specific body of knowledge. This leads to knowledge fragmentation in organizations, which in turn has been attacked by organizational learning advocates as a key reason for low process productivity and quality. Many organizational learning proponents, thus, have focused their efforts on finding ways to stimulate inter-functional knowledge sharing.

A relatively new and unorthodox approach to promote inter-functional knowledge sharing is to have workers participate in process improvement groups. While this has been hinted by early contributors of the organizational learning and total quality management movements, there was virtually no empirical evidence pointing to process improvement as an knowledge sharing catalyst.

This chapter discusses evidence that suggests that the number of knowledge-bearing communication exchanges in improvement processes is much higher than that observed in routine processes. It also shows that the proportion of knowledge content in communication exchanges in improvement processes is approximately 35 percent, compared with approximately 15 percent for routine processes. These findings are particularly significant because process improvement, unlike traditional knowledge transfer activities such as training sessions and committee meetings, has other numerous side effects that are obviously beneficial. Perhaps the most important among them is process improvement itself.

ENDNOTES

[1] This statement is often attributed to John Kenneth Galbraith. Born in 1908 in Iona State, Ontario, Galbraith is an internationally acclaimed economist and scholar whose seminal theoretical work has been influential in several areas of organizational research, including the incipient field of

Information Systems. Given the scope and importance of his theoretical contributions, many question why he never received a Nobel Prize.

[2] In the same way as the terms metalanguage and metadata are used to refer, respectively, to a higher-level language used to talk about other languages, and to higher-level data about other data sets.

[3] Novell Groupwise is a leading commercial groupware product distributed by Novell Corporation.

[4] Note that the last statement is a generic statement that expresses a generalization— "something will always happen at a given time of the year". Although this type of statement may be seen as *knowledge*, because it allows for prediction of the future (however, this is done independently of information about the present), it is inconsistent with my operational definition of knowledge. Since in research it is good practice to stick with operational definitions, statements such as this are not counted as knowledge in my analysis. However, as I will show later in this chapter, this consideration had no effect on the main findings of the analysis.

Chapter 4

The Effects of Collaborative Technologies

Ned Kock
Temple University

WHY *DISTRIBUTED* IMPROVEMENT AND LEARNING?

The information era is characterized by a tremendous explosion in the amount of information flowing within and outside organizations. Information flows internally between organizational functions (or organizational *roles*, usually distinguished by different job titles). Information flows outside the organizations when communication takes place between the organization and one of its suppliers or customers.

As discussed in previous chapters, one of the main reasons why such explosion of information flow is taking place is the specialization of knowledge. As more and more knowledge is produced on a global scale, the scope of knowledge that is possessed by individuals becomes increasing narrower. Individuals strive to hold in-depth knowledge in a very limited number of fields and subjects, or, in other words, they specialize. Specialization is an involuntary phenomenon, and follows from human cognitive and, most importantly, *time* limitations. In the information era, those who do not specialize tend to become less competitive, because they do not have the time to acquire the knowledge and skills needed to compete with others in specific fields of knowledge. If you do not believe me, try to think of anyone who could be a top criminal lawyer and, at the same time, an internationally renowned brain surgeon. Even if we are talking about a super-genius here, time constraints will prevent this from happening, as both specialties require years and years of study and focused practice.

Previously Published in *Process Improvement and Organizational Learning: The Role of Collaboration Technologies* edited by Ned Kock, Copyright © 1999, Idea Group Publishing.

However, as the number of different knowledge specialties increases, so does the need for organizations to hire and manage groups of experts who specialize in different subject areas. A typical mid-sized financial services firm, for example, has to maintain hundreds of experts who specialize in different areas of financial analysis. Each of these areas, e.g. mutual fund management and securities analysis, are themselves made up of dozens of experts who specialize in different economic sectors and industries, e.g. Asian government bonds and domestic high-tech stocks. The existence of such knowledge variety leads organizations into a high degree of departmentalization (Hunt, 1996), or the organization around a heterogeneous structure of work teams (Eason, 1996), to cope with the management complexity that it generates.

Previous studies have shown that a high degree of knowledge specialization and the resulting high degree of departmentalization correlate with an intense flow of information. My own research on this topic suggests the existence of a very strong correlation between the number of functions in a process and the number of information exchanges in it[1]. That is, the trend towards knowledge specialization seen today is also leading to a severe increase in the amount of information that has to be transferred in organizations.

Figure 1: Information exchanges often lead to knowledge exchanges

---

John and Mark are working on the development of a new toothbrush. In order to do so they have to exchange information *and* knowledge. The dialogue below illustrates an initial exchange of information (two first paragraphs) that leads to the need for an ensuing exchange of knowledge (last paragraph).

"John, you told me that the elasticity of the middle section of our tooth-brushes will decrease next year. Why is that?"

"Mark, you're always the last to know things around here, aren't you? It is because we will be using high density polyethylene to manufacture them, instead of the softer low density polyethylene that we use today."

"What? John, can you explain this to me please."

"Well, high density polyethylene is a very strong and hard type of plastic. If we use this type of plastic in our toothbrushes, their middle sections will be much less elastic than they are now."

To complicate the picture painted above, previous research has also pointed to a high correlation between knowledge and information flow[2]. That is, as the flow of information increases, so does the flow of knowledge. In fact, this seems to be caused by another interesting cognitive phenomenon. There appears to be an information exchange threshold above which knowledge *needs* to be exchanged as well. The existence of such threshold can be intuitively understood through the observation of the communication that takes place between pairs of workers engaged in a common process. For example, let us consider two people engaged in the process of developing a new toothbrush, each of them being an expert in their own field (e.g. plastic materials resistance and oral preventive medicine). In the beginning of their interaction, these two people exchange descriptive information so each can reach their own conclusions about their plans for new toothbrush features. However, at a certain point, they will start transferring information that does not make absolute sense to each other—i.e. information that cannot be processed based on the existing body of knowledge that each of these experts possesses. At this point they will have to start exchanging knowledge (see Figure 1).

The need for transferring increasing amounts of information and knowledge in organizations has been compounded by (or combined with) another set of trends.

First, no longer do organizations need to rely on endowment factors (e.g. natural resources, cheap labor) to compete globally. Competitive advantage is now defined by the ability of organizations to acquire and deploy process-related knowledge (Porter, 1980; 1985). A good example of this is provided by Japanese automakers like Toyota and Mazda, which managed to success-fully compete on the global market in spite of Japan's lack of natural resources and of a relatively expensive labor force. Just compare the success of Japan with that of other countries, like Brazil, for example, whose natural resources relevant to the automobile manufacturing industry have always been much more abundant and whose labor force has always been cheaper. It can clearly be seen that global industrial success has very little to do with country endowment factors.

Secondly, process-related knowledge is increasingly found in a geo-graphically dispersed way. People with expertise in processes like pharma-ceuticals research for example, can be found in places as far apart as California, Oregon, Pennsylvania, New Zealand, and Uruguay.

Thirdly, the capitalist principles of free market and competition have been increasingly finding widespread adoption around the world, particularly since the early 1990s. This has intensified competition among organizations in the same industry at a global level.

A sub-product of the above trends has been that organizations are increasingly moving towards what some refer to as the "virtual organization" paradigm (Davidow and Malone 1992; Mowshowitz, 1997). Virtual organizations produce and deliver their products independently of their physical location and structure. Their most important assets are not material, tangible assets, but knowledge assets. Many knowledge-intensive processes rely largely on the transfer of information and knowledge, which can be done through the transfer of data. And, more and more today, data transfer relies heavily on computer networks.

It should come as no surprise, then, that the higher the *degree of virtuality* of an organization, the more likely it is that it will rely on computer networks to support communication among its members. Local and wide area computer networks have the potential to support the acquisition, transfer, storage and use of geographically dispersed process-related knowledge and information.

However, as with more traditional organizations, process teams in virtual organizations also have to cope with process inefficiencies, and the need to share process-related knowledge. And given the distributed nature of such process teams, it becomes increasingly important that process improvement (PI) and organizational learning in virtual organizations be conducted in a distributed, asynchronous (i.e. time-disconnected) manner. Hence the importance of understanding the effects of asynchronous group support technologies on PI groups. After all, PI groups, as I have shown in Chapter 4, can be a powerful tool to achieve both process improvement and organizational learning.

In Chapter 3 I discussed a link between process improvement and organizational learning based on the analysis of a number of PI groups conducted at two New Zealand organizations, namely Waikato University and MAF Quality Management. In this chapter, I will discuss the effects of a type of asynchronous group support technology on these PI groups. The technology used to support group communication was e-mail conferencing. The e-mail conferencing system allowed members to send e-mail messages to a central mailbox, which then automatically distributed the messages to all the other members of the group (e.g. as in Internet e-mail lists, or "Listservs"). Most groups had members who were physically dispersed, either in different offices of the same building or campus, or across different cities or campuses. Most group members belonged to the same process team, that is, they were involved in the execution of the same (typically interdepartmental) process, even though they were usually not co-located.

To facilitate understanding, I split technology effects into three main categories in this chapter. The first category of effects are those on the efficiency of PI groups, that is, on the organizational cost of PI groups and on the total number of simultaneous PI groups that an organization can possibly have at any given time. The second category of effects refers to the impact on the quality of the outcomes generated by the PI groups, i.e. on the quality of process improvement proposals. The third category relates to the effects on learning effectiveness, as perceived by PI group members. Each of these categories of effects is individually discussed next.

EFFICIENCY EFFECTS FROM A GROUP PERSPECTIVE

John Grinder[3] was the national manager of the training and certification arm of MAF Quality Management. He was responsible for ensuring that field inspectors had the training and the certification credentials to do their job, as required by government regulations. As MAF Quality Management had many offices spread throughout New Zealand, John had to rely on local centers to handle training and certification sessions. Such sessions involved government-accredited consulting and training firms, as well as international certification bodies, and MAF Quality Management's field inspectors. Many of these inspectors routinely audited the operations of meat and milk farms, packaged food manufacturers, and livestock enhancement companies, among other food-related organizations.

Spreadsheet-based applications had been developed independently by each local training and certification center to keep track of information about field inspectors and the suppliers of training and certification services. However, due to recent changes in government regulations, John needed to generate periodic reports of the status of training and certification of inspectors nationwide. Moreover, John believed these services could be partially delivered online to MAF Quality Management, through the use of computer networks. John believed that this could potentially improve the quality of training, by allowing full-time access to training material by instructors, and at the same time reduce its cost to MAF Quality Management. John wanted to improve the process he managed.

John could simply hire a team of consultants to redesign the whole process and develop a distributed computer system to integrate data from the several local centers scattered throughout the country. But John knew better than that. If he wanted the new process to work, John knew that he would have to explain to the local centers why it was necessary to change the way training and certification was carried out up until then. He also knew that he would have to give them the opportunity to propose process changes themselves. It was either this, or the local centers would resist any change. *"People don't dislike change,"* John said to himself. *"People dislike change being imposed on them."*

The problem was that, in order to get everyone's input regarding the process change, John would have to bring together a group of at least 20 people, representing each of the various local centers. And he was not sure his quarterly budget would allow him to pay for the travel and accommodation expenses of all these people. Not to mention buyout fees that some offices wanted to charge him to compensate for the hours the staff would spend in the process redesign—MAF Quality Management's administrative structure was highly decentralized, with many departments independently handling their own budgets. He decided to run the whole discussion as a PI group whose members would interact through an e-mail conferencing system. He contacted each of the local centers by phone, and invited 23 people to participate in the e-mail-supported PI group.

The discussion lasted about three months, and the whole group met face-to-face only once at the end of the discussion. John estimates that the use of the e-mail conferencing system has saved him over $60,000 only in travel and accommodation expenses. Also, he did not have to pay for the staff-hours spent in the electronic discussion, as staff did not have to physically leave their offices during the discussion. Moreover, he was pleased with the results. Representatives of local centers proposed and, after some discussion, almost unanimously agreed on adopting a new set of procedures. They went some way towards specifying software and hardware requirements for a computer system to enable the new procedures, which was soon after implemented by a software firm.

Figure 2: Perceptions about computer support impact on group cost

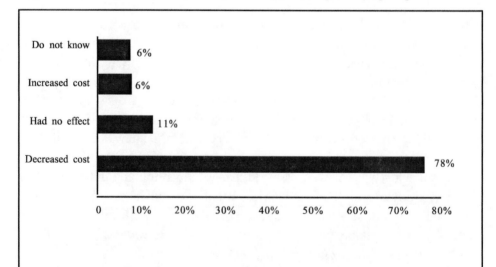

The organizational cost of improvement
groups is reduced

Although the picture painted above may seem a bit too rosy, it is true to the general trend observed in the PI groups I have facilitated and studied (see Appendix B). However, an analysis of the PI group descriptions in Appendix B shows that not all groups were as successful as the group led by John. Some of the groups studied, for example, failed to reach a consensus about process changes, and as a result no changes were either proposed or implemented by these groups. A nutshell discussion of PI group success factors, based on the analysis of the 12 groups described in Appendix B, is provided in Chapter 6. Some considerations on the general quality of computer-supported PI group outcomes are made later in this chapter.

Nevertheless, an important trend that was observed in the twelve computer-supported PI groups conducted at Waikato University and MAF Quality Management is their reduced cost compared with similar face-to-face PI groups. Group members themselves indicated such cost reduction, in interviews. They were asked to compare the computer-supported PI groups with previous face-to-face PI groups in which they had participated.

Twenty-nine out of 46 PI group members at Waikato University, or 63 percent, spontaneously remarked that computer support had reduced the costs of member participation in PI groups. Two main reasons for this cost reduction were mentioned. A reduction in disruption costs, or costs related to staff having to interrupt their routine activities in order to participate in the PI

Figure 3: Perceptions about computer support impact on group lifetime

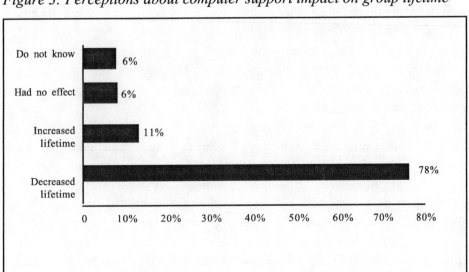

groups, was the reason given by most of the interviewees. The other reason was a reduction in the time each member spent participating, either actively or passively, in the group discussion. When asked about a possible reduction in travel and accommodation costs, all PI group members stated that those cost reductions were very significant in most groups, but too obvious to be mentioned in the interviews. The quote below is from a faculty member who had been involved in a PI group dealing with legal issues related to the provision of academic advice to students:

> It is very hard […] to organize meetings around people's schedules. It was probably a lot quicker to respond to [electronic contributions] than to get together and sit in a face-to-face meeting and talk about other things for a while until you get on with the subject at hand. […] It probably increased the input that you got from other departments.

At MAF Quality Management, structured interviews indicated that approximately 78 percent of the respondents viewed computer-supported PI groups as having cost much less to the organization than face-to-face PI groups. This is illustrated in Figure 2, where the distribution of response frequencies suggests a statistically strong trend[4] in the direction of a collective perception that computer support leads to a reduction in group cost.

At MAF Quality Management, the average time spent by a member of a PI group discussion was estimated at slightly over 20 hours if the discussions had been carried out exclusively through face-to-face meetings. This time was reduced by computer support to about one hour and 30 minutes, which was the average time spent by ordinary group members (i.e. all group members with the exception of the group leader). This amounts to an average reduction of approximately 93 percent. For group leaders, the average time spent in the group discussion went from twenty hours to approximately seven hours, according to direct time measurements. Although less than for ordinary members, this amounts to a 65 per cent reduction in the group leader participation time.

The bottom-line money saving per group was gauged through an absolute dollar amount estimate, which proved to be very attractive. To obtain such estimate I assumed, very conservatively, that a group member costs the organization on average 15 dollars per hour. As the average number of members in a PI group is nine (averaged based on the PI groups at MAF Quality Management), then computer support reduced the cost per group to the organization in at least $2,415. This is the price of a good desktop computer with basic office automation software installed in it. Note that group facilitation (provided by a PI consultant, for example) and travel expense savings have been disregarded in the calculation of this figure.

The lifetime of improvement groups is reduced

Another trend observed in the computer-supported PI groups conducted at Waikato University and MAF Quality Management was an apparently shortened lifetime, in comparison with face-to-face PI groups. And yet, as it will be seen later in this chapter, this reduced lifetime has not led to a decrease in the quality of group outcomes (i.e. the process redesign proposals generated by the groups). PI group lifetime was measured in days, from the inception of the group to its formal cessation.

The lifetime of the PI groups conducted at Waikato University varied from thirty-two to fifty-four days, with an average of about 40 days, and a standard deviation of approximately nine days. At MAF Quality Management, PI group lifetime was slightly shorter. It ranged from ten to 29 days, averaging at 22 days, with a standard deviation of approximately eight days.

At Waikato University, many PI group members voluntarily and consistently noted a perceived decrease of group lifetime as a consequence of computer support, though no frequency distribution analysis was performed. At MAF Quality Management, interviewees' responses displayed a strong trend towards the perception that computer-supported PI groups had been completed in less time, measured in number of days, than face-to-face PI groups. Approximately 78 percent of the interviewees were of this opinion, which indicates a statistically strong trend[5]. This is illustrated in Figure 3, which, coincidentally, is similar to Figure 2.

The main cause for the reduction of group lifetime, according to group members, had been a reduction in what many referred to as "group set up time." This was generally described as the time needed to accomplish group set up activities, such as defining a list of problems (or improvement opportunities) to be discussed by the group, selecting group members, and inviting those members to take part in the group. Many interviewees noted that while the time needed to carry out some of these activities had been curtailed by computer support, the need for other activities more typical of face-to-face meetings had been completely eliminated. Examples of such activities are choosing and preparing a venue for the group meetings, and coordinating member attendance.

Improvement initiatives are decentralized

Managers have long dominated the scene when it comes to changing their organizations. Total quality management tried to turn this picture around a little, by showing that the best prepared to improve processes were those who

Figure 4: Computer support impact on factors influencing group demand for senior leadership

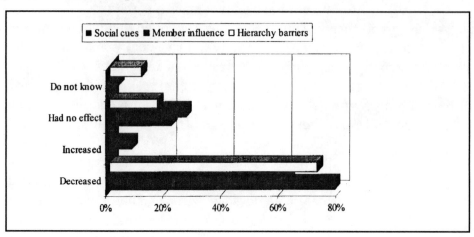

carried them out, not those who managed them. Yet, in spite of this, process improvement has long suffered from an over-reliance on managers. And the business process re-engineering movement, with its top-down change philosophy, somewhat legitimized this situation.

However, managers are just a few when compared with the body of line staff in organizations. And with the current corporate downsizing trend, the manager-to-employee ratio is being steadily reduced, day after day. One management "guru" has been quoted as proudly saying that, "where years ago there was one manager for each seven employees, now there is one for each 100 employees." Obviously, this is an achievement for many organizations, particularly those where management levels are more of an information buffer than anything else. After all, managers, like other support and control entities, do not usually add value to customers.

But as managers grow more and more scarce, they also become busier. Their endless stream of business meetings and improvised interactions (Kurke and Aldrich, 1983; Mintzberg, 1975) becomes more fragmented, and the likelihood that they will want, or have the time to participate in more meetings grows increasingly slim. Such environment, though purportedly more cost-effective in terms of management expenses and utilization, is not a fertile ground for process improvement ventures. Managers, whose leadership and seniority are needed to legitimize and give weight to improvement efforts, are hardly available.

Apparently, computer support reverses the picture above, by reducing the demand for senior leadership in PI groups. At Waikato University, some PI group leaders spontaneously remarked that computer support had made it

Figure 5: Perceptions of computer support impact on process redesign quality

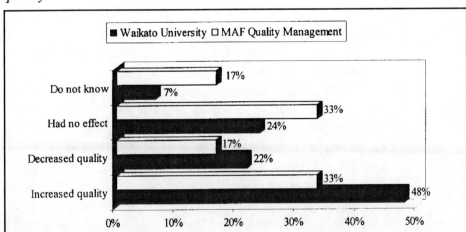

considerably easier for them to lead their PI groups. None of these leaders were the most senior members of their PI groups. One of these group leaders, who was the most junior person in his group, stated that:

> [...] leading a face-to-face meeting [with the same group members] would be considerably more demanding and stressful for me.

His junior status in the organization was perceived by the leader as likely to have considerably hindered him from leading the PI group, had the group been conducted only through face-to-face discussions.

At both Waikato University and MAF Quality Management, similar reasons were put forth by PI group members for the reduction of in-group demand for leadership seniority apparently associated with computer support. The most common reasons were:

- A suppression of social cues by the electronic medium, which could differentiate junior from senior members;
- A reduction in the influence that individual members have on the group, which was seen as likely to increase with seniority in face-to-face groups; and
- A suppression of hierarchy barriers to an open discussion.

Note that these reasons almost imply a sense of partial anonymity in computer-mediated discussions. Yet, none of the PI groups involved anonymous electronic contributions at all. The following quote from a group leader illustrates the member perceptions underlying their explanations:

> Normally if I am in a [face-to-face] situation and with [another member's name - removed], who is my boss, his opinion counts over mine, when I'm sitting in the same room ... on e-mail I feel just as equal—I don't feel that he will influence me or that his opinion will be more important than mine. Because I feel like I can just freely put my ideas on an e-mail and I don't feel threatened by him being above me. You [referring to PI group members in general] are all equals on e-mail ... I definitely don't think about the hierarchy structure when I'm on e-mail, but I do think about it when I'm sitting in a room and I see [names of two other group members - removed] sitting there. And they get a lot more influential because of that, because everybody is a bit more wary of what they say, whereas on e-mail people are more likely to say what they've got to say.

Figure 4 shows statistically significant (according to Chi-square tests) perception trends for members polled across different PI groups that provide majority support for all of these reasons.

The number of possible improvement groups is increased
As demand for senior leadership is reduced by computer support, so does the need to rely on managers to lead PI groups. Ordinary PI group members, as opposed to leaders, do not need to be managers either; they can be anyone within the organization or even come from outside. They can be external customers and suppliers, for example. A direct and obvious consequence of this relaxation in leadership requirements afforded by technology is an increase in the number of possible PI groups that can be run at a given time in the organization. To this, it can be added that the lifetime of PI groups is reduced by computer support, making this effect even stronger. That is, the increase in organizational PI groups capacity is combined with a shorter lifetime to yield a potential expansion in the number of PI groups that can be conducted per unit of time (e.g. per quarter).

This combined effect could be clearly observed at Waikato University. This organization had instituted "official PI days" in which staff and faculty members were expected to engage full-time in PI group discussions during a whole day. PI groups would look into current business processes and related organizational procedures and regulations, and then propose changes aimed at process improvement. Although these group efforts were typically seen as relatively successful by most, their frequency was very low, usually twice every year. As soon as computer support was made available to staff and faculty, five groups were conducted within less than a quarter.

Many PI group members at both Waikato University and MAF Quality Management pointed out that computer support had made it much easier for them to start and conduct their PI discussions with a minimum of disruption for them and their fellow group members. Several of these members spontaneously mentioned a reduction of group set up time as an explanation for their perceptions.

EFFECTS ON GROUP OUTCOME QUALITY

Whatever efficiency gains are obtained through computer support, it would be difficult to justify the use of computer support if it impaired the quality of group outcomes. The main outcome of any PI group is the process change proposal generated by the group. Such outcome is the focus of this section. Here, we are concerned with the impact that computer support has on the quality of process improvement proposals in comparison with that of face-of-face groups.

PI group members were asked to compare their experience in the computer-supported PI group discussion, with that of similar face-to-face situations. An aggregate analysis of their answers indicates an interesting, yet slight trend towards a perceived increase in the quality of process redesign proposals generated by groups. This trend was observed at both Waikato University and MAF Quality Management, and was marginally stronger at the education institution. Figure 5 shows the frequency distribution of answers from PI group members regarding process redesign quality in both organizations.

As in previous analyses of perception frequency distributions, I used a statistical analysis technique called Chi-square test of independence to establish the statistical strength of the perception trend. This test revealed a five-percent probability that the trend observed at Waikato University was due to chance; for MAF Quality Management, the test yielded 63 percent of certainty regarding the perception trend, or a 37 percent probability that the trend was due to chance. In other words, if I was to generalize the findings to other areas (or departments) of either organization, I would be much more confident the validity of such generalization for Waikato University, than for MAF Quality Management.

A decisive trend towards an increase in group outcome quality due to computer support cannot be inferred based on the evidence collected, as there was a considerable number of members who perceived it otherwise. Seventeen percent of the PI group members at MAF Quality Management, and 22 percent at Waikato University, perceived a decrease in quality due to computer support (see Figure 5). Nevertheless, the perception frequency distribution in Figure 5 does suggest a

Figure 6: Perceptions about computer support impact on learning

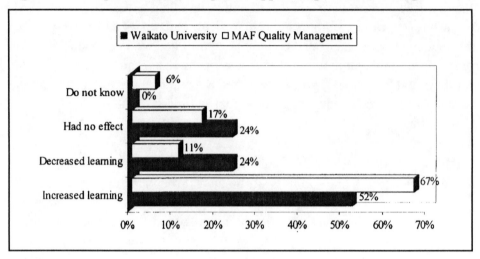

general and statistically strong trend towards a *non-negative* effect on process redesign quality. Seventy-two percent of the respondents at Waikato University perceived either an increase or a null effect in process redesign quality; this proportion was about 66 percent at MAF Quality Management.

Most of the group members who perceived an increase in quality explained it by an improvement in the quality of individual contributions from PI group members interacting through the computer system. That is, they noticed an increase in the quality of individual contributions, which, they reasoned, had led to an increase in the quality of the process redesign proposals generated by their groups. The remarks below, from a PI group member, provide a good illustration of this general perception:

> You think more when you're writing something, so you produce a better quality contribution. Take for example what [member's name - removed] wrote, she wrote a lot and it seemed that she thought a lot about it before she e-mailed it to the group. She wasn't just babbling off the top of her head, she tended to think out what she was writing. I know I did it a lot, specially my first message. I really thought a lot to put it together.

The majority of those who perceived a decrease in process redesign quality believed that it had been caused by inherent characteristics of computer-mediated communication. In these members' judgment, interacting through the computer system increased the ambiguity in the PI group discussion. This was particularly true, according to these PI group members, in the analysis stage of a PI group, where the group analyzes the target process (or processes) for redesign. Group members had to build a shared understanding of the process being analyzed in this stage, so they could later effectively contribute process change suggestions.

Most groups had a multi-departmental composition. Which meant that differences in the technical language used by different members had often become obstacles that had to be removed if the discussion was to proceed successfully. The asynchronous and distributed nature of the computer-supported communication in the PI groups prevented immediate feedback and the use of non-verbal cues (e.g. gestures), which apparently made it more difficult, in the opinion of some members, to remove obstacles to a shared understanding about the process being analyzed.

Still, the percentage of respondents who were of the opinion that redesign quality had been decreased by the use of group technology was comparatively low. This indicates that the higher quality observed in individual contributions might have offset the communication constraints inherent in the electronic medium. As a consequence, a neutral, bending towards positive, overall effect on process redesign quality can be inferred from the evidence collected.

EFFECTS ON ORGANIZATIONAL LEARNING EFFECTIVENESS

Process improvement itself fosters, as a group process, knowledge communication. This conclusion was largely based on content analysis of communication interactions between people carrying out process improvement and routine processes in real organizational settings. In this section our main concern is shifted to the effect that computer support has on the effectiveness of organizational learning. Even though, more knowledge communication is apparently closely linked to the task of improving processes, it is important to establish whether *computer support* does not interfere negatively with the learning process that PI group members undergo when they exchange knowledge and information.

The perception aired by some PI group members that computer support may increase communication ambiguity, which was discussed in the previous section, is consistent with previous research, notably research associated with a very influential theory of media adoption and use known as Media Richness Theory (Daft and Lengel, 1986). Media Richness Theory argues that different communication media possess varied amounts of an abstract property called "richness", which relates to the capacity of the media to convey more or less information and knowledge. According to Media Richness Theory, the richest communication medium is that afforded by face-to-face interaction (Lee, 1994). Media that prevent non-verbal cues from being communicated and which delay feedback, like e-mail, are seen as less rich than media which allow immediate feedback and the communication of non-verbal cues; features that are found in abundance in face-to-face meetings (Daft et al., 1987; Lengel and Daft, 1988). It follows that asynchronous and distributed computer conferencing systems provide a leaner medium for communication than do face-to-face meetings. And, argues Media Richness Theory, lean media are less adequate to the transfer of knowledge and information[6] than rich media.

Given expectations based on Media Richness Theory, pessimistic forecasts about the impact of computer support on learning in PI groups can be reasonably expected. Moreover, the empirical research literature on asynchronous and distributed group support technologies has reported a number of failures of these technologies to support interdepartmental knowledge communication (Kock, 1997). Among other reasons, these failures have been explained by:

- The inherent ambiguity that the electronic medium adds to group communication (Rogers, 1992);
- Social norms and reward systems adopted by firms, that can themselves become obstacles to knowledge sharing (Orlikowski, 1992); and
- The lack of balance between the benefits to those who have to do extra work because of the introduction of a group support system and those who do not (Grudin, 1994).

The perceptions of the PI group members regarding individual learning, however, contradicted the gloomy picture painted by previous theories and empirical research. Group members were consistently positive in their views about computer support impact on individual learning, as shown in the distribution of perceptions depicted in Figure 6. As with previous analyses of frequency distribution, this trend was checked for statistical significance. This revealed that the probability that the trend observed was due to chance is about 2.5 percent for the frequency distribution at Waikato University and 0.5 percent for MAF Quality Management. That is, it can be safely assumed that the trends are not due to chance. My interpretation is that these trends are most likely a result of underlying capabilities of the technology to move group behavior towards learning-conducive situations.

A little unexpected is the explanatory direction pointed at by the evidence, particularly the evidence presented in the previous section. There, group members perceived an increase in the quality of their group outcomes (i.e. process redesign proposals) as resulting from computer mediation. One of the main reasons for this, according to the group members themselves, was the better preparation of individual contributions by group members. Yet, the same members perceived computer mediation itself as having the potential to increase communication ambiguity. What is the direction at which this evidence points in light of the perception trends shown in this section? It appears the answer is that the leanness of the communication medium afforded by computer support has led to an adaptive behavior that overcame, at least partially, the constraints posed by the leaner medium. More knowledge was communicated, which led to higher perceived learning.

When asked to explain their answers regarding computer support impact on individual learning, there was a clear convergence in the answers given by PI group members. Most of the relatively small number of members who perceived a decrease in individual learning, suggested that this was due to a reduction in the degree of interaction caused by computer mediation. That is, less individual contributions are made in computer-mediated than in face-to-face discussions, and thus less learning takes place. The idea that computer mediation leads to reduced group interaction is certainly incorrect for same-time-same-place computer interaction, where the number of contributions per unit of time has consistently been found to have been increased (Dennis et al., 1996, Sheffield and Gallupe, 1993). However, in my study of asynchronous (time-disconnected) and distributed computer-supported groups, partially discussed here, group interaction indeed seemed to have been considerably reduced by computer mediation. Yet, whether this led to reduced information and knowledge exchange is doubtful, since the length of individual contributions and their knowledge content appears to have been considerably increased. This effect may be partly due to computer mediation.

At MAF Quality Management, the two main reasons presented for the perceived increase in individual learning were better quality of and more sincere individual contributions. PI group members linked the increase in sincerity to a sense of personal insulation fostered by the computer mediation. That is, often when members interact via a computer they feel less inhibited to freely express their feelings and ideas. This perception is partially supported by previous studies of e-mail communication in organizational contexts (Sproull and Kiesler, 1986), distributed and anonymous groups (Jessup and Tansik, 1991), and groups composed of introverts and extroverts (Yellen et al., 1995). PI group members at Waikato University gave the same explanations. Yet, they added a new one to our repertoire, which was that member learning was improved by the higher departmental heterogeneity afforded by computer support. According to these members the distributed and time-independent nature of the computer-mediated interaction allowed for a larger number of departments to be represented in each PI group. This in turn brought into the discussion more ideas and individual perspectives that were new to many group members, thus leading to a perception of increased individual learning.

SUMMARY AND CONCLUDING REMARKS

The ever-growing amount of information flowing in organizations, knowledge specialization, and geographical distribution of expertise are among the main factors driving the expansion in the use of computers to support team-based processes. At the same time, these factors also lead to more and more processes being carried by distributed teams. This environment poses obstacles to traditional face-to-face interaction, which, combined with growing competitive forces, drives firms into increasingly using computers for process improvement and organizational learning.

This chapter presents and discusses solid evidence that points to an increase of process improvement group efficiency due to computer support. Efficiency gains are reflected in reduced group cost, lifetime, and reliance on managers. Additionally, the number of simultaneous process improvement groups is increased by computer support.

The evidence also points to increases in perceived group outcome quality and organizational learning effectiveness, as a result of computer support. These findings, combined with those regarding group efficiency, provide a sound basis for the endorsement of asynchronous collaborative technologies as tools for process improvement and organizational learning.

ENDNOTES

[1] The correlation coefficient found was *.86*, using the Pearson product-moment method, which suggests that 86 percent of the variation in the variable *information exchanges* can be explained through functional diversification. The likelihood that such high coefficient of correlation is due to chance was found to be lower than five percent (Kock et al., 1997).

[2] This correlation has been found to be as high as *.75 (Pearson)*. The likelihood that this high correlation is due to chance was found to be lower than five percent (Kock et al., 1997).

[3] As with the rest of this book, names and some situations in this chapter have been disguised to honor confidentiality agreements.

[4] The likelihood that the perception trend observed is due to chance is lower than one-tenth of a percent, as indicated by a statistical test called Chi-square test of independence between frequency distributions.

[5] The likelihood that the perception trend observed is due to chance is lower

than one-tenth of a percent, as indicated by a Chi-square test of independence between frequency distributions.

[6] The theory actually claims that "uncertainty" and "equivocality" reduction are better accomplished through richer communication media. It is my interpretation that uncertainty is reduced through the exchange of information, and equivocality through the exchange of knowledge, according to the definitions of information and knowledge provided earlier in this book. Hence my statement regarding media richness and the communication of knowledge and information.

Chapter 5

The Collaborative Use of Information Technology: End-User Participation and System Success

William J. Doll
University of Toledo, USA

Xiaodong Deng
Oakland University, USA

User participation seems especially important in the development of collaborative work systems where the technology is used by a work group to coordinate their joint activities. Users rather than systems analysts are often the best source of information on how they will use information technology to collaborate. It is almost an axiom of systems development that end users should participate in a broad range of activities/decisions, and that they should be permitted to participate in these decisions as much as they want. Despite these widely held beliefs, research has not focused on the differential efficacy of user participation in collaborative versus non-collaborative applications.

Building upon the work of behavioral scientists who study participative decision making, Doll and Torkzadeh (1991) present a congruence construct of participation that measures whether end users participate as much as they want in key systems analysis decisions. Using a sample of 163 collaborative and 239 non-collaborative applications, this research focuses on three research questions: (1) Is user participation more effective in collaborative applications? (2) What specific decision issues enhance user satisfaction and

Previously Published in the *Information Resource Management Journal, vol.14, no.2,* © 2001, Idea Group Publishing.

productivity? and (3) Can permitting end-users to participate as much as they want on some issues be ineffective or even dysfunctional? The results indicate that user participation is more effective in collaborative applications. Of the four decision issues tested, only participation in information needs analysis predicts end-user satisfaction and task productivity. Encouraging end users to participate as much as they want on a broad range of systems analysis issues such as project initiation, information flow analysis, and format design appears to be, at best, a waste of time and, perhaps, even harmful. These findings should help managers and analysts make better decisions about how to focus participatory efforts and whether end users should participate as much as they want in the design of collaborative systems.

INTRODUCTION

A new era of collaborative organizations characterized by lateral leadership and virtual teams is emerging (Pasternack and Viscio, 1998; Ghoshal and Bartlett, 1997). Firms that compete by developing and deploying intellectual assets are finding that their competitive advantage will depend on developing a superior collaborative capability. Collaboration occurs when two or more people interact to accomplish a common goal. Collaboration means that people who work together support each other by sharing their ideas, knowledge, competencies, and information and/or by coordinating their activities to accomplish a task or goal (Hargrove, 1998). Collaborative work systems are defined as applications where information technology is used to help people coordinate their work with others by sharing information or knowledge. In a longitudinal study, Neilson (1997) describes how collaborative technologies such as Lotus Notes can enhance organizational learning.

Knowledge is a social activity. Complex problems can not be solved by specialists thinking and working in isolation, but in coming together through a process of dialogue, deeply informed by human values and focused on practical problems. Today people from all over the world have the capacity to communicate by e-mail and to participate in electronically distributed meetings. Technology has, in most cases, increased the quantity of interactions people are having. But, has it improved the quality of those interactions? To do this will require a shift in thinking and attitudes towards being more creative and collaborative in systems development (Hargrove, 1998).

Can analysts really design collaborative applications that enhance the quality of human interactions without engaging the application's users in the design effort? In other words, should the design of collaborative applications itself be a collaborative activity? The literature on collaborative systems has focused on: (1) the nature and capabilities of the software, and (2) its application to specific problems requiring collaborative interaction. It has largely ignored the issue of user participation in the design of collaborative applications.

User participation is widely accepted as essential to developing successful information systems (Ives and Olson, 1984; Barki and Hartwick, 1994; McKeen,Guimaraes and Wetherbe, 1994). System analysis decisions have a huge effect on the downstream costs, timing, and on the likelihood of overall system success. Through interviews, surveys or joint application development sessions, the specification of user requirements is thought to improve the quality of design decisions and, thereby, improve the satisfaction and productivity of end-users.

Many analyst and user man-hours and considerable expense can be incurred in making sure that the user requirements are correctly specified. Despite the cost and importance of user participation, we have little knowledge of which decision issues are the most important (McKeen and Guimaraes, 1997). Research on user participation has focused more on the form (Barki and Hartwick, 1994) or degree of user participation (Franz and Robey, 1986) rather than the efficacy of specific decision issues. More emphasis should be placed on identifying the key decision issues and how those issues might differentially relate to satisfaction and productivity.

Few doubt whether users should participate in systems analysis decisions. However, should they participate as much as they want? Studies have shown that most end users want (desire) to participate more than they are actually permitted to participate in the development of applications that they use (Doll and Torkzadeh, 1989). Participatory arrangements, time constraints, and resources often constrain user participation and limit its potential (Doll and Torkzadeh, 1991).

User participation seems especially important in the development of collaborative work systems where the technology is used by a work group to coordinate their joint activities. Collaborative systems are especially difficult to design and require user input. Several interacting users are involved and their collaborative requirements emerge from a changing task context. User experience with the emergent nature of this collaborative activity is essential to effective systems design. In collaborative systems, users rather than systems analysts are often the best source of information on how they will use these applications to coordinate their work.

Managers and systems analysts would like to encourage further end-user participation. However, such efforts can be costly and time consuming, especially when they are not well focused on specific issues. We have little information on what decision areas are the most effective avenues for user participation. Despite the growing importance of collaborative systems, no research studies have specifically focused on: (1) which decision issues are the most effective for improving user satisfaction and task productivity, and (2) whether end users should participate in the development of collaborative systems as much as they want.

COLLABORATIVE APPLICATIONS AND USER PARTICIPATION

The interest in and adoption of collaborative applications is being driven by the needs of organizations to address fundamental business problems, specifically those relating to becoming more flexible organizations, shortening time-to-market, and, above all, becoming more responsive to customers (Marshak, 1994). Historically, information technology was used to support individual users and their needs. Computer systems that were used by groups of people e.g., transaction processing applications, were usually geared toward aggregations of individuals. That is, each user is seen by the system as a discrete unit or a point of input in a sequential process; there is little or no direct interaction, collaboration, or shared work among the users (Johansen, 1988).

In the 1980s, information technology was seen to be a way to support and empower ad hoc teams to meet these needs. Initial applications were aimed at providing a method for these teams to communicate; particular emphasis was placed on teams that could not meet in real time due to organizational or locational differences. Applications such as e-mail, conferencing and bulletin boards provided these teams with the ability to brainstorm, share their findings, and, in some cases, work collaboratively.

For some time now, organizations have turned their focus from supporting teams and groups to looking at their business processes and figuring out how to redesign, support, and manage them to achieve the same overriding goals that has brought attention to teams (Harrington, 1991; Davenport, 1993). Kock (1999) describes how collaborative technologies can facilitate process improvement and enhance organizational learning. Thus, the focus has shifted from the team to the process and, in particular, to the business goal of the process - a satisfied customer and a quality product with short time-to-market.

David Marshak (1994) argues that by the year 2000, collaborative systems will disappear entirely as separate application category. He argues that as applications are redesigned around this process focus and the technologies currently grouped under the umbrella of groupware or collaborative systems become ingrained in the way we work, collaborative systems will simultaneously become transparent and ubiquitous, thus disappearing forever as a separate category of application (Marshak, 1994). If this is true, researchers have to redefine what they mean by a collaborative application.

Paradigms for Defining Collaborative Applications: Design and System-use

Collaborative applications can be defined in terms of a design or a system-use paradigm. The design paradigm is based on the software designer's intentions. Here a collaborative system is viewed as a separate application category whose primary purpose is to provide technical support for collaborative work, whether it is actually used for that purpose or not. In contrast, the system-use paradigm is behaviorally based. Here a collaborative system is defined as any software application that is actually being used by individuals to help them coordinate their work with others, whether it was specifically designed for that purpose or not.

This research adopts the system-use paradigm for several reasons. First, as Schrage (1990) argues in his book entitled *Shared Minds*, the real purpose is not to build collaborative tools but to build collaboration. Second, the real end goals are increased responsiveness to customers, shorter time to market, and increased flexibility. If these end goals are to be achieved, information technology must be used more effectively in the organizational context to help work groups coordinate their joint efforts (Doll and Torkzadeh, 1998). Designer intentions do not, by themselves, contribute to these end goals. Third, if David Marshak is right, many of the software features associated with collaborative systems are already incorporated in much of today's software. Excluding these applications from research on collaborative systems may greatly understate the extent to which information technology has been successfully applied to enhance collaborative work.

This system-use paradigm should have positive effects on the way collaborative systems are designed. It places emphasis on user behavior, rather than designer intentions or technical features. As such, it suggests the need for the analyst to understand not only the technology, but also the dynamic nature of the task context and the changing nature of the relationships between the individuals who use the software. This is information that the analyst can only get from the set of end users who will use the application to help them coordinate their work i.e., stakeholders. This suggests the need for end-user stakeholders to take an active role in development i.e., making system development a collaborative activity between diverse stakeholders and the analyst.

User Participation in Systems Development

Reviews of the participative decision making (PDM) literature have identified six broad dimensions of PDM i.e., rationale, structure, form, decision issues, processes, and degree of involvement (Cotton, Vollrath, Froggatt, Lengnick-Hall, and Jennings, 1988; Dachler and Wilpert, 1978; Miller and Monge, 1986; Locke and Schweiger, 1979; Wagner and Gooding, 1987). Although multiple dimensions have been identified, little systematic theory exists concerning the impact of these diverse dimensions on outcomes (Black and Gregersen, 1997).

Locke and Schweiger (1979) suggest that the key dimension of participation is decision making. The literature on decision issues suggests that both participant satisfaction and productivity or decision quality are, in part, a function of the knowledge or expertise that individuals involved in the decision bring to a particular issue (e.g., Davis, 1963; Derber, 1963; Maier, 1965; Vroom, 1973).

Collaborative applications typically involve a larger and more diverse set of stakeholders than non-collaborative applications used by a single end user. In this collaborative context, user participation involves determining how this more diverse group of stakeholders will use the application to facilitate their joint efforts. Each stakeholder may have insights based on their work experience that will enable them to make creative contributions to the application's design and utilization.

Locke and Schweiger (1979) provide a theoretical rationale for participation's impact on satisfaction and productivity. They argue that three psychological mechanisms – value attainment, motivational, and cognitive – link participation with enhanced satisfaction and productivity. Doll and Torkzadeh (1989) adapted Locke and Schweiger's theoretical rationale for participation to explain how these psychological mechanisms link user participation in systems development with end-user computing satisfaction.

Figure 1 extends Doll and Torkzadeh's work on psychological mechanisms to: (1) incorporate task productivity as well as end-user computing satisfaction as dependent variables, and (2) illustrate differences between collaborative and non-collaborative applications, specifically the enhanced efficacy of cognitive mechanism's path to task productivity in collaborative applications. Figure 1 is not the model being tested; it is presented solely as a theoretical justification of the hypothesized relationships between partici-

Figure 1. Psychological Mechanisms Linking Participation Congruence to Task Productivity and End-User Computing Satisfaction

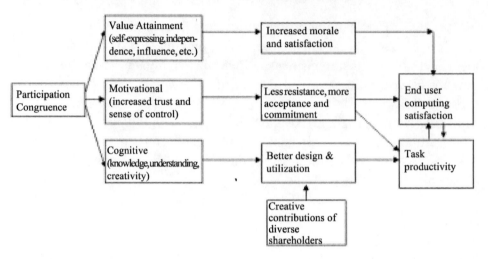

pation congruence and its measurable consequences, end-user computing satisfaction and task productivity.

Participation congruence (i.e., when end-user participate as much as they want) works through value attainment, motivational, and cognitive mechanisms to bring about benefits. Value attainment refers to whether individuals get what they want (accomplish their objectives or attain their values) through participation. Value attainment leads directly to morale and satisfaction and, through increased satisfaction, it affects end-user computing satisfaction. Enhanced end-user computing satisfaction may also improve task productivity. The value attainment mechanism should be equally effective in both collaborative and non-collaborative applications.

Motivational mechanisms reduce resistance to change and enhance acceptance of and commitment to decisions and changes. These benefits of user participation are attributed to greater trust, greater feelings of control, greater ego involvement or identification with the organization, and higher goals, resulting in enhanced end-user computing satisfaction and improved task productivity. The motivational mechanisms should be equally effective in both collaborative and non-collaborative applications.

Cognitive mechanisms refer to increases in information, knowledge, understanding and creativity that user participation can bring to bear on the task of systems development. In the development of both collaborative and non-collaborative systems, the stakeholders in systems development (i.e., users) make cognitive contributions that improve design or system utilization.

Cognitive mechanisms are expected to be more effective in collaborative applications. Collaborative applications are unique in that diverse users who have varied roles and responsibilities greatly enhance the potential for creative contributions of information, knowledge and understanding. The creative contributions of diverse stakeholders can greatly enhance design, facilitate collaborative use, and improve task productivity.

Since improved task productivity is expected to improve end-user computing satisfaction, we hypothesize:

H1A: User participation is more closely associated with user satisfaction in collaborative than in non-collaborative applications.

However, this hypothesis of a differential association between participation and satisfaction is only supported by the contention that more productive end users are more satisfied with their application.

The association between user participation and task productivity might be expected to be stronger in collaborative applications because of the creative cognitive contributions of diverse stakeholders. Thus, we hypothesize:

H1B: User participation is more closely associated with task productivity in collaborative than in non-collaborative applications.

Decision Issues in Systems Analysis

Reviews of the literature on participative decision making (PDM) generally recommend that managers encourage broad-based participation in a variety of decision making issues (Locke and Schweiger, 1979). Individuals typically have different interests and differing areas of knowledge/expertise. Encouraging broad-based participation enables individuals to participate on issues important to them (i.e., where they desire to participate) and/or where they have the knowledge/ expertise necessary to improve the quality of decision making. Locke and Schweiger contend that PDM may be a waste of time or even harmful to decision quality or productivity if the focal individual has significantly less knowledge/expertise than others. PDM research typically focuses on participation's impact on the quality of decisions and, through better decision making, its resultant impact on employee satisfaction and productivity.

End-user participation in systems analysis activities represents a different context than that normally assumed in the PDM literature. First, the range of possible participatory activities focuses on decisions related to the development of a particular application and is, thus, more constrained. Second, the dependent variables of interest are application specific measures of end-user satisfaction or productivity. Third, within the constrained set of systems analysis activities, end-users are not always the best source or only source of knowledge/expertise. In this context, it may be wise to focus participatory efforts on decision issues where end users have superior knowledge/expertise.

Kendall and Kendall (1995) describe the system development life cycle (SDLC) as consisting of seven phases. The first four phases, often referred to as system analysis activities, include: (1) identifying problems, opportunities, and objectives; (2) determining information requirements; (3) analyzing system needs (e.g., information flow analysis), and (4) the logical designing of the information system. Several researchers (Edstrom, 1977; Doll and Torkzadeh, 1989; 1990) have suggested that user participation may be most effective in these system analysis stages where decisions are made on system objectives, user information needs, information flows, and initial input/output screens/formats.

This research identifies four key decision issues for user participation that roughly correspond to Kendall and Kendall's stages in systems analysis. These key decision issues are referred to as project initiation, information needs analysis, information flow analysis, and format design. Shelly, Cashman, Adamski, and Adamski (1995) describe project initiation as the first stage where the problems and opportunities are identified and objectives for the system are set. In the logical design stage, users participate in prototyping to validate the user interface i.e., decisions concerning input/output formats or screens. Table 1 describes how the items used by Doll and Torkzadeh can be grouped by Kendall and Kendall's four stages in system analysis.

These key decision issues arise at different times during systems analysis and require different expertise/knowledge. Users may participate in some of these decisions, yet not be available or otherwise occupied when other decisions are made. Also, user participation in each of these decision issues may not be equally effective. Where managers or systems analysts rather than end users have the knowledge/expertise necessary to improve the quality of decision making, encouraging end users to participate as much as they want may be ineffective or dysfunctional i.e., resulting in lower quality decisions.

Managers or systems analysts may have a broader view of the organization's business activities/needs and be in a better position to make decisions concerning the initiation of new projects and the determination of project objectives. Determining system needs can require technical skills or knowledge of related systems beyond the scope of the job responsibilities of a particular end user. A skilled professional may be necessary to trace information flow from source to end user and be sure the "right" information is being used for decision making. End users should be able to judge whether

Table 1: Decision Issues in Systems Analysis

Label for Decision Issues (Items X1 thru X8)	Kendall and Kendall's Decision Stages	Doll and Torkzadeh's Measurement Instrument
Project Initiation	Identifying problems, opportunities, and objectives	X1. Initiating the project X2. Determining system objectives
Information Needs Analysis	Determining information requirements	X3. Determining the user's information needs X4. Assessing alternative ways of meeting the user's information needs
Information Flows Analysis	Analyzing system needs (e.g., information flow analysis)	X5. Identifying sources of information X6. Outlining information flows
Format Design	Logical design*, especially the validation of user interface requirements (e.g., prototyping)	X7. Developing input forms/screens X8. Developing output format

Note: * Logical design includes the design of data entry procedures, user interface, files or databases, and controls and backup procedures. Of these, the validation of user interface requirements via prototyping is, perhaps, the best opportunity to involve users.

they find a particular format design useful or easy to understand, but they would not normally be as knowledgeable as a systems analyst about the range of possible alternative design formats.

Information needs analysis is a decision issue that is dominated by the end users rather than the analyst. Here the end users have on-the-job experience/ expertise and best understand how the application will actually be used to get their work done and to coordinate their activities with others. In a changing job context, these patterns of collaborative work must remain flexible. Collaborative applications must be designed to support this on-going refinement of how they are used.

Organizational or staffing changes can also affect the relationships between users and how they coordinate their activities. Users of the same application often have different information needs due to differences in their job responsibilities, decision context, or the scope of their personal influence. Even when standard software packages are being installed, differences in the way firms do business may require "work arounds" or modifications to meet the needs of users in a particular firm. Systems analysts typically recognize user expertise in this area by conducting user interviews to determine "what decisions they make" and "what information they need to make those decisions".

User participation is more likely to improve user satisfaction and productivity for those decision issues where the end-user has superior expertise or knowledge (Locke and Schweiger, 1979). In both collaborative and non-collaborative applications, end-user expertise is unquestioned in making decisions about information needs. In the other decision issues, line management or information systems professional may have more expertise or knowledge. Thus, the researchers suggest the following hypotheses:

H2A: Participation in information needs analysis is more effective in improving user satisfaction than participation in other decision issues (i.e., project initiation, information flows analysis, and format design).

H2B: Participation in information needs analysis is more effective in improving task productivity than participation in other decision issues (i.e., project initiation, information flows analysis, and format design).

RESEARCH METHODS

Mindful of Marshak's (1994) argument that, as applications are redesigned around a process focus, technologies currently grouped under the umbrella of collaborative systems will become ingrained in the way we work, the researchers employed the system-use paradigm rather than a design paradigm to define a collaborative application. This methodology also enabled the researchers to assess to what extent information technology is currently being used for collaborative purposes. The system-use paradigm influenced both the sampling methods and the means for classifying collaborative versus non-collaborative applications.

The Sample

The researchers gathered a sample of 402 end users from 18 organizations including 8 manufacturing firms, 1 retail firm, 2 government agencies, 2 utilities, 2 hospitals, 2 educational institutions, and one "other." This was half of the firms contacted. In each firm, the MIS directors were asked to identify their major applications and the major end-users for each application. They also consulted with the heads of user departments to identify important end-user applications and their users. A list of respondents was compiled and surveys were distributed via inter-office mail. Responses were obtained from 63 percent of those surveyed.

Respondents were asked to identify their position within the organization; they responded as follows: 20 top level managers, 80 middle managers, 75 first level supervisors, 140 professional employees without supervisory responsibility, and 87 operating personnel. The sample consisted of 139 different applications including profit planning, engineering analysis, process control, budgeting, CAD, CAD-CAM, customer service, service dispatching, manpower planning, financial planning, inventory control, production planning, purchasing, quality analysis, sales analysis, accounts payable and receivable analysis, work order control, general ledger, order entry, payroll, and personnel.

To identify collaborative versus non-collaborative applications, the researchers used a four-item summed scale recently published by Doll and Torkzadeh (1998) to measure horizontal integration i.e., the extent that information technology is used to coordinate work activities with others in one's work group. The items were:

- My work group and I use this application to coordinate our activities.
- I use this application to exchange information with people in my work group.
- I use this application to communicate with other people in my work group.
- I use this application to coordinate activities with others in my work group.

These items used a five point scale (1=not at all, 2=at little, 3=moderately, 4=much, and 5=a great deal). In this sample, the scale has a reliability of .90. The sample of 402 respondents was divided into two groups based upon this four-item scale: 239 non-collaborative applications i.e., respondents with a score of less than 12; and 163 collaborative applications i.e., a score of 12 or higher.

The collaborative respondents were substantially more likely to be using a decision support application. The breakdown of the sample by type of application is depicted in Table 2. Sixty-three percent of the collaborative systems were decision support; only thirty eight percent of the non-collaborative applications were classified as decision support. Forty eight percent of the non-collaborative applications were transaction processing while only twenty five percent of the collaborative systems were used to process

Table 2: Collaborative and Non-collaborative Respondents by Type of Application

Application Type	Non-collaborative Applications		Collaborative Applications	
	Sample Size	Percentage	Sample Size	Percentage
Decision Support	90	38%	103	63%
Database	35	14%	20	12%
Transaction Processing	114	48%	40	25%
Total	239	100%	163	100%

transactions. Many of the collaborative transaction process applications represented tasks such as service dispatching or customer service that, while transaction processing in nature, required extensive use of the computer to coordinate the activities of the work group.

The 139 names of the applications were sorted alphabetically for both collaborative and non-collaborative applications. A comparison between the two lists revealed that, in almost all cases, the same application names appeared on both lists. This indicated that the key issue was not the nature of the application, but rather how the technology was used by the individuals. This observation further supported the system-use paradigm for defining collaborative applications.

Measurement Instruments

In the literature on user participation in systems development, there are two validated instruments: (1) the Barki and Hartwick (1994) instrument which focuses on identifying the structure and form of user participation, and (2) the Doll and Torkzadeh (1990) instrument which focuses on decision issues. Doll and Torkzadeh's instrument is used in this research because it identifies thirty-three decision issues in systems development that are grouped into three factors—system analysis, system implementation, and administration.

Predictive validity analysis (Doll and Torkzadeh, 1990) suggests that only one factor—user participation in systems analysis issues—is effective for improving user satisfaction. System implementation and administration factors had spurious correlations with user satisfaction. Doll and Torkzadeh's research suggests that user participation's effectiveness may be limited to a specific and somewhat narrow set of decision issues in systems analysis.

To measure whether users participate as much as they want in systems analysis, the researchers used a participation congruence instrument developed by Doll and Torkzadeh (1991). To scale participation congruence, respondents are asked how much they desired (wanted) to participate in specific systems analysis decisions and how much they actually did participate using the items X1 to X8 illustrated in Table 1. For each item, the difference between desired and actual participation provides a direct measure of whether the end user participate as much as they want. These differences are summed over the eight items to provide a single measure of participation congruence. The scale is reversed; thus, high participation congruence exists when an individual's desire to participate in a specific decision activity equals to their actual (i.e. perceived) level of participation.

The congruence instrument assumes a unidimensional construct consisting of a variety of systems analysis activities that have the same or nearly the same impacts on dependent variables such as user satisfaction and task performance. It seems plausible that project initiation, determining information needs, analyzing information flows, and designing input/output formats may require different end-user skills or expertise and that, thus, each of these activities may not be equally effective.

The eight-item congruence instrument is reliable (Torkzadeh and Doll, 1994), distinguishable from its components (i.e., actual and desired participation), and a better predictor of end-user computing satisfaction than perceived participation (Doll and Torkzadeh, 1991).

The eight-item participation congruence scale had a reliability (alpha) of .95 in this sample. The project initiation, information needs, information flows, and format design subscales had reliabilities (alpha) of .92, .89, .88, and .89, respectively. These results suggest that the eight-item scale and each of the subscales have adequate reliability.

Participation is considered effective if it improves user satisfaction with the resultant application or the user's task productivity. To explore the efficacy of the eight-item participation instrument as well as the initiation, information needs analysis, information flow analysis, and format design subscales, the researchers used the 12-item end-user computing satisfaction scale (Doll and Torkzadeh, 1988) and a 3-item task productivity scale. In this sample, the end-user satisfaction instrument has a reliability (alpha) of .93.

The task productivity scale measures a user's perception of a specific application's impact on his/her work. The task productivity items are: "This application increases my productivity", "This application allows me to accomplish more work than would otherwise be possible", and "This application saves me time." A five-point scales is used (1=not at all, 2=a little, 3=moderate, 4=much, 5=a great deal). In this sample, the task productivity scale has a reliability (alpha) of .93.

Methods for Testing Substantive Hypotheses

H1A and H1B are tested by examining the correlations between the eight-item congruence instrument and the dependent variables - end-user computing satisfaction and task productivity - for both collaborative and non-collaborative respondents. A test of the difference in correlation coefficients between independent samples (Ferguson, 1966) was used to determine whether differences between collaborative and non-collaborative groups were statistically significant.

H2A and H2B are tested in a similar manner using the four subscales for project initiation, information needs analysis, information flow analysis, and format design. However, the four subscales are highly correlated with each other, suggesting the need to test for spurious correlations. For example, the correlations between project initiation and information needs, information flows and format design are .7542, .7303, .7088, respectively. Information needs correlation with information flows and format design are .7966 and .7702, respectively. Information flows also has a .7427 correlation with format design. Thus, correlations between project initiation, information flows, and format design on one hand and satisfaction or productivity on the other might be an artifact of these variables' high correlation with information needs analysis. Thus, even where the correlations were not significantly different, the researchers checked for spurious correlations.

Previous research has shown that the effective range of participation decisions did not include factors such as participation in implementation and project administration. These factors had spurious correlations with user satisfaction i.e, correlations that were an artifact of their correlation with participation in systems analysis decisions (Doll and Torkzadeh, 1990). Due to this prior evidence of spurious correlation, the researchers felt that they should also examine the subscales measuring project initiation, information needs, information flow, and format design for spurious correlations with satisfaction and task productivity. Partial correlation analysis was used to provide a simple and effective test for spurious correlations.

RESULTS

The collaborative and non-collaborative subgroups are compared in Table 3. The mean scores of overall participation congruence as well as the project initiation, information needs, information flows and format design were not significantly different between collaborative and non-collaborative applications. This indicates that the gap between actual and desired participation is not effected by whether the application is used for collaborative purposes. A reasonable inference is that systems analysts are not making special efforts to encourage user to participate as much as they want in the development of collaborative applications.

The mean scores for end-user computing satisfaction and task productivity are significantly higher for collaborative applications. The biggest change is in task productivity which changed from 9.7 to 12.1, almost a 25 percent increase. The researchers wanted to examine whether the higher satisfaction and productivity scores reported in Table 3 for collaborative

Table 3: Analysis of Collaborative and Non-collaborative Subgroups

Dimension	Non-collaborative Applications M (SD)	Collaborative Applications M (SD)	p-value of the difference between means
Overall participation (X1 thru X8)	29.560 (8.922)	29.683 (9.398)	.4509
Project Initiation (X1 & X2)	7.425 (2.477)	7.608 (2.628)	.2492
Information Needs Analysis (X3 & X4)	7.050 (2.518)	7.316 (2.541)	.1601
Information Flows Analysis (X5 & X6)	7.792 (2.316)	7.533 (2.446)	.1529
Format Design (X7 & X8)	7.136 (2.630)	7.213 (2.626)	.3902
End-user Computing Satisfaction	46.778 (8.566)	49.247 (7.905)	.0022
Task Productivity	9.703 (3.861)	12.104 (2.799)	.0000

applications are an artifact of differences in application mix between the collaborative and non-collaborative categories. If users evaluated decision support application more favorably than the other types, the higher satisfaction or productivity scores for collaborative applications might be due to having a greater percentage of decision support applications in the collaborative category.

Table 4: Analysis of Collaborative and Non-collaborative by Application Type

Application Type	End-User Satisfaction			Task Productivity		
	Non-Collab. M (SD)	Collab. M (SD)	p-value of difference between means	Non-Collab. M (SD)	Collab. M (SD)	p-value of difference between means
Decision Support	49.78 (7.83)	49.88 (7.67)	.9292	10.97 (3.82)	12.46 (2.34)	.0016
Database	45.89 (8.74)	47.30 (10.31)	.6084	8.80 (4.16)	11.50 (3.62)	.0154
Transaction Processing	43.57 (9.14)	46.58 (9.64)	.0904	8.98 (3.56)	11.50 (3.24)	.0002

Table 4 compares satisfaction and productivity scores by type of application for both collaborative and non-collaborative applications. For each type of application (decision support, database, transaction processing) the end-user satisfaction scores are not significantly (p <.05) higher for applications that are used collaboratively. This suggests that the higher satisfaction scores for collaborative applications, as reported in Table 3, is an artifact of differences in application mix. However, differences in application mix do not explain the higher task productivity scores for collaborative applications. For each type of application the task productivity scores are significantly (p <.05) higher for applications that are used collaboratively than for the same type of application that is not used collaboratively. When applications are used to enhance collaborative work, information technology's potential for improving productivity is enhanced.

Results for Hypotheses H1A and H1B

The results for H1A and H1B are depicted in Table 5. Overall participation congruence has a significant (p <.01) correlation with end-user computing satisfaction among non-collaborative and collaborative applications, .3622 and .3679, respectively. This difference is non-significant. Thus, H1A, the hypothesis that participation is more effective at improving user satisfaction in collaborative applications, is rejected.

Overall participation congruence has a non-significant correlation with task productivity (r=.0511) among non-collaborative applications. However, it has a significant (p <.01) correlation with task productivity (r=.2533) among collaborative applications. This difference is significant at p < .0212. Thus, H1B, the hypothesis that participation is more effective at improving task productivity in collaborative applications, is not rejected.

This means that, from the perspective of improving user satisfaction, permitting end users to participate as much as they want in systems analysis decision is equally effective in both collaborative and non-collaborative applications. If the goal is satisfied users, user participation works regardless of the nature of the application.

More interestingly, these results suggest that permitting end users to participate as much as they want in systems analysis decisions is ineffective at improving productivity among non-collaborative applications. A significant participation-productivity relationship is only present among collaborative applications. If the goal is more productive users, user participation appears to work in collaborative applications. The evidence suggests that user participation's power to enhance productivity is more limited among non-collaborative applications.

Table 5: Correlations Between Participation Congruence Dimensions and Dependent Variables

Participation Congruence Dimension	End-User Satisfaction				Task Productivity			
	Overall (n=402)	Non-Collab. (n=239)	Collab. (n=163)	p-value #	Overall (n=402)	Non-Collab. (n=239)	Collab. (n=163)	p-value #
Overall Participation (X1 to X8)	.3629***	.3622***	.3679***	.4744	.1178**	.0511	.2533***	.0212
Project Initiation (X1,X2)	.2682***	.2544***	.2832***	.3809	.0927	.0067	.2364***	.0111
Information Needs (X3,X4)	.3551***	.3238***	.3943***	.2145	.1625***	.0927	.2764***	.0312
Information Flows (X5,X6)	.2916***	.2691***	.3502***	.1903	.0743	.0332	.2149***	.0354
Format Design (X7,X8)	.3202***	.3329***	.3022***	.3694	.0839	.0256	.2000**	.0418

Note. * indicates significant level at .10; ** indicates significant level at .05; and *** indicates significant level at .01.
p-value is for test of differences in correlations between collaborative and non-collaborative groups

Socio-technical (Pasmore and Sherwood, 1978; Pasmore, 1995) systems theory provides a possible explanation of these results. This theory says that, to optimize productivity, both the social system and the technical system must be considered in the design of work. Systems that are optimized for technology, but do not consider the collaborative social environment of work, will be less productive. Collaborative applications are complex social and technical systems. The team or work group can achieve its goals in many ways. User participation enables the analyst to understand how the work group wants to use information technology to get their job done. It enhances both design and utilization by incorporating the creative contributions of diverse stakeholders.

Socio-technical systems theory may also be applicable to non-collaborative applications. However, the low use of these systems to coordinate work with others suggests that these jobs have not, as yet, been redesigned from a process perspective that emphasizes lateral relationships. Here user participation may enhance design, but the design may focus narrowly on the requirements of one user or category of user. Design and utilization do not benefit from the creative contributions of diverse stakeholders. Thus, participation's potential for productivity improvement is limited.

Results for Hypothesis H2A and H2B

Table 5 indicates that project initiation, information needs analysis, information flow analysis, and format design have significant correlations with end-user satisfaction, .2682, .3551, .2916, and .3202, respectively. While information needs has the highest correlation with satisfaction, it is not significantly higher that the others. Information needs analysis has a significant ($p < .01$) correlation ($r = .1625$) with task productivity while the others have nonsignificant correlations. Again, information need's correlation with task productivity is not significantly higher than project initiation's ($r=.0927$), information flows ($.0743$) or format design ($.0839$). Thus, without examining partial correlations, H2A and H2B would be rejected.

Because the participation subscales are highly correlated with each other, the researchers conducted a partial correlation analysis using the overall sample of 402 respondents. In Table 6a, the participation congruence dimensions are correlated with user satisfaction and task productivity while controlling for the impact of information needs analysis. With the effect of information needs partialed out, overall participation scale as well as the participation scales for project initiation, information flows, and format design have nonsignificant correlations with user satisfaction. With the effect of information needs partialed out, overall participation scale as well as the

Table 6: Partial Correlations Between Participation Congruence Dimensions and Dependent Variables

Congruence Dimension	End-User Satisfaction	Task Productivity
a. Partial Correlation Analysis Controlling for Information Needs (X3,X4)		
Participation Congruence Dimension		
Overall Participation Congruence (X1 to X8)	.0237	-.0963**
Project Initiation Congruence (X1,X2)	-.0030	-.0520
Information Flows Congruence (X5,X6)	-.0219	-.1391***
Format Design Congruence (X7,X8)	.0546	-.0622
b. Information Needs Partial Correlations With Dependent Variables		
Congruence Dimension Controlled		
Controlling for Project Initiation (X1,X2)	.2429***	.1373***
Controlling for Information Flows (X5,X6)	.2558***	.2183***
Controlling for Format Design (X7,X8)	.2075***	.1515***

Note.* indicates significant level at .10; ** indicates significant level at .05; and *** indicates significant level at .01.

participation scales for project initiation, information flows, and format design have negative partial correlations with task productivity. Two of these negative partial correlations are statistically significant, -.0963 for overall participation (p < .05) and -.1391 for information flows (p <.01).

Table 6b reports information need's first-order partial correlations with user satisfaction and task productivity while controlling for each of the other participation subscales. While partialling out the effects of project initiation, information flows, and format design participation, information needs retains significant (p <.01) positive partial correlations with both end-user satisfaction and task productivity.

These results provide strong support that participation in information needs analysis is the only active causal agent that predicts end-user satisfaction and task productivity. The researchers conducted this analysis for both the collaborative and the non-collaborative subsamples with almost identical results to those reported in Tables 6a and 6b. In both subsamples, information needs was the only active causal agent predicting satisfaction and task productivity. The significant positive correlations reported in Table 5 between project initiation, information flow analysis, and format design on one hand and user satisfaction or task productivity on the other, appear to be spurious.

On the basis of this partial correlation analysis, the researchers failed to reject hypothesis H2A and H2B. The results suggest that, unlike participative decision making where a broad range of decision issues might be effective, the range of effective decision issues in the development of collaborative or non-collaborative applications appears to be limited to narrow set of decision issues surrounding the assessment of information needs where users have special expertise by virtual of their work experience and training. User participation in project initiation, information flows analysis, and format design appear to be "ancillary" in that they are additional decision activities that might clarify, supplement or embellish our understanding of user information needs. The significant negative partial correlation between information flow analysis and task productivity suggests that permitting end users to participate as much as they want in technical issues where they may not possess unique skills or training may be dysfunctional.

CONCLUSIONS

In this new area of collaborative organizations, information technology offers substantial promise for improving productivity. This sample of major applications at 18 firms reveals that information technology already plays an important role in enhancing productivity by facilitating collaborative work. The key to achieving further productivity gains is to remember that the real goal is not to build collaborative systems, but to use information technology to enhance collaboration. The system-use paradigm is fundamental to this effort.

This study indicates that user participation is more effective in enhancing productivity in the context of collaborative work systems. This suggests that the design of collaborative work systems should itself be a collaborative activity between analysts and users. Moving the analyst-user relationship from participation to collaboration requires a common goal. By focusing both users and analysts on using information technology to enhance collaborative work rather than building collaborative systems, the system-use paradigm provides the common goal necessary to support this transition.

This study suggests that users should be encouraged to participate as much as they want in the development of collaborative applications. While the extent of participation should not be limited, the range of participatory issues should focus on supporting collaborative work by determining the information needs of a broad network of stakeholders who might improve how they work together. Encouraging too much user participation on technical issues such as information flow analysis where users do not have special expertise can be dysfunctional. The results suggest that the range of decision issues that are effective in improving user satisfaction or productivity are narrow and focused around information needs analysis.

This study uses reflective measures of actual and desired user participation obtained after implementation. Scores obtained after implementation may differ from those obtained during the process. Future research efforts might cross validate these findings using participation measures obtained just after the user engages in project initiation, information needs analysis, information flows analysis, and format design.

REFERENCES

Barki, H., and Hartwick, J. (1994). Measuring user participation, user involvement, and user attitude. *MIS Quarterly, 18*(1), 59 – 82.

Black, S., and Gregersen, H. (1997). Participative decision-making: An integration of multiple dimensions. *Human Relations, 50*(7), 859 – 878.

Cotton, J., Vollrath, D., Froggatt, K., Lengnick-Hall, M., and Jennings, K. (1988). Employee participation: Diverse forms and different outcomes. *Academy of Management Review, 13*(1), 8 – 22.

Dachler, H., and Wilpert, B. (1978). Conceptual dimensions and boundaries of participation in organizations: A critical evaluation. *Administrative Science Quarterly, 23*(1), 1 – 39.

Davenport, T. (1993). *Process innovation: Reengineering work through information technology.*, Boston, MA: Harvard Business School Press.

Davis, K. (1963). The case for participative management. *Business Horizons, 6,* 55 – 60.

Derber, M. (1963). Worker participation in Israeli management. *Industrial Relations, 3,* 51 – 72.

Doll, W. J., and Torkzadeh, G. (1988). The measurement of end-user computing satisfaction. *MIS Quarterly, 12*(2), 259 – 274.

Doll, W. J., and Torkzadeh, G. (1989). A discrepancy model of end-user computing involvement. *Management Science, 35*(10), 1151 – 1171.

Doll, W. J., and Torkzadeh, G. (1990). The measurement of end-user software involvement. *Omega, 18*(4), 399 – 406.

Doll, W. J., and Torkzadeh, G. (1991). A congruence construct of user involvement. *Decision Sciences, 22*(2), 443 – 453.

Doll, W. J., and Torkzadeh, G. (1998). Developing a multidimensional measure of system-use in an organizational context. *Information and Management, 33*(4), 171 – 185.

Edstrom, A. (1977). User influence and the success of MIS projects: A confirmatory approach. *Human Relations, 30*(7), 589 – 607.

Ferguson, G. (1966). *Statistical analysis in psychology and education.* New York: McGraw-Hill.

Franz, C., and Robey, D. (1986). Organizational context, user involvement, and the usefulness of information systems. *Decision Sciences, 17*(3), 329 – 356.

Ghoshal, S., and Bartlett, C. A. (1997). *The Individualized Corporation*. New York, NY: HarperBusiness.

Hargrove, R. (1998). *Mastering the art of creative collaboration*. New York: McGraw-Hill.

Harrington, H. J. (1991). *Business process improvement: the breakthrough strategy for total quality, productivity, and competitiveness*. New York: McGraw-Hill.

Ives, B., and Olson, M. (1984). User involvement and MIS success: a review of research. *Management Science, 30*(5), 586 – 603.

Johansen, R. (1988). *Groupware: Computer support for business teams*. New York, N.Y: The Free Press.

Kendall, K., and Kendall, J. (1995). *Systems analysis and design* (3rd ed.). Upper Saddle River, NJ: Prentice Hall.

Kock, N. (1999). *Process improvement and organizational learning: the role of collaborative technologies*. Hershey, PA: Idea-Group Publishing.

Locke, E. A., and Schweiger, D. M. (1979). Participation in decision making: One more look. *Research in Organizational Behavior, 1*, 265 – 339.

Maier, N.R.F. (1965). Group decision in England and the United States. *Personnel Psychology, 15*, 75 – 87.

Marshak, D. (1994). The disappearance of groupware. In P. Lloyd (Eds.), *Groupware in the 21st century: Computer supported cooperative working towards the millennium* (pp. 24 – 28). Westport, CT: Praeger.

McKeen, J., and Guimaraes, T. (1997). Successful strategies for user participation in systems development. *Journal of Management Information Systems, 14*(2), 133 – 150.

McKeen, J., Guimaraes, T., and Wetherbe, J. (1994). The relationship between user participation and user satisfaction: An investigation of four contingency factors. *MIS Quarterly, 18(*4), 427 – 451.

Miller, K., and Monge, P. (1986). Participation, satisfaction, and productivity: A meta-analytic review. *Academy of Management Journal, 29*(4), 727 – 753.

Neilson, R. (1997). *Collaborative technologies and organizational learning*. Hershey, PA: Idea-Group Publishing.

Pasmore, W. (1995). Social science transformed: the socio-technical perspective. *Human Relations, 48*(1), 1 – 21.

Pasmore, W. A., and Sherwood, J. J. (Eds.). (1978). *Sociotechnical systems*. La Jolla, CA: University Associates.

Pasternack, B., and Viscio, A. (1998). *The centerless corporation*. New York, NY: Simon and Schuster.

Schrage, M. (1990). *Shared minds: the new technologies of collaboration.* New York, NY: Random House.

Shelly, G., Cashman, T, Adamski, J., and Adamski, J. J. (1995). *Systems analysis and design* (2nd Ed.). Danvers, MA: Boyd and Fraser Publishing Company.

Torkzadeh, G., and Doll, W.J. (1994). The test-retest reliability of user involvement instruments. *Information and Management, 26*(1), 21 – 31.

Vroom, V.A. (1973). A new look at managerial decision making. *Organizational Dynamics, 3*(1), 66 – 80.

Wagner, J., and Gooding, R. (1987). Shared influence and organizational behavior: A meta-analysis of situational variables expected to moderate participation-outcome relationships. *Academy of Management Journal, 30*(3), 524 – 541.

Chapter 6

Promoting Collaboration among Trainers in the National Weather Service

Victoria C. Johnson[1] and Sherwood R. Wang
Cooperative Program for Operational Meteorology, Education and Training

BACKGROUND

In the last several years, the National Weather Service (NWS) has undergone a *massive* modernization and reorganization effort, substantially changing the organization's structure and the technologies used to produce forecasts. When the reorganization is completed in the year 2000, the NWS will have approximately 120 local weather forecast offices throughout the country (plus Puerto Rico and Guam), with over 1000 forecasters.

The new technological systems (such as Doppler radars and upgraded satellites) have produced a flood of data that requires forecasters to have up—to—date scientific knowledge, computer skills, and cognitive tools for synthesizing the vast amount of information available. Early in the modernization process, the NWS recognized the need for a strong training program to help its forecasters effectively use the new technologies and data to better predict deadly weather events. Toward that end, the NWS developed a unique peer training system and created a new position, the Science Operations Officer (SOO), in each forecast office to lead it.

Many organizations use peer training, primarily for short—term, focused training on a skill or knowledge (Bergeron, 1994; Ginger et al., 1996; Carr, 1992) or to fill gaps when training budgets have been cut (Howe, Dawson, & Gaeddert, 1991). Businesses and other organizations usually bring employees to a corporate

Previously Published in *Challenges of Information Technology Management in the 21st Century* edited by Mehdi Khosrow-Pour, Copyright © 2000, Idea Group Publishing.

training facility, teach them fundamental instructional skills and theories (Nilson, 1990) such as adult learning theory (Filipczak, 1993), and then provide them support in terms of both materials and mentoring (Trautman & Klein, 1993). Once the training need is over, the peer trainers frequently return to their previous jobs.

The NWS' training program is considerably different from the above model. First, SOOs are responsible for all aspects of training in their office, not just a single course or topic. They do not return to their 'real' jobs when the training need is over — training is a continuing responsibility. Second, most SOOs do not have prior experience in training, and many have had no training in how to be a trainer. Third, although nationally developed training materials are provided, SOOs must tailor them to address their local needs and forecast problems.

In recent years, SOOs have been assigned additional responsibilities, decreasing the time available for their training and research duties. For those with little experience or incentive to do training, other job duties can quickly take higher priority. Even for SOOs who enjoy doing it, finding time to develop and deliver training is problematic.

The NWS funds a variety of training activities, including our own program, the Cooperative Program for Operational Meteorology, Education and Training (COMET®). The COMET Program provides both on-site courses and distance learning materials. SOOs make up a substantial portion of the students attending our residence courses, but the classes focus on advances in meteorology. Neither the COMET Program or the other NWS training organizations have traditionally provided much support to SOOs in their functions related to developing and delivering training.

In the absence of training experience and a support facility, SOOs do have one major asset each other. Many SOOs have been in their jobs for several years and have learned what works and what doesn't, at least for their staffs. Those most active in training have developed dozens of local training packages that others could use, either entirely or as development templates. However, with the SOOs scattered throughout the country and reduced travel budgets, they have few opportunities to share their experiences and the materials they have developed.

IMPROVING COLLABORATION USING TECHNOLOGY

As part of the COMET Program's efforts to improve NWS training, we wanted to help SOOs share training materials and other resources they have found useful. In addition, we hoped to provide learning opportunities for those unfamiliar with educational theory, instructional design, and other components of training. A final goal was to foster a community in which best practices could be shared and more experienced members could mentor newer members.

To accomplish these goals, we developed a Web-based Training Resource Center (TRC) that consists of three main pages: Catalogue, Forum, and Other Resources (http ://meted ucar. edu/resource/soo/index . htm). The Catalogue page provides links to descriptions of locally produced training materials. The Forum page hosts threaded discussions on various topics identified from a survey as being of interest to the trainers. The Other Resources page contains miscellaneous resources pertinent to conducting an effective training program. Each of these three pages is described in more detail below.

The Catalogue page contains links to other HTML pages describing locally developed training materials. The Catalogue does not contain the training materials themselves; it merely stores descriptive information, such as information about how to acquire the product, a short description, key words, etc. A 500 (or other forecaster) who has developed a training package accesses an online form on the Catalogue page, fills in the descriptive fields, and then submits the form electronically. A CGI script automatically generates an HTML page that essentially duplicates the form. Every catalogue entry is then linked under each of five main categories (topic, location, format, presentation setting, and type) and any relevant subcategories.

The Web-based catalogue has proven to be very successful. Similar attempts to create paper-based catalogues several years ago failed, but the online catalogue apparently provides the immediacy and simplicity that the trainers require. Eight months after the TRC Web site opened, the Catalogue page had 63 entries posted by 26 different SOOs. Nineteen of 36 SOOs responding to a survey at the end of the trial period indicated that they had used the Catalogue to access a copy of at least one training product.

The Other Resources page, while not used as extensively as the Catalogue, has also been quite popular. This page contains a variety of resources, including copies of training plans developed by SOOs who are considered by their peers to be good trainers, links to resources about developing presentations, teletraining schedules, etc. One small disappointment, however, is that no SOO or other NWS employee has ever recommended some piece of information for inclusion on the page. While it would be nice to believe that we correctly identified all of the relevant materials that should be on this page, it would be better if the SOOs took more ownership by furnishing their own materials and suggestions.

The Forum page is intended as the place for discussions that we feel are key to building the community of practice among the SOOs. Initially our software engineers convinced us to use a newsgroup reader for the discussions, a tool they use frequently and feel quite comfortable with. However, in a preliminary test with a small group of SOOs, none could get the reader to work correctly without a great deal of troubleshooting on our part. Ultimately, the newsgroup reader was abandoned in favor of a shareware threaded discussion product (Matt's Script Archive at http ://www .worldwidemart.com/scripts/wwwboard. shtml). Four threaded discussions were held over an 8-month period. Two of the topics related to "best practice" suggestions, while the other two were instructional pieces (one on instructional design and the other on developing and delivering teletraining lectures).

The discussions were less successful than the Catalogue in that many people apparently observed them (according to the Web use report), but few chose to participate. The discussions may have simply been the victims of bad timing because, at the same time they were being held, all of the NWS offices were installing new computer systems that resulted in significant upheavals in daily functions. Many SOOs indicated that the installation had limited the amount of time they could spend on nonessential activities, but that they hoped to participate in discussions more fully once the installation was complete in 2000.

LESSONS LEARNED

The TRC, and particularly the Catalogue page, is a good example of an idea that had to wait for the right technology. Previous attempts to establish a paper-based catalogue of training materials had failed, mainly because 1) the submission process was too cumbersome, 2) the updated results were not immediately available, and 3) the catalogue never attained the visibility it needed. The immediacy of the Web solved all three problems. We processed every entry form within 48 hours of receiving it or, if the entry could not be posted by that time, we e-mailed the SOO with the date it could be expected to appear on the Catalogue page. This assured the SOOs that their efforts to contribute to the catalogue were valued. We also e-mailed all the SOOs whenever a new submission was received, which served to give them regular reminders to use the Catalogue and to submit their own entries. This kept the Catalogue visible in a way that had been impossible with the earlier paper-based systems.

Our main recommendation to others who want to establish a similar resource facility is to first ensure that it meets a well-defined need and has enough support from the users to assure its viability. The Catalogue clearly met those criteria. Another important factor in the catalogue's success was having enough materials already in place in the facility so that the users could see from the beginning how it could benefit them. Early acceptance is an important key to success.

In addition to the poor timing, we believe that the Forum was less successful because it did not meet the criteria of having a well-defined need. While we who instigated the TRC (and a few of the SOOs) believed in the benefits of using technology to foster community and collaboration, the majority of the users probably saw it as just one more thing to take time away from dealing with more pressing problems. We did not find a topic that was compelling enough to rise to the top of the priority list in the SOOs' daily activities. Comments from the SOOs also suggest that the technology itself may have been a drawback for some, especially those who were convinced they could learn something meaningful only through face—to-face interactions.

Other recommendations for a project of this nature are described below.

I. Enlist the active support of others who deal with the target community. We worked only with the SOOs themselves. However, there were several others at the regional and national levels in the NWS with SOO—related responsibilities, and it would probably have been beneficial if we had involved them more directly in the creation and implementation.

2. Maintain high visibility. No more than 2 weeks should go by without the users receiving some sort of message, and that message should usually announce something new on the site.

3, Maintain a network of contacts within the user community and elsewhere to identify materials needed for the site. Because the SOOs were so absorbed with the computer installation, we felt we should be as unobtrusive as possible. In the absence of that complication, however, it might have been better to work with key individuals (both experts and novices) to identify materials and to build ownership.

4. Threaded discussions should be on topics the users identify as important and are willing to commit to participating in. The timing of the discussions should take into consideration what else might make participation difficult. Also, we might have attracted a larger audience if we had had topics that involved demonstrations, prototype projects, or some other activities that actively engaged users beyond simply reading information.

5. Contributors to the Catalogue should be encouraged to develop materials that can be accessed immediately by others. Accessing most of the Catalogue entries requires contacting the originator who then sends out paper copies or computer disks. If all the materials were available on the Web or via ftp, circulation of the materials would be easier for all concerned.

6. Use simple technological tools. Any new technology can be intimidating, even when used by a computer-savvy group, such as the SOOs. If the audience gets frustrated, they often will not try again.

7. Recognize that building a community and encouraging collaboration via technology requires a great deal of hands-on support, encouragement, cajoling, and marketing.

NOTE

[1] Doctoral candidate, Nova Southeastern University. The project described was conducted by the lead author in partial fulfillment of degree requirements.

REFERENCES

Bergeron, R. (1994, August). The cascade approach: How to train 2,288 employee Lsic] in two years. ffim33, 46-47.

Carr, C. (1992). *Smart training: The manager's Guide to training for improved performance*. New York: McGraw-Hill, Inc.

Filipczak, B. (1993, June). Frick teaches Frack. *Training, 30*, 30-34.

Ginger, K. M., Moran, J. M., Weinbeck, R. S., Geer, I. W., Snow, J. T., & Smith, D. R. (1996). Project ATMOSPHERE 1995 teacher enhancement programs. *Bulletin of the American Meteorological Society, 77*, 763-769.

Howe, M. A., Dawson, C. L., & Gaeddert, D. (1991, March). Expert training that's free. *Personnel Journal, 70*, 59-63.

Nilson, C. (1990). *Training for non-trainers: A do-it-yourself guide for managers*. New York: AMACOM.

Trautman, S., & Klein, K. (1993, July). Ask an Expert. *Training & Development, 48*, 45-48.

Chapter 7

A KM-Enabled Architecture for Collaborative Systems

Lina Zhou & Dongsong Zhang
University of Arizona, Tucson, USA

Driven by the collaborative technology, COllaborative SYstems (COSY) facilitate information management in the organizations. In face of the dynamic and information-overloaded age, knowledge management (KM) has been recognized as an effective solution in the past few years. Thus, merging the force of COSY and KM will be very promising in increasing the competitive advantages of the organizations.

This paper proposes a KM-enabled architecture for COSY. Some research issues related with KM in the new architecture are discussed. It is shown from applying the architecture to a virtual global business company that the architecture could support and integrate COSY and KM effectively.

INTRODUCTION

With the commercialization of the collaborative systems and the popularity of Internet, COllaborative SYstems (COSY) facilitate information management in the organizations. In essence, COSY provide an environment for information collection, exchanging, and sharing, etc. They break the physical barrier of "distance" or even "time" concerning asynchronous systems and create a virtual collaborative environment. However, pure collaboration can't tackle the problem of information overload. Concerning the overwhelming information repositories remain untapped, knowledge management (KM) has been recognized as an effective solution to make sense out of the collected information. How to merge the force of COSY and KM is an emerging issue to explore. It is essential to create, organize and discover knowledge and allow it to thrive and grow across the entire

Previously Published in *Challenges of Information Technology Management in the 21st Century*
edited by Mehdi Khosrow-Pour, Copyright © 2000, Idea Group Publishing.

enterprise or organization. In this paper, we are going to design a KM-enabled architecture for COSY.

KNOWLEDGE MANAGEMENT AND COLLABORATIVE SYSTEMS
Knowledge and Knowledge Management (KM)

Figure 1: Knowledge & Knowledge Management (IME, 1998)

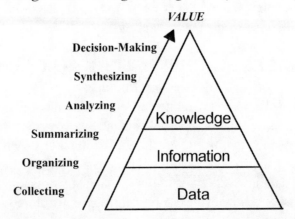

The relation between knowledge and KM has been illustrated in Figure 1. From large amount of data to concise knowledge, its value is gradually added along the KM process on the upper-left arrow. Up to date, KM has been approached from different perspectives in the discipline of business management:

- Activity view: KM consists of activities focused on gaining knowledge from its own experience and from the experience of others by an organization, and on the judicious application of that knowledge to fulfill the mission of the organization (Wenig, 1996).
- Asset view: KM is an audit of "intellectual assets" that highlights unique sources, critical functions and potential bottlenecks that hinder knowledge flows to the point of use (Grey, 1996).
- Process view: KM is a systematic process for acquiring, creating, synthesizing, sharing and using information, insights and experiences to achieve organizational goals (Andersen Consulting, 1996).

Apparently, one of the primary goals of these views is to make knowledge accessible and reusable to the enterprise.

COSY
Faced with the dispersion of expert knowledge as well as the increasing turnover rate of qualified personnel, many organizations are turning to COSY to foster

and distribute their corporate knowledge. COSY can be divided into the following categories (Kraut & Scherlis, 1998):

- Group Decision Support Systems (GDSS)
- Organizational Memory Systems
- Video Conferencing Systems
- Systems for creating virtual spaces
- Workflow and other systems to structure interaction.

COSY enhances productivity, promotes creativity, lowers costs, and most importantly, creates a central repository for the work completed and lessons learned (Nunamaker & Briggs, 1996-97).

A KM-ENABLED ARCHITECTURE FOR COSY
4-Tier Architecture

The traditional client/server architectures will not scale well because the data access, and system administration and efficiency will degrade rapidly with the increase of user connection. To address the above limitations, many development groups are moving to 3-tier architecture. The idea is to offload the code bloat on the client or the database server, centrally manage business logic and get more flexibility out of working with the database instead of just stored procedures and triggers (Kim, 1998).

To extend KM capability of the 3-tier architecture, a four-tier architecture[1] is proposed in the paper. It is implemented by attaching a KM-server tier to the data-server tier and extending the functionality of the data-server tier.

Extended Client-tier

It is responsible for presenting data, receiving user events and controlling the user interface. We extend the function of this layer to include more complex processes of presentation, such as automatic speech recognition and machine translation, and so on.

Scalable Application-server-tier

Business objects that implement the business rules "live" here, and are available to the client-tier (Kim, 1998). Extensible multithreading in this level improves the scalability of the application.

Centralized Data-server-tier

This tier is responsible for data storage. Besides the widespread relational database systems, existing legacy systems databases are often reused here (Kim, 1998). It becomes the other middle layer in the new architecture.

Figure 2: 4-tier KM-enabled Architecture for COSY

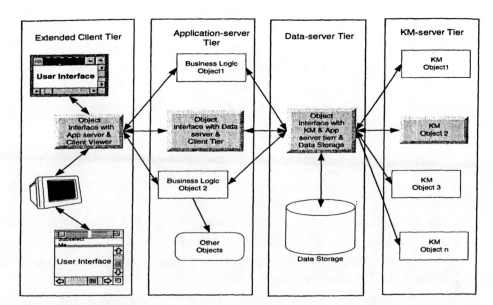

Intelligent KM-server-tier

Fed with the information from the third tier, this new end layer will further organize and discover knowledge, and add intelligence value to the available information.

Since the first 3 tiers are similar to those in the typical 3-tier architecture. We will focus on the KM-server-tier in the following discussion.

Related Research Issues

A number of research issues, fundamental to building the KM-tier of the architecture, will be briefly summarized. The term "*information*" or "*knowledge*" in the rest of the paper will be restricted to the information in text format that is required to support decision making or business processes. However, most of the following issues also fit for other type of information.

Information extraction

Information Extraction (IE) is to analyze unrestricted text in order to extract specific types of information. It can play an important role in transforming the raw material, refining and reducing it to a germ of the original document (Cowie & Lehnert, 1996). The basic approach has been to use a variety of natural language processing and statistical techniques to extract predetermined types of facts for a specific domain.

Information clustering

Information clustering can be used to group discrete similar objects for different applications. There are many different algorithms and approaches for document clustering, such as minimal spanning tree, self-organizing map and nearest neighbors, etc. It is typically based on pairwise comparisons of objects with a similarity measure. There are many variations of the similarity measures, but most of them are normalized versions of simple matching coefficient or inner product for weighted terms.

Summarization

Summarization can be used for both undirected browsing and directed browsing (Callan, 1998). It can be one of the two categories:
• Document-based: summarize the entire document
• Subject-based: summarize the parts about a particular subject.

Various methods have been developed for summarization: statistical method, linguistic method, knowledge-based method, and generation from data. Natural language processing has the potential to generate higher quality summary, but some issues like reference resolution, tense agreement, and filling quantifier, are still challenges in this area.

Information retrieval and reuse

If there is a way of automatic indexing and retrieval of the information or knowledge, people would really benefit from reusing other's experience. The retrieval techniques include exact-match retrieval, basic probabilistic retrieval model, vector space model, and Latent semantic indexing (Yang & Liu, 1999). Clustering makes it possible to retrieve documents that may not have many terms in common with the query. Collaborative information filtering (Billsus & Pazzani, 1998) is another way to reuse the old information or knowledge. Information filtering can use such methods as exact match, user profile, vector space model or Bayesian network model. Among many other important issues related with KM, there are information visualization, knowledge representation, and KM performance evaluation. Next, we are going to apply the new architecture to a virtual global business company.

EXAMPLE STUDY UNDER THE KM-ENABLED COLLABORATIVE ARCHITECTURE

In the global economy age, a typical business company will need distributed collaboration among its branches, customers, suppliers around the world. As is shown in Figure 3, various COSY and KM components are useful for this scenario.

Figure 3: A collaborative architecture design for a virtual global business company

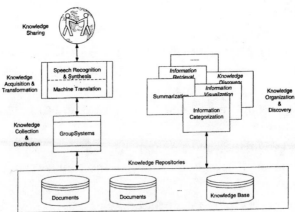

Components of the system

Since the 3-tier collaborative technology is relatively new, few of the existing COSY have adapted to the new framework. Thus, we will make use of one of the 2-tier COSY –GroupSystems to explain the architecture.

GroupSystems

GroupSystems comes with a Standard Tools set, which uses group processes such as brainstorming, information gathering, voting, organizing, and consensus building (Ventana Corporations, 1996). The Electric Brainstorming activity and the Categorizer activity have been selected in this sample system.

Machine translation (MT)

MT systems can be built based on syntax, semantics or pragmatics (Nida & Taber, 1969). There has been some success in machine assisted human translation and translation between particular language pairs or in particular domains, such as Systran (SYSTRAN, 1999).

Speech recognition and synthesis

Automatic speech recognition (ASR) is concerned with building systems that can convert speech into words, while speech synthesis can convert the text sentence into computer-generated speech. Dragon Systems Inc. is a leading worldwide supplier of speech and language technology.

Processes involved in the virtual system

1) Users directly input their ideas into the computer or speak to ASR system. Then, the input text will be fed into MT system, which could translate the text

from the user's preferred language into the language the GroupSystems can accept, say English.

2) The Brainstorming in GroupSystems acquires knowledge from all the users and save it in the knowledge repository.

3) Knowledge organization and discovery includes the following two steps:

a) Cluster the comments collected from Brainstorming into different groups.

b) Generate short summarization for each group.

4) The Categorizer in GroupSystems reads the classified results and displays them to all the users.

5) MT system could translate the English text in the Categorizer into the user's preferred language. Finally, the translated text will be synthesized and broadcast to the participants.

6) Participating users start to share the knowledge.

DISCUSSION AND FUTURE RESEARCH

The proposed architecture for KM-enabled COSY adds a KM-server layer to the regular 3-tier architecture, which enriches the KM capability for the traditional COSY in a large degree. It not only adapts the COSY to the emerging KM requirements, but also helps users make better sense of the collaboration results. Finally, it is expected to improve decision-making, retain corporate memory, increase innovation and support the conversion of information into knowledge (IME, 1998). It is shown from the study of a virtual global business company that the new architecture could meet KM needs in the collaborative situation effectively. Many other applications under the new paradigm are worth to explore in the future.

[1] Since there might be more than one middle tier, so 4-tier really means at least 4-tier architecture.

REFERENCES

Andersen Consulting (1996).URL:http://www.ac.com/services/knowledge/km_home.html.

Billsus, D., & Pazzani, M. (1998). Learning Collaborative Information Filters. In Machine Learning: *Proceedings of the 15th International Conference.*

Callan, J. (1998). Document Summarization, URL: http://ciir.cs.umass.edu/cmpsci646/Notes/Summarization/index.htm.

Cowie, J., & Lehnert, W. (1996). Information Extraction. *Communications of the ACM*, 39(1), 80-91.

Grey, D. (1996). What is knowledge management? Newman, B.D (ed.). The Knowledge Management Forum. URL: http://www.km-forum.org/what_is.htm.

IME (1998). Information Management & Economics, Inc. URL: http://home.istar.ca/~ime/knowledge.htm.

Kim, T. (1998). Looking for a 3-Tier App Builder. Java Developer's Journal. SYS-CON Publications, Inc. 3(1).

Kraut, R. & Scherlis, W. (1998). Computer Supported Collaborative Work. URL: http://www.cs.cmu.edu/afs/cs/user/wls/www/cscw.

Nida, E., & Taber, C. (1969). The theory and practice of translation, Leiden: Brill.

Nunamaker J. F, & Briggs, R. O., et al. (1996-97). Lessons from a dozen years of group support systems research: a discussion of lab and field findings. *Journal of Management Information Systems*. 13(3). 63-207.

SYSTRAN (1999). Systran Translation Software. URL: http://www.systransoft.com/.

Ventana Corporations (1996). URL: http://www.ventana.com/html/overview.html.

Wenig, R. G. (1996). Knowledge Management. Newman, B.D (ed.). The Knowledge Management Forum. URL: http://www.km-forum.org/what_is.htm.

Yang, Y., & Liu, X.(1999). A re-examination of text categorization methods. *ACM SIGIR Conference on Research and Development in Information Retrieval (SIGIR)*. 42-49.

Chapter 8

Computer-Mediated Inter-Organizational Knowledge-Sharing: Insights from a Virtual Team Innovating Using a Collaborative Tool*

Ann Majchrzak
University of Southern California

Ronald E. Rice
Rutgers University

Nelson King
University of Southern California

Arvind Malhotra
University of North Carolina at Chapel Hill

Sulin Ba
University of Southern California

How does a team use a computer-mediated technology to share and reuse knowledge when the team is inter-organizational and virtual, when the team must compete for the attention of team members with collocated teams, and when the task is the creation of a completely new innovation? From a review of the literature on knowledge sharing and reuse using collaborative tools,

Previously Published in the *Information Resource Management Journal, vol.13, no.1*, Copyright © 2000, Idea Group Publishing.

three propositions are generated about the likely behavior of the team in using the collaborative tool and reusing the knowledge put in the knowledge repository. A multi-method longitudinal research study of this design team was conducted over their ten-month design effort. Both qualitative and quantitative data were obtained. Results indicated that the propositions from the literature were insufficient to explain the behavior of the team. We found that ambiguity of the task does not determine use of a collaborative tool; that tool use does not increase with experience; and that knowledge that is perceived as transient (whether it really is transient or not) is unlikely to be referenced properly for later search and retrieval. Implications for practice and theory are discussed.

How does a team use a computer-mediated technology to share and reuse knowledge when the team is inter-organizational and virtual, and when the task is the creation of a completely new innovation?

This is an important set of interrelated questions because of the increasing use of *virtual inter-organizational collaboration* and the development and diffusion of *collaborative technologies* (CT) to facilitate the collaboration process (Allen & Jarman, 1999; Coleman, 1997; Haywood, 1998; Lipnack & Stamps, 1997). Dow, Ford, Chrysler and British Petroleum are well-known examples of companies diffusing CTs to facilitate their work (Ferranti 1997; Hamblen 1998). A Gartner Group (1997) study went as far as to say: "Real-time collaboration use will change from virtually nothing to ubiquity by 1999" (p.26).

The use of CTs is fundamental to making virtual teams work. A CT, also referred to as a virtual workplace, should be able to record, at a minimum, the process of the group, an agenda, libraries of solutions and practices, different forms of interaction, meta-information (such as date, sequence, author of contributions), and provide shared information storage, access and retrieval (Ellis et al., 1991; Field, 1996; Ishii et al., 1994; Kling, 1991; Nunamaker et al., 1993, 1995; Romano et al., 1998; Thornton & Lockard, 1994).

Critical, then, for knowledge-sharing and reuse with CTs is that the CT includes not just a mechanism for exchanging information (such as e-mail), but a mechanism for creating a knowledge repository and a mechanism for accessing the knowledge repository. In this paper, we report results from a 10-month field study of an inter-organizational virtual engineering design team and describe how a CT is used with respect to knowledge-sharing. The two questions we address are: (1) When do members of a virtual, distributed, inter-organizational team designing an innovative new product use a CT to collaborate? (2) When and how do team members reuse the knowledge once it is shared in the knowledge repository of the CT?

LITERATURE REVIEW AND RESEARCH PROPOSITIONS

The criticality of CTs to collaborative work has been well-recognized in the literature (see Eveland & Bikson, 1989; Galegher & Kraut, 1990; Hiltz & Turoff, 1993; Johansen, 1988, 1992; Olson & Atkins 1990; Rice & Shook, 1990; Romano et al., 1998; Schrage, 1990). Among the many factors affecting the use of CTs suggested by these studies, two are of primary concern to us in this study: 1) *experience* with the CT and 2) *task* being accomplished using the CT.

Experience with a CT is a critical factor because, typically, teams use face-to-face media to share crucial knowledge on the extant norms, habits, and political relationships, in addition to content (Ehrlich, 1987; Kraut et al., 1998; Markus, 1992; Perin, 1991; Rice & Gattiker, 1999; Saunders & Jones, 1990). Over time, however, teams have been observed to gradually adjust to conveying richer information through the collaborative tool (Hiltz & Turoff, 1981; Orlikowski et al., 1995; Walther, 1992).

In addition to experience, studies have also found that not all tasks that a team might undertake to accomplish its objective are best suited for use with CTs. Several theories provide foundations for this perspective: "information richness" theory, "social presence" theory (Daft & Lengel, 1986; Rice 1984, 1987; Short et al., 1976), and the task circumplex model (McGrath & Hollingshead, 1993). These theories argue that organizational information-processing activities are differentially supported by various media; the attributes of certain media match the information processing requirements of some activities better than others. Because of the kind of information they can transmit (nonverbal cues, etc.), some channels (face-to-face, videoconferencing, etc.) are particularly suited for tasks that are not analyzable, non-routine, equivocal and involve manageable amounts of information. Nonanalyzable tasks that teams might perform include strategic direction-setting, brainstorming, and conflict resolution. For such tasks, the theories predict that, given the option, teams will opt to use what can be called "interpersonal" methods of sharing knowledge since such methods provide the most context-rich capability. The most personal of these methods is the face-to-face meeting. For distributed team members, dyadic phone conversations are not nearly as interpersonal, but they provide at least the opportunity to share information in a one-on-one setting with aural cues. In contrast to these interpersonal methods are computer-mediated collaborative tools that share the information with the entire team. Collaborative tools are generally considered less likely to be used for ambiguous tasks because their public text-based computer-mediated nature makes it more difficult to share the context-rich information needed to understand the task.

Sharing knowledge and putting the shared knowledge into a knowledge repository are an important start in knowledge-sharing and the basis for organizational memory (Davenport et al., 1996; Huber, 1991; Walsh & Ungson, 1991). The repository alone is insufficient, however. For shared knowledge to be meaningfully used, the knowledge needs to be coupled with mechanisms for organization, retention, maintenance, search and retrieval of the information (Stein & Zwass, 1995). Such mechanisms are often computer-based, ranging from simple keyword organizing principles to complex intelligent agents and neural networks that grow with the growth of the knowledge repositories (Ellis et al., 1991; Johansen, 1988; Maes, 1994). Common among all these mechanisms is that they are established at the outset of a project (such as keywords) and are not generally modified during use. Thus, the literature indicates that these mechanisms, if established at the outset to promote knowledge reuse, will generally succeed at promoting knowledge reuse.

Although past research has yielded these important suggestions for the use of CTs, the literature on the use of CTs identifies a whole host of individual, technology, organizational, and group process factors that can also affect the use of CTs in sharing and reusing knowledge (DeSanctis & Gallupe, 1987; Furst, Blackburn & Rosen, 1999; Hibbard, 1997; Rice & Gattiker, 1999; Sambamurthy & Chin, 1994). Because of the many factors that affect the knowledge-sharing and use process, we contend it is difficult to determine which conclusions from the literature apply in all situations. Others (e.g., Kraemer & Pinnsonneault, 1990) have made similar arguments.

One aspect of a situation that has been little studied is the use of CTs among highly creative teams. Most studies of virtual team knowledge-sharing have been conducted on teams working on defined tasks such as software development. We believe that the decision process for creating an entirely innovative design, such as is called for in "discontinuous technology developments" (Iansiti, 1995; Tushman & Anderson, 1986), is fundamentally different than making decisions about problems for which there is a known solution or process because the brainstorming is neither anonymous nor non-evaluative, the knowledge to be shared is highly contextualized and reliant on informal opportunities of physical proximity, and knowledge-sharing involves not just synthesizing information but dissecting and recreating that knowledge in fundamentally different ways (Allen, 1985; Davis, 1984; Kraut et al., 1990).

Given these characteristics of knowledge-sharing in creative contexts, conclusions about how CTs are used to share knowledge among team members with more routine tasks may not apply. For example, for creative tasks, the theories noted above all suggest that knowledge-sharing be performed face-to-face. However, for a creative design team, this would mean that most if not all their work be done face-to-face. Such a conclusion seems too extreme and negates the purpose of virtual design teams.

In sum, then, a situation that has particularly been under-studied is the use of CTs for knowledge-sharing among: a) distributed team members b) working collaboratively c) across organizations d) via a collaborative tool to e) create a revolutionary new product. As a starting point, we used the suggestions from the literature on using CTs for knowledge-sharing and knowledge reuse as propositions to be examined for this special population of virtual teams.

We examined two propositions for using CTs to share knowledge:

Proposition #1: A distributed virtual team will initially show little use of CT, but its use of CT will increase over time as the members gain more experience with it.

Proposition #2: When a distributed virtual team performs highly ambiguous tasks, the members will use person (face-to-face or phone) more than CT-based media; but when the task is less ambiguous, the members will use the CT more..

We examined one proposition for using CTs to reuse knowledge:

Proposition #3: Establishing technology features and mechanisms for knowledge reuse at the beginning of a project will prompt the virtual team to reuse knowledge during the course of the project.

RESEARCH DESIGN
Site, Sample, and Project

We explored these three propositions through a longitudinal research study of an engineering design team for the ten months during its conceptual design process. The team involved eight engineers spending a small (<15%) fraction of each of their total work time from three different companies (RocketCo, 6SigmaCo, and StressCo as pseudonyms); the project was referred to by the code name for the product, "Slice". Their goal was to design a new form of a rocket engine thrust chamber. The engineers were organized into a traditional concept development team consisting of a project team leader, conceptual designer, lead design engineer, design engineer, stress analyst, aerothermal analyst, combustion analyst, and a producibility analyst.

The Slice team's design task was a highly innovative one: to design a high-performance rocket injector using combustible fluids that had not been used together previously in RocketCo, at a manufacturing cost that was a significant reduction over what had been previously achieved. The innovation of using a different combination of fluids meant that knowledge of fluid dynamics and combustion behavior acquired from previous designs could not be applied directly to this one. As a result, the design process became more iterative than usual, one in which ideas were generated, analyses performed, guesses made, and ideas thrown out when people didn't seem convinced of the idea's feasibility or analysis results.

In addition to the product innovation, the team was tasked with the explicit objective of innovating in the use of a collaborative tool among geographically dispersed team members; this also represented an innovation for the company. As a result, they saw that part of their effort was not only to design a product (a rocket thrust chamber), but to develop a new process (use of a collaborative tool). Finally, the fact that three companies were involved in this early stage of concept development was new, especially for RocketCo, which considered rocket engine design its core competency. The other companies were included because they had core competencies in producibility engineering and stress analysis, which are crucial components in the initial development of a rocket engine.

Despite all the complexities faced by the team and a poor mid-project review by senior technical managers, by the end of the project, the team was judged by the senior managers in RocketCo as successfully achieving its objectives. The team designed a thrust chamber for a new rocket engine with only six parts instead of the traditional hundreds, with a predicted quality rating of 9 sigma (less than one failure out of 10 billion) instead of the traditional 2 to 4 sigma, at a first unit cost of $50,000 instead of millions, and at a predicted production cost of $35,000 instead of millions. The team was able to achieve all of this with no member serving more than 15% of his time, within the development budget, with total engineering hours 10 times less than traditional teams, using a new collaborative technology with several partners having no history of working together. Finally, senior management has been sufficiently impressed with the design to approve it for the next step in the development process: a cold flow test assessing the validity of the assumptions of liquid flow through the parts.

Thus, this study provides an excellent opportunity to observe a highly successful virtual team using a CT to accomplish its task.

Description of the Collaborative Technology

Team members had two types of communication channels available to them: interpersonal (which included face-to-face for a few members in RocketCo, three team-wide meetings, and the telephone for all members), and the collaborative tool (e-mail was infrequently used).

The collaborative tool available to them was called The Internet Notebook ("Notebook"). This CT allowed team members access to a project knowledge repository, which was housed on a centralized server located at the tool vendor's site. The Notebook was typically launched as a helper application from an HTML browser. Each time a team member would log-on to the central server, he could either just view the notebook without launching the Notebook application, or he could launch the full application. Launching the application provided the engineer with both the knowledge repository as well as such useful capabilities that permitted authoring new documents (called entries), commenting on entries in the notebook, sorting entries by date, keyword or reference links, navigating to find entries, creating sketches using a whiteboard, "snapshotting" and hot-linking screen displays from other applications, creating a personal profile for e-mail notification of relevant entries, using templates for frequent team activities (such as minutes, agendas), and vaulting documents requiring configuration control.

Team members could use the CT asynchronously or synchronously. Asynchronous use of the Notebook meant that a team member could make an entry into the Notebook with appropriate team members automatically notified of the entry, and then those notified members could comment on the entry and republish it. Team members also used the Notebook for synchronous team meetings which they called "teleconferences". These meetings consisted of the application-sharing Notebook for data only, and audioconferencing on a separate channel, supplemented with the Notebook's full functionalities. This is referred to by the Gartner (1997) group as the "down and dirty" approach to synchronous communication.

Data Collection Methodology

Since virtual teams evolve through different phases depending on the stages of the design project, we used a multi-method longitudinal study design (Menard, 1991):

1. Ethnographic observation (Geertz, 1973; Harvey & Myers, 1995; Hughes et al,. 1992; Orlikowski & Robey, 1991) of all 89 one-hour teleconferences and three in-person team meetings (at the kickoff, at mid-project, and at the end).

2. Panel questionnaire surveys of the eight team members at the three stages in the project: inception, for each of the 40 weeks during, and at the project,

end to collect data on team members' background, use of communication media, attitudes toward communication media, and satisfaction with team process. Standardized instruments were used and are available upon request.

3. Weekly communication network diaries completed by team members.
4. Interviews with team members after critical events.
5. A "Lessons Learned" group meeting conducted with the team members at the end of the project.
6. Weekly logs of electronic traffic using the Notebook among team members.

FINDINGS FOR PROPOSITIONS FOR USE OF CT IN KNOWLEDGE-SHARING

Findings on Proposition 1: CT Use Will Increase Over Time

Across the entire project, the team members collaborated with others 61% of their time, with the rest of the time spent in activities they could perform themselves (e.g., drawing, analysis, report-writing, etc.). We observed the choices the team members made on whether to use interpersonal media (such as face-to-face or phone) or collaboration tool support when they collaborated with others. Following our initial expectation and that of the literature's, we anticipated that the use of interpersonal media would be high initially and reduce over time while the use of the collaborative tool would be low initially and gradually increase over time.

Figure 1 presents the weekly data over the course of the 10 months of the project. While on the average, across the time-span of the project, the team members used interpersonal methods (face-to-face and phone) 37% and the

Figure 1: Percent Collaboration Conducted through Computer-mediated Communication by Week (Remaining Percent Conducted through In-person and Telephone)

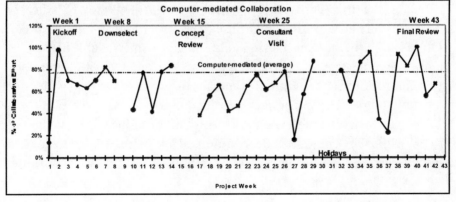

collaboration tool 63% of the time, there were wide fluctuations in use. Instead of a gradual increase in CTuse, we found that the members quickly learned the tool and began to use it at a moderate level of use, with enormous peaks and valleys throughout the project, but never showing a consistent trend of increasing. Thus members did not increase their usage over time compared to more interpersonal media of face-to-face and phone.

Findings for Proposition 2: CT Use Will be Less for Ambiguous Tasks

The literature had suggested that face-to-face was more likely to occur with strategic direction-setting, creative brainstorming, and conflict resolution on the design concept. Table 1 shows the results of the questionnaire given to the members at the end of the project asking them to indicate which communication media they actually used primarily and secondarily. Apparent from Table 1 is that, as expected, the team members indicated that they tended to use face-to-face or phone for the more ambiguous tasks of managing external relationships and conflicts (including obtaining resources or information outside of the team, resolve design conflicts with others outside the team, and clarify project objectives and priorities with those outside the team, get appropriate team members to participate), brainstorming (e.g., quickly generate new ideas, transform concept sketch into a thrust chamber drawing), and strategic direction-setting (e.g., move project forward when stalled, clarify project objectives). Also, as expected, they tended to use the synchronous CTs for the more routine tasks of analysis (e.g., comparing competing concepts, examining design tradeoffs, focus analysis on important design issues), and project statusing (monitor program status and documentation, get up to speed on current concept, and recall technical specs and constraints).

In addition, however, the questionnaire data indicated that the CT was used for more ambiguous tasks as well. Such tasks as clarify project objectives, change project objectives, learn about unfamiliar parts of the concept, and understand the design concerns of other team members — clearly non-routine tasks — were performed by the team members, on the average, using the CT 69% of the time (versus face-to-face or phone). This clearly indicates that members were able to adjust to the use of CTs for more ambiguous tasks.

Observations of the team also indicated that the team was able to use CTs for more ambiguous tasks. In particular, the intense, creative "grab-the-pen" variety of brainstorming was initially accomplished only through a face-to-face meeting, but later in the project was accomplished using the CT.

Why was the team able to do brainstorming using the CT at the end of the project while they couldn't at the beginning? We believe it had to do with the artifacts and the shared language that came about from the earlier efforts.

Table 1: Modes of Communication

| | Primary Method | | Secondary Method | | Mean % Personal | Mean % Public |
	Personal FtoF + Phone	Public TeleConf + Notebook	Personal FtoF + Phone	Public TeleConf + Notebook	Primary & Secondary	Primary & Secondary
1 ...clarify team members' roles and relationships.	38%	63%	38%	63%	38%	63%
2 ...clarify project objectives and priorities within the team.	13%	88%	50%	50%	31%	69%
3 ...clarify project objectives and priorities with those outside the team.	75%	25%	83%	17%	79%	21%
4 ...change project objectives, priorities, or specification.	13%	88%	50%	50%	31%	69%
5 ...recall technical specifications and constraints.	0%	100%	25%	75%	13%	88%
6 ...sketch out ideas for injector concept.	50%	50%	50%	50%	50%	50%
7 ...transform concept sketch into injector drawing.	50%	50%	67%	33%	58%	42%
8 ...learn about unfamiliar parts of the concept.	25%	75%	38%	63%	31%	69%
9 ...understand the design concerns of other team members.	13%	88%	50%	50%	31%	69%
10 ...get up to speed on current concept.	13%	88%	25%	75%	19%	81%
11 ...share own design expertise with others.	25%	75%	71%	29%	48%	52%
12 ...identify areas requiring more detailed evaluation.	25%	75%	50%	50%	38%	63%
13 ...quickly generate new ideas.	38%	63%	75%	25%	56%	44%
14 ...compare competing concepts.	0%	100%	13%	88%	6%	94%
15 ...focus analysis on important design issues.	13%	88%	38%	63%	25%	75%
16 ...examine design tradeoffs.	0%	100%	25%	75%	13%	88%
17 ...jointly author a document or joint analysis.	25%	75%	63%	38%	44%	56%
18 ...quickly identify disagreements.	13%	88%	88%	13%	50%	50%
19 ...quickly resolve conflict over design approach.	25%	75%	75%	25%	50%	50%
20 ...determine next steps in the design process.	38%	63%	50%	50%	44%	56%
21 ...coordinate activities within the team.	0%	100%	88%	13%	44%	56%
22 ...get appropriate team members to participate.	75%	25%	63%	38%	69%	31%
23 ...move project forward when stalled.	29%	71%	86%	14%	57%	43%
24 ...resolve design conflicts with others outside the team.	88%	13%	75%	25%	81%	19%
25 ...obtain resources or information outside of team.	88%	13%	100%	0%	94%	6%
26 ...monitor program status and documentation.	0%	100%	13%	88%	6%	94%

asking: "To what extent do you believe that ..."

At the only face-to-face brainstorm, the team members came up with a first-cut design which, even though was very different from the final design, was instrumental in establishing an artifact around which team members could now work virtually. They used that artifact to explain the underlying physics of combustion and to explain the fundamentals of their disciplines to other team members. In addition, during the earlier meetings, experts spent time explaining the technical reasons for rejecting concepts, which paid off later in the project when other team members detected similar problems encountered earlier. Nonaka and Takeuchi (1995) stress the importance of such shared understanding for enabling knowledge transfer among collaborators.

What created this shared language? Certainly the first two face-to-face meetings provided an important medium. In fact, several members commented that more in-person meetings to resolve conflicts would have been helpful. However, we believe that the ability of the team to create a shared language was also partially attributable to the departure of the initial combustion analyst and conceptual designer — a turnover that eventually led to a more homogeneous team. In a sense, the brainstorming at the beginning was over fundamental differences of opinion, while the brainstorming at the end accepted certain fundamental assumptions. As a result, brainstorming at the end could focus on idea-generation and critique rather than resolution of inherently unresolvable conflicts over assumptions and approaches. Note that in this instance, the richer face-to-face medium can be seen as exacerbating the divergent group norms, while the leaner CT can be seen as facilitating the use of a convergent group norm.

In sum, we learned that sharing knowledge virtually using a CT is not determined solely by the ambiguity of the task but rather by the identification of a common language and artifacts through face-to-face communication. Once the commonality is created, even ambiguous tasks such as creative brainstorming can be performed using CTs. In addition, the use of a CT does not increase as experience with the tool increases, but rather varies with the task at hand, and not necessarily because of task ambiguity.

Findings for Proposition 3: CT Features Will Prompt Knowledge-reuse

Team members were very interested in encouraging reuse of the knowledge generated by the team. Therefore, at the outset of the project, selected members of the team spent significant time developing a Coordination Protocol that identified ways to use features of the CT that would increase team members' ability to reuse knowledge. This protocol encouraged the use of reference links and keywords when entering knowledge into the CT; using templates for meeting agendas, decisions, action items, and meeting minutes;

and being automatically notified when entries relevant to a members' interest were created. The members who created the Protocol obtained concurrence from the team to use the protocol and then trained all team members in its use. Thus, we proposed that these features and the protocol would succeed in creating reuse among the team.

Again, the team fooled us. Although in the beginning the members agreed to the standards for keyword use, as the design effort began in earnest, keyword-use and reference links quickly fell to the wayside. Only 37% of the entries had two or more keywords and only 27% of the entries had three or more. Members turned off their notification profiles, because, when an entry was republished many times, they would receive too many e-mail notifications (e.g., 621 notifications generated for the keyword "design" in the first two weeks of the project). The variety of templates available were not used as often as expected, with only the "meeting minutes" template still being used midway through the project. Finally, members rarely used the more sophisticated navigation features of the tool (such as the ability to view networks of entries in accordance with the frequency with which they referenced each other); instead most relied on finding entries by reviewing them in their chronological order (looking at those that had arrived since they last looked into the Notebook) with only occasionally even doing a quick top-level keyword search (e.g., search on the keyword "minutes" to find the minutes of a meeting missed).

The questionnaire data from the team members provide additional insight into the use of the CT's features for search and retrieval. Team members were asked the frequency with which they used various features of the CT. Table 2 shows the frequency of use for each. The only feature used relatively frequently (slightly more than 2-3 times a month) was the documen-

Table 2: Frequency of Notebook Usage during Project

Feature	Mean	Std Dev
Documentation in public notebook	4.5	1.4
Documentation in personal notebook	2.9	2.0
Navigator	3.3	1.8
Reference Links/Hot Links	3.6	1.2
Templates	2.1	0.9
Snapshot	3.4	1.7
Sketching via Notebook tools	2.4	1.5

Note: Scale consisted of "1" - Never during project, "2" - Less than once a month, "3" - Once a month, "4" 2-3 times a month, "5" - Once a week, "6" - 2-3 times a week, "7" - Daily.

tation of work in the public notebook. In sum, the team made little use of the supposedly powerful organization, search, and retrieval mechanisms provided by the CT.

What explains the team's use of the knowledge repository in this way? We found that the design process was so unpredictable that most of the members had no clue as to whether or not the knowledge they were putting into the database would be of value later on and thus those entries did not warrant attempts at categorization and organization. Since designs were changing almost biweekly (with over 20 design concepts generated during the ten months represented in 60 entries), analysis results relevant to a particular design might be obsolete a week later. Since management was seen as changing their directions throughout the project, entries of discussions of strategy and goals were often of limited value a month later. Since drawings were often being redesigned, a drawing might or might not have features and dimensions that would be of use in later designs. We believe that the fact that some knowledge may be perceived to only have what we call "transient utility" has an effect on what gets entered and how it gets entered and recalled.

In other words, because information was changing so rapidly, team members didn't bother to waste their time to attach keywords or reference links. As a result, keyword searches and networks of linked documents quickly became useless. Moreover, because the information was transient, it was hard for them to even see a pattern to the entries in order to suggest new keywords. In fact, at the end of the project, one team member suggested wistfully: "You know, it would have been a good idea if we had created a new keyword for each new concept so that we could search easier"; even this suggestion at structure was critiqued by another member, who pointed out: "How could we? We often didn't even know when we were doing a new concept rather than just a revision to the existing concept".

Was the lack of organization a problem for retrieving needed information? Despite members believing that virtually all entries were transient, in reality, many entries were referenced in conversations later on. By the end of the project, there were almost 1000 entries: 661 generated by the design team, with the remaining for notebook administration, testing, and pre-kickoff discussions. To look for previous entries, then, took significant amounts of time during a meeting. Moreover, even though reference links were used only 19% of the time, the team members reported, in Table 3, that when the reference links were created, they were the most useful features for finding information quickly since they helped to trace back to those documents that were the most relevant to their search needs.

Table 3: Usefulness of Notebook Features in Finding Relevant Information Quickly

Feature	Mean	Std Dev
Authoring Notebook entries	3.6	1.3
Snapshot	3.6	1.3
Sketching	2.8	1.2
Navigator	2.8	0.8
Notify via email of new/changed entries	3.5	1.3
Reference Links	4.6	0.7
Hot Links	4.8	0.4
Template	2.3	1.2
Remote access	3.8	1.3

Note: Scale anchored from "1", definitely useless, to "5", definitely useful.

Given that the links were considered as having the most potential use for finding information quickly, what barriers need to be removed for engineers to consider using them, especially for what might appear, at first sight, to be "transient knowledge"? To address this question, we asked the team members, at the end of the project, to indicate their agreement with a series of assumptions that tool vendors make about how engineers might use CTs to facilitate their collaboration (Ellis et al., 1991; Grudin, 1988, 1994; Ishii et al., 1994; Johnson-Lenz & Johnson-Lenz, 1982; King & Majchrzak, 1996; Kling, 1991; Malone et al., 1987; Nunamaker et al., 1993). Table 4 shows these results. While team members agreed that a CT and an accessible knowledge repository are valuable assets to their work, such assets will have limited value for knowledge re-use unless such knowledge search mechanisms as reference links require less discipline by the team member to maintain, and quickly provide more information to facilitate a search process, and the bulk of knowledge is not of transient utility.

In sum, both the questionnaire and observational data suggest that knowledge reuse by a team using CT is not facilitated with existing mechanisms for search and retrieval when the knowledge informant considers the knowledge to be transient; can not be aided by a set of keywords created in the abstract prior to actual use of the CT; and can not be aided by user-governed reference-linking mechanisms, which impose too much burden on the user.

CONCLUSIONS

From our detailed and longitudinal examination of how members of a distributed, virtual, inter-organizational creative design team shared and reused their knowledge using a collaborative tool, we found that propositions

Table 4: Assumptions about Use of Electronic Notebook

Item	Mean	Std Dev
Engineers need not only a collaborative tool, but also a personal knowledge storage tool.	5.9	0.9
Engineers need to access their own documents while traveling or away from their desk.	5.5	1.7
Engineers want to quickly access old documents.	6.0	1.0
Engineers want to see the connections (links) among old documents.	5.5	1.0
The data structure represented by the links helps engineers understand the content of the document before opening it.	3.3	1.6
When an author publishes a document, he/she will choose the appropriate keywords.	3.4	1.5
Set of selected keywords are accurate classifications of the document content.	2.6	1.0
Engineers can easily determine which documents should be linked together.	3.5	1.7
Engineers will make an effort to make (link) the connections among documents.	3.0	1.5
Templates help engineers organize their thoughts.	2.5	1.6
Templates help engineers collect structured data.	3.1	1.8
Engineers want to be automatically informed when documents of interest are published (or changed).	5.8	0.8
When engineers specify their personal profile, they understand the exact meaning of the keywords.	3.3	1.2

Note: 1 to 7 anchored scale from "1" - Not at all to "7" great extent, from the literature were insufficient to inform either theory or practice on the use of collaborative tools.

The information-sharing literature must begin seriously considering the contingent conditions involved in the novel setting of a virtual distributed inter-organizational creative team (such as organizational context, team structure, group composition, team norms, building team identity, trust, team cooperation and heterogeneity, process losses, social loafing, groupthink, criteria for group process effectiveness, and material group resources — Furst, Blackburn & Rosen, 1999). However, in spite of the lack of frequent informal or face-to-face interactions, this team was extraordinarily innovative and successful. Very little of the communication here was of the "formal" type (i.e., reports, documents, articles) even if for the simple reason that there were few precedents for the designs, so most of it involved sharing between individuals through attempts at direct solutions. Thus CT designs for such groups should not over-emphasize formal channels, even when technologically possible, and should allow ways to incorporate more "rich" forms of interaction even though the CT itself. Further, it is clear that a fair amount of "mutual expectations" and shared understandings had to be developed before the group could move into a period of focused design process (Krauss & Fussell, 1990; Schrage, 1990).

In addition to the rejection of commonly-accepted propositions in the literature for more routine work environments, our study demonstrated that although most CTs claim to support the exchange of ideas, opinions, and preferences within the group, the document database features that are currently available in most collaborative tools mainly serve as an information repository, not a gateway to the right information, or a process for developing shared cognition. Most navigation tools (search by keywords or links, for example) are not sufficient enough to achieve the purpose. One possible solution to this problem is to create a Knowledge Management role on the team. By organizing the information and collectively monitoring various information sources to ensure information integrity and accuracy, within the rich and transient contexts of the group and the project, the knowledge manager can lower knowledge gathering and monitoring costs of each team member. The fact that early studies of computer conferencing arrived at the same general conclusion — the need for a human process mediator to help support, motivate, and essentially reinforce the group identity and purpose (Kerr, 1986) — reinforces the validity of this suggestion.

REFERENCES

Allen, G. & Jarman, R. *Collaborative R&D: Manufacturing's New Tool*. NY: Wiley, 1999.

Allen, T. (1985). *Managing the flow of technology, technology transfer and the dissemination of technological information with the R&D organization*. Cambridge, MA: MIT Press.

Coleman, D. (1997). Knowledge management: The next golden egg in groupware. *Computer Reseller News*, March 31.

Daft, R., & Lengel, R. (1986). Organizational information requirements, media richness and structural design. *Management Science, 32*(5), 554-571.

Davenport, T., Jarvenpaa, S.L., & Beers, M.C. (1996). Improving knowledge work process. *Sloan Management Review, 37*(4), 53-65.

Davis, T. (1984). The influence of the physical environment in offices. *Academy of Management Review, 9*(2), 271-283.

DeSanctis, G., & Gallupe, R.B. (1987). A foundation for the study of group decision support systems. *Management Science, 33*(5), 589-609.

Ehrlich, S. (1987). Strategies for encouraging successful adoption of office communication systems. *ACM Transactions on Office Information Systems, 5*(4), 240-357.

Ellis, C.A., Gibbs, S.J., & Rein, G. (1991). Groupware: Some issues and experiences. *Communications of the ACM, 34*(1), 39-58.

Eveland, J.D., & Bikson, T. (1989). Work group structures and computer support: A field experiment. *ACM Transactions on Office Information Systems, 6*(4), 354-379.

Ferranti, M. (1997). Automaker aims for companywide collaborative standards. *Computing*, December 11.

Field, A. (1996). Group think. *Inc., 18*(13), Sept 17.

Furst, S., Blackbrun, R., & Rosen, B. (1999). Virtual teams: A proposed research agenda. Paper presented to Academy of Management, Chicago, August. Chapel Hill, NC: University of North Carolin Kenan-Flagler Business School.

Galegher, J., & Kraut, R.E. (1990). Technology for intellectual teamwork: Perspectives on research and design. In J. Galegher, R.E. Kraut, & C. Egido (eds.) *Intellectual teamwork: The social and technological bases of cooperative work.* (pp. 1-20.) Hillsdale, NJ: Erlbaum.

Gartner Group. (1997). Matter: Summer/Fall 1996 – the future of collaboration. *Gartner Group strategic analysis report*, April.

Geertz, C. (1973). *The interpretation of cultures.* New York: Basic Books.

Gerwin, D., & Moffat, L.K. (1997). Withdrawal of team autonomy during concurrent engineering. *Management Science, 43*(9), 1275-1287.

Grudin, J. (1988). Why CSCW applications fail: Problems in the design and evaluation of organizational interfaces. In *Proceedings of the Second Conference on Computer-Supported Cooperative Work.* (pp. 85-93.) New York: Association for Computing Machinery.

Grudin, J. (1994). Groupware and social dynamics. *Communications of the ACM, 37*(1), 93-105.

Hamblen, M. (1998). Netmeeting cuts Dow travel expenses. *Computerworld,* March 9, 20.

Handy, C. (1995). Trust and virtual organization. *Harvard Business Review, 73*(3), 40-50.

Harvey, L., & Myers, M. D. (1995). Scholarship and practice: The contribution of ethnographic research methods to bridging the gap. *Information Technology & People, 8*(3), 13-27.

Haywood, M. (1998). *Managing Virtual Teams.* Boston: Artech.

Hibbard, J. (1997). Knowledge management – knowing what we know. *Information Week,* 653(October 20).

Hiltz, S.R., & Turoff, M. (1993). *The network nation: Human communication via computer, 2nd ed.* Reading, MA: Addison-Wesley.

Huber, G.P. (1991). Organizational learning: The contributing processes and literatures. *Organization Science, 2*(1), 88-115.

Hughes, J. A., Randall, D., & Shapiro, D. (1992). Faltering from ethnography to design. in *CSCW '92: Proceedings of the 1992 ACM Conference on Computer-Supported Cooperative Work: Sharing Perspectives.* (pp. 115-123.) New York: Association for Computing Machinery.

Iansiti, M. (1995). Technology integration - managing technological evolution In a complex environment. *Research Policy, 24*(4), 521-542.

Inkpen, A.C. (1996). Creating knowledge through collaboration. *California Management Review, 39*(1), 123-140.

Ishii, H., Kobayashi, M., & Arita, K. (1994). Iterative design of seamless collaboration media. *Communications of the ACM, 37*(8), 83-97.

Johansen, R. (1988). *Groupware: Computer support for business teams.* New York: Free Press.

Johansen, R. (1992). An introduction to computer-augmented teamwork. In R. Bostrom, R. Watson and S. Kinney (eds.) *Computer-augmented teamwork: A guided tour.* (pp. 5-15.) New York: Van Nostrand Reinhold.

Johnson-Lenz, P., & Johnson-Lenz, T. (1982). Groupware: The process and impacts of design choices. In E. B. Kerr, and S.R. Hiltz (eds.) *Computer-*

mediated communication systems: Status and evaluation. (pp. 45-55.) New York: Academic Press.

Kerr, E. (1986). Electronic leadership: A guide to moderating online conferences. *IEEE Transactions on Professional Communications, PC29*(1), 12-18.

King, N.E., & Majchrzak, A. (1996). Concurrent engineering tools: Are the human issues being ignored? *IEEE Transactions on Engineering Management, 43*(2), 189-201.

Kling, R. (1991). Cooperation, coordination, and control in computer-supported work. *Communications of the ACM, 34*(12), 83-88.

Kraemer, K., & Pinnsonneault, A. (1990). Technology and groups: Assessment of the empirical research. In J. Galegher, R.E. Kraut, and C. Egido (eds.) *Intellectual teamwork: The social and technological bases of cooperative work.* (pp. 375-405.) Hillsdale, NJ: Erlbaum.

Krauss, R. & Fussell, S. (1990). Mutual knowledge and communicative effectiveness. In J. Galegher, R.E. Kraut, and C. Egido (eds.) *Intellectual teamwork: The social and technological bases of cooperative work.* (pp. 111-144.) Hillsdale, NJ: Erlbaum.

Kraut, R., Egido, C., and Galegher, J. (1990). Patterns of contact and communication In scientific research collaboration. In J. Galegher, R.E. Kraut, and C. Egido (eds.) *Intellectual teamwork: The social and technological bases of cooperative work.* (pp. 149-171.) Hillsdale, NJ: Erlbaum.

Kraut, R., Rice, R.E., Cool, C. & Fish, R. (1998). Varieties of social influence: The role of utility and norms in the success of a new communication medium. *Organization Science, 9*(4), 437-453.

Lipnack, J. & Stamps, J. (1997). *Virtual Teams.* NY: Wiley.

Maes, P. (1994). Agents that reduce work and information overload. *Communications of the ACM, 35*(11), 30-40.

Malone, T., Grant, K., Turbak, F., Brobst, S., & Cohen, M. (1987). Intelligent information sharing systems. *Communications of the ACM, 30*(5), 390-402.

Markus, M.L. (1992). Asynchronous technologies in small face-to-face groups. *Information Technology & People, 6*(1), 29-48.

McGrath, J.E., & Hollingshead, A.B. (1993). Putting the 'group' back in group support systems: Some theoretical issues about dynamic processes in groups with technological enhancements. In L.M. Jessup and J.S. Valacich (eds.) *Group support systems: New perspectives.* (pp. 78-96). New York: Macmillan.

Menard, S. (1991). *Longitudinal research.* Newbury Park, CA: Sage Publications.

Nonaka, I., & Takeuchi, H. (1995). *The knowledge creating company*. New York: Oxford University Press.

Nunamaker, J., Dennis, A., Valacich, J., Vogel, D., & George, J. (1993). Group support systems research: Experience from the lab and field. In L. Jessup and J. Valacich (eds.) *Group support systems: New perspectives*. (pp. 123-145.) New York: Macmillan Publishing.

Nunamaker, J., Jr., Briggs, R., & Mittleman, D. (1995). Electronic meeting systems: Ten years of lessons learned. In D. Coleman and R. Khanna (eds.) *Groupware: Technology and applications*. (pp. 149-193.) Englewood Cliffs, NJ: Prentice-Hall.

Olson, G. & Atkins, D. (1990). Supporting collaboration with advanced multimedia electronic mail: The NSF EXPRES project. In J. Galegher, R.E. Kraut, and C. Egido (eds.) *Intellectual teamwork: The social and technological bases of cooperative work*. (pp. 429-451.) Hillsdale, NJ: Erlbaum, Hillsdale.

Orlikowski, W. J., & Robey, D. (1991). Information technology and the structuring of organizations. *Information Systems Research, 2*(2), 143-169.

Orlikowski, W., Yates, J., Okamura, K., & Fujimoto, M. (1995). Shaping electronic communication: The metastructuring of technology in the context of use. *Organization Science, 6*(4), 423-443.

Perin, C. (1991). Electronic social fields in bureaucracies. *Communications of the ACM, 34*(12), 75-82.

Rice, R.E. (1984). Mediated group communication. In R.E. Rice and Associates (eds.) *The new media: Communication, research and technology*. (pp. 129-154.) Beverly Hills, CA: Sage.

Rice, R.E. (1987). Computer-mediated communication and organizational innovation. *Journal of Communication, 37*(4), 65-94.

Rice, R.E., & Gattiker, U. (1999). New media and organizational structuring of meanings and relations. In F. Jablin and L. Putnam (eds.) *New handbook of organizational communication*. (in press.) Newbury Park, CA: Sage.

Rice, R.E., & Shook, D. (1990). Communication, collaboration and voice mail. In J. Galegher, R.E. Kraut, and C. Egido (eds.) *Intellectual teamwork: The social and technological bases of cooperative work*. (pp. 327-350.) Hillsdale, NJ: Erlbaum.

Romano, N. Jr,. Nunamaker, J., Briggs, R., & Vogel, D. (1998). Architecture, design, and development of an html/javascript web-based group support system. *Journal of the American Society for Information Science, 49*(7), 649-667.

Sambamurthy, V., & Chin, W. W. (1994). The effects of group attitudes toward alternative gdss designs on the decision-making performance of computer-supported groups (group-decision support systems). *Decision Sciences, 25*(2), 215-241.

Saunders, C., & Jones, J. (1990). Temporal sequences in information acquisition for decision making: A focus on source and medium. *Academy of Management Review, 15*(1), 29-46.

Schrage, M. (1990). *Shared minds: The new technology of collaboration.* New York: Random House.

Short, J., W.E., & Christie, B. (1976). *The social psychology of telecommunications.* New York: Wiley.

Stein, E.W., & Zwass, V. (1995). Actualizing organizational memory with information systems. *Information Systems Research, 6*(2), 85-113.

Thornton, C., & Lockhart, E. (1994). Groupware or electronic brainstorming. *Journal of Systems Management, 45*(10), 10-12.

Tushman, M. L., & Anderson, P. (1986). Technological discontinuities and organizational environments. *Administrative Science Quarterly, 31*(3), 439-465.

Walsh, J. P., & Ungson, G. R. (1991). Organizational memory. *Academy of Management Review, 16*(1), 57-91.

Walther, J. (1992). Interpersonal effects in computer-mediated interaction: A relational perspective. *Communication Research, 19*(1), 52-90.

* The authors would like to thank the following individuals who generously offered their time and energy throughout this research: Robert Carman, Vern Lott, Hal Buddenbohm, Dave Matthews, Linda Finley, Steve Babcock, Hollis Bostick, Dennis Coston, Bob Corley, Li-Kiang Tseng, Terry Kim, Dave Bremmer. The research was funded by ARPA.

Chapter 9

Alignment of Collaboration Technology Adoption and Organizational Change Findings from Five Case Studies

Bjørn Erik Munkvold
Agder University College, Norway

The chapter presents an analysis of the alignment process of the adoption of collaboration technology and related organizational change identified in a multiple case study in five organizations. Special emphasis is put on the sequential relationship between technology adoption and organizational change, and the question of whether successful adoption of collaboration technology requires the pre-existence of a collaborative organizational culture. Findings from the case studies imply that successful adoption of collaboration technology can follow different patterns, and that contextual factors can be equally important in explaining adoption as characteristics of the technology and implementation project. The case studies also illustrate how elements of learning and maturation in the implementation process can help in overcoming barriers to adoption.

INTRODUCTION

Collaboration technology has now come of age. Over the last decade it has developed from something exotic and esoteric, to become a vital element in many organizations' IT architecture. The main driving force behind this has been the increasing focus on organizational learning, knowledge management and virtual organizations. Collaboration technology is seen to provide the necessary infrastructure to realize these organizational strategies (e.g., Kock, 1999; Neilson, 1997). The term collaboration technology is here used in a broad sense, including all forms of IT that enable communication, coordination and collaboration within and between organizations.

The need for alignment of technology and organization for effective implementation of IT is well acknowledged (McKerzie and Walton, 1991). However, the nature and dynamics of this alignment process is still a question for debate. Due to the potential impact of collaboration technology on organizational work and social relations, the relationship between this technology and organizational change is believed to be of crucial importance for successful adoption of the technology. Several recent studies have addressed the dynamics related to the adoption of collaboration technology (e.g., Bardram, 1996; Ciborra, 1996; Karsten and Jones, 1998; Orlikowski, 1996). These studies show that this adoption process involves a complex interplay between characteristics of the technology and the organizational routines and social processes into which it is assimilated. An example of a question that is still open for debate, is whether collaboration needs to be established prior to the technology implementation, or whether the technology can serve as the catalyst for a change towards collaborative work practices. In general, this research is still in an early stage, and several authors have argued for the need for more field studies of the adoption of collaboration technology in different organizational settings (e.g., Grudin and Palen, 1995; Karsten and Jones, 1998), to be able to develop a more detailed understanding of different adoption patterns and their implications for implementation strategy.

This chapter presents an analysis of the alignment process of the adoption of collaboration technology and related organizational change identified in a multiple case study in five organizations. The organizational context in these cases is common in that each organization comprises several semi-autonomous units, implying a decentralized adoption process. The focus here is mainly on adoption at the level of the organizational units. Thus, this research can be seen to contribute to the accumulation of knowledge related to the adoption of collaboration technology in different organizational settings.

The chapter is structured as follows: The next section presents a brief overview and discussion of previous research on adoption of collaboration technology and the relationship with organizational change. Section three describes the methodological approach and provides a brief description of the technology adoption in the five case studies, as a basis for cross-case comparison in section four. The findings are discussed in section five, and the final section presents conclusions and implications for practice and further research

PREVIOUS RESEARCH ON COLLABORATION TECHNOLOGY AND ORGANIZATIONAL CHANGE

So far, most of the research on this topic has been conducted under the 'umbrella' of CSCW (Computer-Supported Cooperative Work) and groupware. In general, most of the field studies related to CSCW and groupware have focused on identifying factors that are important for successful adoption and use of the technology. In addition to the 'usual suspects' such as user support, project champions and top management involvement, several factors that are more specific for collaboration technology have been identified. These include the potential disparity in work and benefit among different adopters (Grudin, 1994), the users' mental models of the technology (Orlikowski, 1992), the need for a supportive technological and behavioral infrastructure (Grudin and Palen, 1995) and training that also emphasizes the collaborative nature of the technology (Bratteteig, 1998; Orlikowski, 1992).

Fewer studies can be identified, that explicitly address the adoption of collaboration technology and the relationship with organizational change. In the following, a brief overview of some of this research is presented. This is structured according to a framework of alignment patterns developed by McKerzie and Walton (1991). This framework consists of three different patterns of alignment, that differ in the sequential relationship between technology implementation and organizational change:

- Organizational change followed by IT implementation
- Simultaneous implementation of organizational change and IT
- New technology as catalyst for organizational change and alignment

Although this framework may seem somewhat crude and deterministic, it serves to distinguish between different adoption contexts related to the sequence of organizational change and technology implementation. Further, it may also be applied as a basis for classifying different alignment patterns identified in the research on the adoption of collaboration technology.

The first of these patterns represents an 'organizational pull' situation, where the conditions favorable to effective IT utilization are established prior to the technology implementation. Thus the technology is 'pulled into place' by the users as a result of the need for technology supporting the new routines. This is often considered to be a favorable adoption pattern, and is corresponding to a commonly held view in groupware implementation research that effective implementation of groupware requires the pre-existence of a collaborative culture in the organizations (Bratteteig, 1998; Orlikowski, 1992). However, a recent study by Karsten and Jones (1998) challenges this view, by showing how other aspects of the organizational context (e.g., recession in national economy, and changes in roles and work practices) may exert stronger influence on the implementation of collaboration technology than the existence of a collaborative culture.

The second alignment pattern involves a process of mutual adaptation between technology and organization, and can thus be traced back to the socio-technical perspective. This pattern can be seen to constitute the basis for much of the recent research on the dynamics of the adoption of collaboration technology and organizational change. For example, in presenting a series of case studies of groupware implementation in large, complex organizations, Ciborra (1996) describes the implementation processes as *"variable, context-specific and drifting"* involving frequent shifts in the role and function of the technology compared to the planned objectives. In a similar vein, Orlikowski (1996) argues for a *situated change perspective*, in which organizational change results from the ongoing improvisation enacted by the organizational actors in experimenting with and adapting the technology to their local work practices. Although contributing to an increased insight into the nature of the process of collaboration technology adoption, it can be argued that these studies provide few explicit implications for practice related to the adoption of collaboration technology. A more practice-oriented study is that of Bardram (1996), presenting a participative design approach termed *organizational prototyping*. This approach addresses the problems of prototyping in the context of collaboration technology, and specifies a scenario-based method facilitating the mutual adaptation of technology and social organization of work.

In the third pattern in the McKerzie and Walton (1991) framework, the technology is implemented first, with existing organizational arrangements left in place. Organizational changes are subsequently attended to on a responsive or adaptive basis. This strategy emphasizes getting started and later moving to more powerful uses of the technology made possible by organizational change. Previous studies show that this pattern is most frequent in the adoption of collaboration technology (e.g., Bratteteig, 1998). While it may be argued that this pattern often will result in the full potential of the technology not being realized, situations exist where technology implementation is a prerequisite for organizational change, for example the implementation of collaborative work in distributed organizational settings.

CASE STUDIES

Table 1 gives an overview of five case studies on adoption of collaboration technology, conducted in the period from 1994 to 1996. A multiple case study design enables the study of variations in the phenomena in focus between different settings. The aim of this research is thus to contribute to an *"explanatory typology"* (McPhee, 1990). The cases were selected on the basis that they represented distributed contexts where the technology was implemented for supporting

Table 1: Overview of cases

Case	Type of organization	Goal of impl. project	Informants
Implementation of an integrated communication system in NNB	Organizational network of four companies in building construction	Make the tendering process more effective	CEO, users in each organization, members of implementation team
Implementation of Lotus Notes in Telenor	Norwegian state-owned telecommunications group	Support product development process	Project leader, potential users, members of implementation team
Implementation of Lotus Notes in ABB Corporate Research	Eight research labs in six countries - part of the ABB engineering group	Support all stages of research projects conducted across research labs	Process owner, information officer, program manager
Implementation of a global area network in Kvaerner	Multinational engineering group	Support increased communication, coordination and collaboration among Kvaerner companies	Project advisor, design manager and IT manager in member organization, vendor's representative
Implementation of Lotus Notes in Statoil	Norwegian state-owned oil company	Support core business processes, increased communication and collaboration	Project advisor, project leader

collaboration within and between the different units in the organization. However, as will be discussed, the role of the technology implementation in the transition towards more collaborative work practices has varied between the cases.

The primary method used for data collection was semi-structured interviews with key actors in each implementation project (listed in Table 1), with interviews lasting from 0,5 to 2,5 hours. Additional data were collected through document analysis (meeting minutes, project plans and design specifications), and in two of the projects (NNB and Telenor) the possibility for conducting observation of different project activities (charting in organizational units, training of users) was also exploited. A longitudinal design was applied, with the time frame for data collection in the cases varying from 6 to 21 months. However, depending on the time of entry in the cases some of the data collection has been of a retrospective nature.

The format of this paper does not allow for a "thick" description of each case. Instead, a brief description of the technology adoption in each case is provided, as a basis for further analysis and cross-case comparison in the next section. A more detailed description of the cases is provided in Munkvold (1999, 2000).

NNB (North-Norwegian Building group)

This organizational network was formed in 1989 to compete with larger organizations in the building industry, through obtaining economies of scale in tendering, production and marketing. The network succeeded in winning a major contract for building the media village of the Lillehammer Winter Olympic Games in 1994. A virtual LAN based on ISDN was implemented offering integrated e-mail, computer-supported telephony, file sharing and fax. However, problems with immature ISDN services and incompatibility between the NNB virtual LAN and existing LANs in each organization caused major delays in the implementation. As a result, the installation and training of the technology did not take place until after the major activities in the Lillehammer project had been completed. Thus, without new collaborative projects scheduled the incentives for using the technology were lacking. This also coincided with a boom in the local markets for two of the member companies, resulting in priority being given to individual projects. As a result of not winning any new contracts, the member organizations terminated the collaborative arrangement.

Telenor

The Lotus Notes implementation in Telenor took place as part of a major reengineering project initiated in 1993, where the entire company was restructured into a process-based organization. Due to the organizational changes made in this process the Lotus Notes implementation actually was conducted in the form of three successive projects, supporting the following processes: document management, distributed collaboration and product development. A general problem in this implementation was to define routines and responsibilities in a new organization that had still not 'settled'. The adoption process in each unit was slow as the decision-makers had problems with relating to technology support for organizational routines not yet established. The adoption did not gain momentum until after the new distributed process had been implemented and the users started experiencing the need for technological support.

ABB Corporate Research

The organization of the Asea Brown Boveri (ABB) group consists of a complex matrix structure, comprising more than 1300 separate operating companies that are all legal entities. In general, this type of organizational structure creates a need for a standard communication-sharing platform for all units, and ABB has chosen Lotus Notes as the common infrastructure. In 1990, ABB Corporate Research was reorganized into fifteen research programs running across eight research labs in six different countries. During 1995 a Lotus Notes based application was developed and implemented for supporting all stages in the workflow of the research projects. Although the adoption process was slow at first, a year later this project support application had become the major work tool for the employees.

Kvaerner

The implementation of the global area network in Kvaerner was originally initiated for saving communication costs through establishing a common infrastructure supporting voice, e-mail and data communication. However, the scope of the implementation gradually expanded to also include increasing collaboration and coordination among the different companies in Kvaerner, for example related to resource deployment and experience transfer. The vision from the Kvaerner top management of increased collaboration in the group was not shared by all subsidiaries, and adoption was slow in many companies. While companies that already were engaged in collaborative activities saw the potential in this technology, others found it too expensive and without a real benefit. The implementation team thus had to create incentives for adopting the network. This was done both by sponsoring the establishment of regional hubs for reducing the costs of linking to the network, and by using the network to establish a corporate intranet that provided vital information not available through other communication channels. Through these strategies a critical mass of adopting units was finally established, and use of the technology has since increased gradually. Over a period of 1,5 year since the start of the project in 1995, the network has reached the status of being characterized as "mission critical" by members of the Kvaerner staff.

Statoil

In Statoil the Lotus Notes implementation spread out from a local initiative among managers in one department. After a few pilot studies, a company-wide implementation project was launched in 1995, involving a "toolbox" of seven different Notes applications supporting asynchronous collaboration and coordination. During a two-year period the implementation covered all employees in the organization. Thus, measured by the number of users and frequency of use the implementation has been a success. However, the acceptance of the different applications has varied. While tools for distribution of information (e-mail, group calendar and news databases) have been widely adopted, the adoption of applications requiring each user to produce input to the databases has been slower. Thus, the system has mainly been used for automating existing processes rather than supporting new collaborative work practices. Statoil has since launched follow-up projects intended for establishing more effective use of the technology, and this process still continues as part of the ongoing work of improving the information infrastructure in Statoil.

COMPARISON OF ALIGNMENT PATTERNS

Table 2 summarizes the relationship between organizational change and technology implementation in each case, according to the McKerzie and Walton (1991) framework. For each case, the major contextual influences identified in the adoption process are also listed.

Table 2: Alignment patterns and contextual influences

Case	Relationship between groupware implementation and org. change	Major contextual influences
NNB	Organizational change follow-ed by IT implementation	Immature technology, local market conjunctures, tempor-ary nature of organizational network
Telenor	Simultaneous implementation of organizational change and IT	Lack of organizational stability, uncertainty in roles and routines
ABB Corporate Research	Organizational change follow-ed by IT implementation	Immature technology, local variations in workflow management
Kvaerner	New technology as catalyst for organizational change	Lack of incentives for collaboration
Statoil	New technology as catalyst for organizational change	Lack of incentives for information sharing

The cases represent different alignment patterns related to the sequential nature of the relationship between technology adoption and organizational change. In *NNB*, the technology implementation was a direct response to the experienced need for supporting the time consuming routines of information exchange among the member companies in the development of new tenders. Thus, the implementation was intended for supporting a collaborative arrangement already established. In that sense, the users were able to relate the technology to existing work practices, and the user representatives from each organization participating in the collaborative arrangement were motivated to use the technology and saw large potential benefits from the implementation project. However, delays in the project resulting from the immature stage of ISDN technology at that time, and the succeeding failure in winning new contracts, resulted in the incentives for adopting the technology diminishing. Although the project resulted in the implementation of a system meeting the original requirements, when measured in frequency of use the project must be considered a failure as the technology never was taken into regular use before the termination of the collaborative arrangement.

In the four other cases, the technology implementation can be considered a success in that use has increased steadily since the initial adoption. However, the alignment patterns observed in these cases are varying, e.g. related to the degree to which the organizations have succeeded in realizing the full potential of the technology.

In *Telenor*, the technology implementation took place simultaneously with the organizational restructuring of the company. The organizational instability surrounding the implementation was found to result in uncertainty about the roles and routines in the new organization. There was also a lack of continuity in the implementation project, and problems of providing funding and support for the project. In general, it proved difficult to argue for the adoption of technology intended to support a form of work that had not yet been established. Although the formal structure of the new organization had been laid out, the adoption of the technology among the intended users was slow until they actually started experiencing the need for technological support as a result of the new way of working. Important in this process was the mutual learning between those responsible for the implementation and those in charge of the business processes, making it possible to identify how the technology could support specific needs related to each business process.

Similar to the NNB case, the technology implementation in *ABB Corporate Research* was initiated for supporting collaborative work practices already established. However, in contrast to the NNB case, this work structure was highly operational and the felt need for technology support was strong. Thus, this implementation project also stands out as the most successful, in that during a relatively short time period this system has become of vital importance throughout the organization. The major challenges in this implementation project have been technological problems resulting from the very advanced nature of this Lotus Notes application, and the adaptation of roles and responsibilities in the workflow to the local culture of each research lab.

In both *Kvaerner* and *Statoil*, the implementation of the technology was intended as a catalyst for a transition toward more collaborative work practices. The adoption process thus had the character of internal marketing, where the implementation team presented the technology together with the vision of increasing collaboration. However, in both cases the process of reaching this goal has been slow, as incentives for collaboration have been lacking. Thus, those responsible for the implementation have had to stimulate adoption and effective use of the technology through different sponsoring strategies and follow-up projects.

DISCUSSION

The cases studied in this research illustrate examples of different alignment patterns. These patterns vary regarding the role of the technology in the organizational change toward increasing collaboration. In the cases where new collaborative work practices already had been established, the technology has served as the necessary support for making these practices effective. In one case study, the technology and new organizational routines have been developed in parallel. In the third type of alignment pattern, the technology has served as a catalyst for the transition towards increasing coordination and collaboration.

In general, it is not possible to explain the variations in relative success of the different implementation projects only through factors related to the technology and the conduct of the implementation projects (Karsten and Jones 1998). Several additional factors related to the organizational context were found to be of influence. For example, in the NNB case the boom in the local markets for two of the member companies resulted in lower priority being given to the collaborative arrangement and the implementation project. Further, the project-based nature of this organizational network resulted in a "one shot only" implementation situation, whereas in the other cases the implementation was a continuous activity over a longer period.

For all three types of patterns, adoption has been dependent upon a felt need among the users for technology support in their work. In the situations where the technology has been implemented for enabling new work practices (Telenor, Statoil, Kvaerner), there have been problems with lack of incentives for adopting the technology. This has also been the case in NNB, where the lack of new collaborative projects resulted in limited interest in the technology. Thus, this can be described as a "Catch-22 situation," where the adoption of the technology is slow because of the lack of collaborative activity, while the process of establishing collaborative work practices is hampered because of the lack of adoption and use of the technology.

From this it would be easy to conclude that the "organizational pull" pattern has advantages over the others, through the users requesting the technology and being motivated for adoption. However, this cannot be reduced to a simple conclusion that adoption of collaboration technology will succeed only in these situations. Except for the NNB network that terminated during the implementation project, adoption has finally taken place in all the cases studied, although at a slower pace than first expected. This can largely be explained by the *learning* and *maturation* taking place in the implementation process in these cases. In all five cases, the implementation project studied represents the organization's first experience with this form of collaboration technology. As the organizations gain experience with these technologies, they improve their understanding of how to manage this process. This involves a process of mutual learning between those in charge of the technology implementation and the intended adopters responsible for the business processes in focus. The adoption process in the cases of Kvaerner and Telenor may serve as an illustration of the maturation taking place in this process. In these projects the implementation teams experienced that the "sales arguments" that originally were rejected by the users as insufficient grounds for adoption became generally accepted after some time. Thus, the vision of increased collaboration through groupware adoption seemingly needed time to mature and "sink in." Important in this was the development of a mutual understanding of how the technology could support specific business needs.

For emerging collaboration technologies, maturity is also an important issue. In the cases studied, several of the implementation problems can be seen as a result of the technology being at a relatively immature stage. As these technologies become more stable and commonly used, these barriers can be expected to decrease.

In general, the technology adoption has been slower and more resource demanding than expected at the outset. In all these cases there are examples of *technological drift* (Ciborra, 1996) in the form of deviations from the original plans, both regarding process and content of the implementation. This has also required various forms of *improvisation* (Orlikowski, 1996) from the actors involved in the implementation projects. However, while these concepts originally have been related to the flexible nature of technologies like Lotus Notes, in some of the case studies these phenomena can also be seen as a result of immature technologies and the dynamic and 'drifting' nature of the organizational context. Examples of this are the problems related to immature ISDN services in the NNB case, and the continuous organizational change in the Telenor case.

CONCLUSION AND IMPLICATIONS

Through analysis and discussion of the alignment of collaboration technology adoption and organizational change in five case studies, this research contributes to an increased understanding of the process of adopting collaboration technology and the relationship with organizational change. The case studies represent examples of different alignment patterns. While adoption of the technology seemingly was most successful when collaborative work practices were operational prior to the implementation, examples have also been provided of how adoption has succeeded without this condition being fulfilled. This has been ascribed to the learning and maturation taking place as part of the adoption process. The relative success of the adoption in these cases shows that collaboration technology can also be used effectively in contexts where a collaborative culture does not exist prior to the implementation, thus supporting Karsten and Jones (1998). Indeed, in several of the cases the move towards new collaborative work practices could not have been realized without the new technology. This is especially relevant for distributed settings, where increased collaboration is dependent on a technological infrastructure for communication and information exchange.

Further, the study also illustrates the influence of different contextual factors on the adoption process, that only to a limited extent have been addressed in previous research. For example, the implementation project in the NNB network illustrates how technology implementation in virtual-like organizations can be challenging, due to the fragile nature of these organizational arrangements.

In general, this research corroborates the argument made in previous studies that in trying to understand the process related to the adoption of collaboration technology in an organization, it is necessary to take into account the nexus of contextual factors (Ciborra, 1996) and situated change practices (Orlikowski, 1996) particular for this organization. However, by applying the simple framework of McKerzie and Walton (1991) this research contributes to the development of a typology of different alignment patterns, that may aid further inquiry into the nature of organizational adoption of collaboration technology. Future research should focus on detailing this typology further, by studying how specific characteristics of different types of collaboration technology may influence the nature of the adoption process and related organizational change, in different organizational settings. In this pursuit, the different contextual factors influencing the technology adoption also have to be addressed, thus requiring longitudinal, field-based research.

REFERENCES

Bardram, J. E. (1996). Organisational Prototyping: Adopting CSCW Applications in Organisations, *Scandinavian Journal of Information Systems,* 8(1): pp. 69-88.

Bratteteig, T. (1998). The Unbearable Lightness of Grouping: Problems of introducing computer support for cooperative work, *Proceedings of NOKOBIT '98*, Oslo, pp. 99-113

Ciborra, C. U. (ed.) (1996). *Groupware & Teamwork. Invisible Aid or Technical Hindrance?* Wiley, Chichester.

Grudin, J. (1994). Groupware and Social Dynamics: Eight Challenges for Developers. *Communications of the ACM,* 37(1): pp. 92-105.

Grudin, J., and Palen, L. (1995). Why Groupware Succeeds: Discretion or Mandate?, in H. Marmolin et al. (eds.), *Proceedings of ECSCW '95*, Kluwer, Dordrecht, September, pp. 263-278.

Karsten, H., and Jones, M. (1998). The Long and Winding Road: Collaborative IT and organisational change, *Proceedings of CSCW '98*, Seattle, November, pp. 29-38.

Kock, N. (1999). *Process Improvement and Organizational Learning: The Role of Collaboration Technologies*, Hershey, PA: Idea Group Publishing.

McKerzie, R. B., and Walton, R. E. (1991). Organizational Change, in M. S. Scott Morton (ed.), *The Corporation of the 1990's: Information technology and organizational transformation*, NY: Oxford University Press, pp. 245-277.

McPhee, R. D. (1990). Alternate Approaches to Integrating Longitudinal Case Studies, *Organization Science,* 1(4): pp. 393-405.

Munkvold, B. E. (1999). Challenges of IT implementation for supporting collaboration in distributed organizations, *European Journal of Information Systems* (8), pp. 260-272.

Munkvold, B. E. (2000). *Implementing Collaboration Technologies in Industry: Case Examples and Lessons Learned*. London: Springer-Verlag.

Neilson, R. (1997). *Collaborative Technologies and Organisational Learning*. Hershey, PA: Idea Group Publishing.

Orlikowski, W. J. (1992). Learning from Notes: Organizational Issues in Groupware Implementation, *Proceedings of CSCW '92*, Toronto, November, pp. 362-369.

Orlikowski, W. J. (1996). Improvising Organizational Transformation over Time: A Situated Change Perspective, *Information Systems Research,* 7(1): pp. 63-92.

Chapter 10

Information Retrieval Using Collaborating Multi-User Agents

Elaine Ferneley
Information Systems Institute
Salford University, Manchester

INTRODUCTION

Informal channels for the exchange of information have long been recognised as important (Menzel, 1959; Wilson, 1981; Kuhlthau, 1991; Root, 1988; Kraut and Galegher, 1990). Typical examples of informal information exchange activities are conferring with peers and consultation with a subject librarian (Taylor, 1968; Kuhlthau, 1991; Fox, Hix, Nowell, Brueni, Wafe, Heath and Rao, 1993). If Information Communication Technologies (ICTs) are to become truly user-centred then they must support such informal collaborative activity. The recent interest in knowledge management has, in part, been stimulated by the recognition that valuable information is transferred during informal collaborations (Nonaka & Takeuchi, 1995). To bring some formality to the process organisations are investing in document management software, intranets and groupware technologies (Kiesler, 1997). However, these technologies rely largely on the user actively searching out information and assume that the user can formulate their information needs into an appropriate query. Additionally, such systems tend towards failure in the longer term if users are not motivated in augmenting the knowledge base (Skyrme, 1999).

As stated by Schrage (1990, pp.111-112): *"We need to shift away from the notion of technology managing information and toward the idea of technology as a medium of relationships"*. Technology should be proactively supporting the user in their query formulation and information retrieval activities and facilitating the social interaction processes that have resulted in serendipitous information retrieval. Bates (1979a, b) identified a number of, usually collaborative, infor-

Previously Published in *Challenges of Information Technology Management in the 21st Century*, edited by Mehdi Khosrow-Pour, Copyright © 2000, Idea Group Publishing.

mal interactions undertaken during information gathering that promoted serendipity. These can be summarised as:

- *consultation* whereby a specific colleague is asked for help. With reference to ICT retrieval this can be equated to emailing a specific colleague
- *wandering* whereby a range of information sources are consulted in an unplanned manner. This can be equated to the computer supported browsing activity where information searching is opportunistic, reactive and unplanned the aim of which may be uncertain and evolve during the browsing process (Marchionini, 1995);
- *brainstorming*, in ICT retrieval terms this is synonymous with discussions that ensue as a result of queries posted to discussion groups or special interest mailing lists;
- consulting a bibliography, referred to as *bibbling*. With reference to ICT retrieval this can be compared with consulting on-line bibliographies (e.g., the Endnote libraries that are being placed in the public domain).

Such informal collaborative information exchanges are important, yet few systems have been developed to support said activities. Indeed information technology can be seen as a barrier to such exchange processes, hampering social interaction, hindering initiative and creativity (Mantovani, 1996). Additionally, due to the amorphous nature of network communities it may be difficult to establish information exchange relationships between users (Kautz, Selman and Shah, 1997).

This paper recognises the importance of serendipitous discovery via informal collaborations during information retrieval. A model which supports collaborative information retrieval from a range of information sources is presented. The model has an agent-based architecture which is founded on the principles of connectionist information retrieval but with the advantages that it does not require explicit training and is not influenced by individual user use (Belew, 1989). The system consists of a set of co-operating agents which provide both a technical and psychological solution. From the technical perspective the agents manage user interests, engage in information searches and provide a uniformed interface to disparate datasets. From the psychological perspective the agents adopt an anthropomorphic role acting as a user facilitator, they can proactively co-operate to identify additional subject areas, sources and other users with similar interests. Additionally they actively augment and refine search criteria based on their derived knowledge of previous successful searches (Berney & Ferneley, 1999). The system, known as CASMIR, has been implemented as a set of co-operating Java agents communicating in KQML. This paper uses the definition of as software agent as proposed by Huhns (1998):

"an agent is an active, persistent computational entity that can perceive, reason about, and act in its environment, and can communicate with other agents."

Additionally, over time agents *learn*, usually by direct instruction, observation of their human *owner's* actions or by instruction or observation of other agents. Such learning allows agents to fulfil a number of different roles:

- predict desired actions as a result of new situations being presented to them;
- provide a buffer between their owner and complex tasks;
- act as an owner educator;
- facilitate user collaboration;
- proactively inform when changes of state occur in domains that are of interest to their owner.

Evaluation is ongoing, initial results are extremely promising. The results presented here are derived from evaluating the system using the North West Film Archive's (NWFA) catalogue and associated queries. This evaluation was chosen as the dataset is extremely specialist, the archivists have in depth knowledge of the material available and the search criteria is often vague. The catalogue holds references to slightly over 3000 historical records of life in the North West of England in a range of multimedia formats. Requests for material from the archive are usually vague, for example: *'I want a funny rural scene involving farm animals and the landed gentry', 'I need a still illustrating poverty during the depression'*. A number of indexing schemes have been trialled with limited success, the in depth knowledge that the NWFA's librarians have is heavily relied on. However, even with a relatively small collection our research highlighted that the librarians would select significantly different records when presented with the same query. Therefore, this dataset was chosen as one of the evaluation sets as in depth analysis could be undertaken with the librarians. Additional evaluations are ongoing, the reader may participate in the evaluation by downloading CASMIR and trialling it themselves (URL1).

CASMIR DESIGN AND IMPLEMENTATION

CASMIR's architecture consists of 3 types of agent. Firstly, the *User Agent* which manages a user's profile as sets of interests that consist of weighted keywords. Secondly, the *Search Agent* which manages a search. Finally, various *Document Agents* which manage sets of documents. The document agent presented here manages the NWFA dataset, additional document agents have been implemented for a range of datasets including HTML documents, EndNote libraries, various specialist databases and Email. Figure 1 provides a UML sequence

Figure 1: UML Sequence Diagram of Agent Interaction

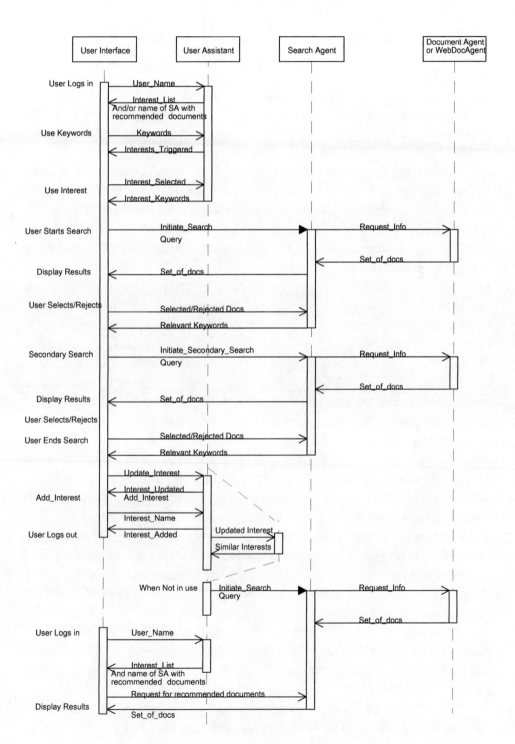

diagram representation of the interactions that occur between the various agents when a search is initiated on a single dataset.

The various agents and user interface are represented as rectangles when they are active and dotted lines when inactive. Communication between the various agents and the interface are represented as arrows with supporting labelling.

Collaboration Scenarios

Four basic types of collaboration scenarios are illustrated which are either initiated by an agent volunteering information it believes will be relevant to other agents or making an explicit request for information that it needs.

The first type of collaboration is whereby a user presents a query to the system by entering keywords and associated weights. The system will firstly attempt to match the presented query with the user's current set of interests. If the query does not trigger one of the user's existing interests (or the user is using the system for the first time) then the query is broadcast to other user agents, the *wandering* activity is initiated (Bates, 1979a, b). Interests and keywords can be weighted by the user to reflect their relative importance in the retrieval process. Interests returned from other user agents may be retained for future use if they are deemed, by the user, to be relevant. User agents providing relevant interest sets may be contacted in future *consultation* scenarios. When an appropriate query has been formulated, or previous query identified as relevant, it is passed to a search agent.

The second type of collaboration is when the user has specified search criteria and a search agent collaborates via various document agents in an attempt to satisfy that query. The search agent initiates a particular plan dependent on the search criteria and then requests information which satisfies the search criteria from the set of document agents proposed in the chosen plan. By consulting a specific plan this retrieval strategy can be viewed as analogous to *bibbling* (Bates, 1979a, b). The search agents operate autonomously in that their specific search strategy is left to their own discretion using a multi-threaded polling scheme. The current implementation specifies a single document agent per database per machine. Document agents calculate a document's relevance relative to requested keywords by the application of a simple algorithm (sum of the products of the document keywords and query keywords). The weights of the keywords relating to specific documents are predefined.

The third type of collaboration is when a search agent presents a set of results back to the user. Based on the selection and rejection process a secondary search can be initiated by the user, this selection/rejection/search process can be iterated repeatedly until an appropriate set of documents have been retrieved. This approach is analogous to individual *brainstorming* (Bates, 1979a, b). At the end of such a cycle the user agent updates the user interest profile, either by augmenting an existing interest or creating a new interest. Because the agent collaboration mechanisms for such a secondary search are the same as the initial result feedback collaboration scenario they are not presented as distinct collaboration scenarios in Figure 1.

The final type of collaboration is when user assistants collaborate to identify users with similar interests. The user can explicitly initiate such collaboration or the user agents can take on a proactive role and initiate collaboration when they are idle. Such directed collaboration is comparative to *consultation* as defined by Bates (1979a, b). If the user initiates such a collaboration scenario then they may define specific *sharing constraints*, thus allowing users to maintain interest confidentiality. Additionally, the user assistant may act proactively when the system is idle, user assistants can generate meta-searches based on aggregations of all keywords across interest sets (confidentiality constraints are maintained), this may be regarded as analogous to *brainstorming*. The search agent which undertakes the user agent generated meta-search holds the search results until the user next logs-in, the user is then free to retrieve the results of the search, refine the search results and generate a new query, update their user profile with the results or delete the search results without viewing them.

Information Retrieval Model Architecture

CASMIR's information retrieval model is based upon a connectionist approach and represents documents and keywords as *nodes* joined by weighted links (Doszkocs, Reggia and Lin, 1990). In retrieving documents, the perceived relevance of a document to a query is calculated by summing the weights of the query keywords with those of the matching keywords within the document. This approach allows partial queries to retrieve documents as well as allowing negative

Figure 2: Document Retrieval Process

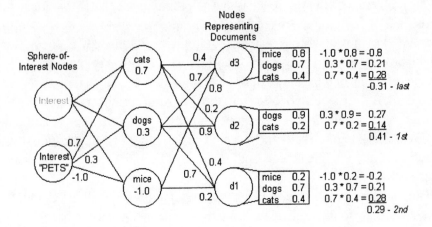

(Boolean NOT) relationships to be represented by negatively weighted keywords. Figure 2 shows documents being retrieved using 3 keywords where the user has specified that they are interested in dogs and cats but NOT mice.

CASMIR aims to support many users hence a novel user-specific layer has been introduced which represents a particular user's interests as *sphere-of-interest* nodes. This is distinct from a single user system where a user profile could simply be expressed as adjustments to the weights within the keyword-document network. Within CASMIR the weights within the user-specific layer are adjusted to reflect a user's behaviour, without affecting the state of the network common to all users. The user names sets of weighted keywords, these sets are known as *interests*. These interests are created and updated based upon feedback from the user via a two stage process. Firstly the user can combine relevant sets of keywords into an interest. Secondly an existing interest can evolve as the user adds and deletes keywords from the interest's set of keywords. The learning system follows a punishment-reward scheme, whereby relevant keywords are strengthened and irrelevant keywords weakened within the interest sphere. Additionally, the user names these interest nodes themselves, allowing their own ideas on subject naming to influence the system.

Within an interest each keyword is assigned a user specified weighted to reflect the respective importance of each keyword within an interest. By using a weighting mechanism CASMIR can produce context-sensitive options during the query process. As keywords are entered, the user agent tries to match these with a local existing interest and, in the same manner as document retrieval, returns extra keywords which are added to the original query to enhance precision.

Following a search CASMIR provides the functionality to automatically update user interests by considering the keywords that were associated with the documents selected or rejected during the search process; existing interests can be modified or new interests created.

One problem with this approach is that of assigning weights to document keywords. Initially, cataloguers were asked to assign weights to documents as they were added to the data-set. However, cataloguer reluctance was encountered and the process proved to be highly subjective. The approach presented here allocated a weight of 0.6 if the term was extracted from the index term pertinent to that record, 0.7 if the term occurred in the description field and 0.8 if the term occurred in the title field. This weighting scheme was devised in consultation with the NWFA's cataloguing staff and is therefore domain specific. Additionally, the Term Frequency/Inverse Document Frequency (TF/IDF) approach is currently under evaluation.

Although users specify particular keywords at initial search the documents retrieved which are found to be relevant are frequently indexed using both the specified keywords and other terms. It is the identification of additional keywords that facilitates *serendipitous discovery*. The relevance of user defined keywords and identification of additional useful keywords in a particular retrieved document is determined in three stages. Firstly, the user assigns a relevance weighting to each document retrieved following the search process, this can range form –1 to +1. Secondly, the weight associated with each keyword, whether user specified or not, in the retrieved document is multiplied by the document relevance weight as specified by the user. Thirdly, because the same keywords usually occur in many of the documents a mean weight for each occurring keyword is derived.

This is the basic keyword weighting approach used in this research and is referred to as *simple positive reinforcement*. Two alternative keyword weighting schemes have also been evaluated Firstly, *negative reinforcement* - this approach assigns negative ratings to those keywords that are common to documents deemed irrelevant by the user. Such keywords are then ORed with the positive keyword set providing positive and negative relevant keywords. Secondly, *query keyword override* - keywords in the original query are not necessarily taken into account when the *relevant* keywords are gathered. An option has thus been included to force the inclusion of the original query terms even if they do not appear in the relevant keyword set as specified once a search has been undertaken. Additionally, original keywords can be included when either positive or negative reinforcement is being used.

EVALUATION

The evaluation presented here has been conducted in association with the NWFA and has concentrated on CASMIR's user profiling subsystem, this consists of two primary activities: interest updating and interest retrieval. Document data supplied by NWFA has been used which consisted of 340 film descriptions, each comprising the fields *'Title'*, *'Description/Synopsis'*, *'Accession number'*, *'Dates'*, *'Index terms'* and keyword weights based upon their presence in the Index, Title and Description fields. A sample of actual queries made against the NWFA film catalogue were used to test the system. 25% of the queries had 2 'relevant' documents associated with them, 25% - 3 'relevant' documents, 25% - 4 'relevant' documents, 12.5% - 1 'relevant' document and 12.5% - 5 relevant documents. The queries were split into two sets, with 10% of the associated queries being the same, thus simulating two users with some complete commonality between interest sets. Iterative use of CASMIR by a user or users was undertaken by a *simulated* user. This simulation was implemented as, at the time of writing, the longitudinal evaluation using the NWFA's data and their extensive client base is not completed.

The first evaluation of interest is that of user interest updating. If the system is a success then serendipitous discovery of addition keyword terms would occur with system use. During the trial the test data and simulated user, documents were given relevance ratings on a scale of -1.0 to 1.0 dependent on whether they were deemed irrelevant or relevant by the simulated user. This cycle was repeated 10 times for each test. During the trial the average number of relevant documents was calculated, the desired result would be a movement of relevant documents from the fourth through to third, second and finally first quartile, indicating an increase in precision. Four different approaches to this task were evaluated. Firstly, *Simple Positive Reinforcement* - keywords are only gathered from documents deemed relevant by the user. Secondly, *Simple Positive Reinforcement with Query Keyword Overriding* - the original query keywords are also added to those gathered. Thirdly, *Positive and Negative Reinforcement* - keywords from irrelevant documents are also gathered but are assigned negative values. Finally, *Positive and Negative Reinforcement with Query Keyword Override* - keywords from irrelevant documents are also gathered but are assigned negative values and the original query keywords are also added to those gathered. All variations of positive reinforcement learning offered an increase in precision when retrieving documents, after approximately 5 iterations the increase in precision was not so marked. Negative reinforcement approaches performed poorly. The most effective approach was positive reinforcement with query keyword override. The results are presented in Graph 1.

The second evaluation of interest is that of the success of collaborative user interest updating. This is concerned with interest sharing which can be undertaken either to increase the learning efficiency of the system or to *unite* users with similar

Graph 1: User Interest Updating Results

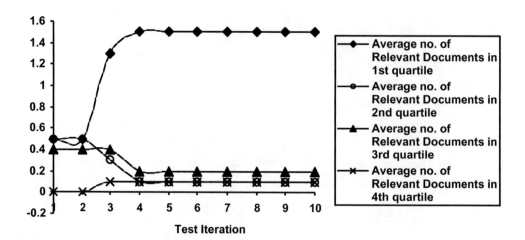

Graph 2: Collaborative Information Retrieval Results

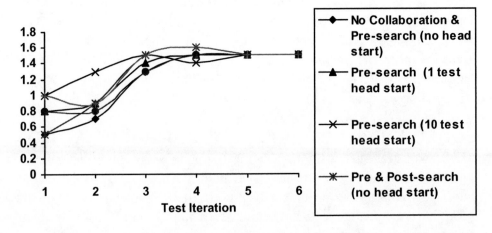

interests. Two *simulated* users (Daisy and Tom) were developed and a number of experiments were undertaken. Firstly, Daisy and Tom worked concurrently for 10 test iterations with them both started their searching at the same time and the whole experiment proceeded concurrently. Secondly, Daisy and Tom worked step-concurrently for 11 test iterations (Daisy with a head-start of 1 iteration), the remainder of the experiment proceeded concurrently. Thirdly, Daisy and Tom worked step-concurrently for 20 test iterations (Daisy with a head-start of 10 iterations), again, the remainder of the experiment proceeded concurrently. Two approaches were evaluated. Firstly, *Pre-search Request Based Collaboration* - user assistants who can not satisfy a search independently collaborate with other user assistants. The initiating user assistant prioritizes responses from other user assistants and chooses whether to retain similar interests for future use. Secondly, *Post-Search Informing* - when not in use user assistants broadcast their interest sets to find other user assistants that are responsible for similar interests. The user may define sharing parameters and constraints on when their interest sets may be automatically augmented.

The results presented are all based upon the performance of Tom's view of the system and indicate the average number of relevant documents in the top 5 of those retrieved for each iteration and for each collaborative approach. Each user's sharing constraint was set to collect similar interests (the lower threshold being set to 0.65). Note that these tests were performed using positive reinforcement learning and that as the results remain constant after six iterations, iterations 7 to 10 have been omitted for clarity.

As can be seen from Graph 2, with Daisy and Tom operating the system concurrently there was no increase in learning efficiency and the results were exactly as for *no-collaboration* - hence only one line is drawn on the graph to represent both scenarios. However, when Tom was able to request information from Daisy with just a single test iteration head start, there was a marked increase in its performance, more so if Daisy had been through 10 iterations. These results clearly demonstrate that Tom was able, as predicted, to build a profile more quickly by collaborating with Daisy.

CONCLUDING REMARKS AND FUTURE DIRECTION

The work presented in this paper aims to support *serendipitous information discovery* with the use of agent-based technology. The advent of isolated computerized searching has meant that the process of social interaction during the information retrieval process has been lost (Bishop & Star, 1996). The agent-based model presented in this paper aims to support serendipity by facilitating *consultation, wandering, brainstorming* and *bibling* (Bates, 1979a, b). An overview of the CASMIR system has been provided which has focussed on the information retrieval model and the user profiling system. Preliminary evaluation results have also been presented. A number of conclusions are drawn:

* the connectionist information retrieval model allows the views of many users to be represented and, because pre-set document weights are used, there is not need for lengthy training;
* the preliminary evaluation shows promise with a high learning rate and an increase in relevant document retrieval over time;
* of the algorithms tested, simple positive reinforcement performed best with query keyword overriding providing a marked increase in precision;
* the use of collaboration in the user profiling provided a marked increase in the learning rate.

Additional evaluation is underway across a range of information sources, the reader is encouraged to participate in this process (URL1).

REFERENCES

Bates, M.J. (1979a). Information search tactics. *Journal of the American Society for Information Science, 30(4),*205-214.

Bates, M.J. (1979b). Idea tactics. *Journal of the American Society for Information Science, 30(5),*281-289.

Belew, R.K. (1989), Adaptive Information Retrieval : Using a Connectionist Representation to Retrieve and Learn About Documents. In Belkin, N.J., van Rijsbergen, C.J. (eds.) *Proceedings of the ACM SIGIR 12th Annual Conference on Research and Development in IR*, June 25-28, Cambridge, MA.

Berney, B. & Ferneley, E.H. (1999). CASMIR: Information Retrieval Based on Collaborative User Profiling, *Proceedings of the 4th International Conference on The Practical Application of Intelligent Agents and Multi-Agent Technology*, 41-56, London.

Bishop, A.P. & Star, S.L. (1996). Social informatics of digital library use and infrastructure, *Annual Review of Information Science and Technology, 31,* 301-401.

Doszkocs, T.E., Reggia, J. & Lin, X., (1990), Connectionist Models and Information Retrieval, in *Annual Review of Information Science and Technology*, 25.

Fox, E.A., Hix, D., Nowell, L.T., Brueni, D.J, Wafe, W.C., Heath, L.S., & Rao, D. (1993). Users, user interfaces, and objects - Envison, a digital library, *Journal of the American Society for Information Science, 44(8)*,480-491.

Huhns, M.N. (1998). Agent Foundations for Cooperative Information Systems, *Proceedings Third International Conference on the Practical Application of Intelligent Agents and Multi-Agent Technology,* London.

Kautz, H., Selman, B. & Shah, M. (1997). Referral Web: Combining social networks and collaborative filtering. *Communications of the ACM*, 40(3),63-65

Kiesler, S. (Ed.) (1997). *Culture of the internet*, NJ: Erlbaum.

Kraut, R.M., & Galegher, J. (1990). Patterns of contact and communication in scientific research collaboration. In J. Galegher, R.M. Krauss, & C. Egido (Eds.) *Intellectual Teamwork: social and technological foundations of cooperative work*, 149-171: Lawrence Erlbaum Associates.

Kuhlthau, C.C. (1991). Inside the search process: information seeking from the user perspective. *Journal of the American Society for Information Science, 42(5)*,361-371.

Mantovani, G. (1996). *New Communication Environments: From Everyday to Virtual,* Taylor & Francis.

Marchionini, G. (1995). *Information seeking in electronic environments*, Cambridge, UK, Cambridge University Press.

Menzel, H. (1959). Planned and unplanned scientific communication. *Proceedings of the International Conference on Scientific Information, 1,* 199-243, National Academy of Sciences.

Nonaka, I. & Takeuchi, H. (1995). *The knowledge-creating company*, Oxford University Press.

Root, R. W. (1988). Design of a multi-media vehicle for social browsing. *Proceedings of the Conference on Computer Supported Cooperative Work*, 25-38, Portland.

Schrage, M. (1990). *Shared Minds: The New Technologies for Collaboration,* New York: Random House.

Skyrme, D. (1999). *Knowledge Networking: creating the collaborative en-*

terprise, Butterworth-Hienmann.

Taylor, R.S. (1968) Question-negotiation and information seeking in libraries. *College of Research Libraries,* 29(3),178-194.

URL1 http://www.salford.ac.uk/isi/staff/ef/.

Wilson, T. D. (1981). On user studies and information needs. *Journal of Documentation, 37(1),* 3-15.

Chapter 11

A Framework for the Implementation of a Collaborative Flexible Learning Environment for Academic Institutions

R. K-Y Li, S. T. Cheng and R.J. Willis
Monash University, Australia

INTRODUCTION

Over the past few years the enormous advances in multimedia and Internet technology have started to affect how we live, play, enjoy and conduct our businesses. At the same time, these technologies have begun to creep into our learning and training environments.

Many educational institutions are experimenting with the use of the new technology to enhance existing teaching methods. The traditional instructor-centric method of teaching is giving way to the learner-centric model of learning in which information is interpreted rather than merely received by the students and new knowledge is created (Lotus Corporation, 1997).

In the learner-centric model, students learn through discovery. The traditional textual and verbal-based learning method is becoming less acceptable. The new learning model is often driven by interactive multimedia which gives the learner full control over the learning process and hence, the focus is on what the learner does not already know. Interactiveness increases the student's motivation and rate of retention (Bielenberg & Carpenter-Smith, 1997). The term *flexible learning*, a contemporary buzzword, is often used to describe the above-mentioned model.

Previously Published in *Managing Information Technology in a Global Economy*, edited by Mehdi Khosrow-Pour, Copyright © 2001, Idea Group Publishing.

Flexibility can be introduced in difference forms, which include:

- *Time:*
The course materials and resources are kept up-to-date and are available on demand at any time that is convenient to the learner (just-in-time).

- *Place:*
Students can access the materials from any place in the world where the course can be delivered. Consistent materials are delivered regardless of the access point.

- *Delivery mode:*
The delivery modes include On-line, Off-line (including VCD/DVD) or the hybrid approach with push technology (Louey, 1997).

- *Curriculum:*
Students are given the opportunity to take greater responsibility for their learning and to be engaged in learning activities and opportunities that meet their individual needs. The courses are flexible in terms of entry and exit points.

- *Pace:*
Learners decide how fast or how slowly they should learn. Students proceed through the course at their own pace, respond actively to each step in the sequence, and receive immediate feedback before proceeding to the next step.

- *Payment*:
Charges are related to the resources that a learner uses and the syllabus he/she chooses to cover.

In the student-centric model, teachers are facilitators who help the students with self-teaching (Reid, 2000). The model provides a rich learning environment in which the student can receive new experiences, promote knowledge acquisition activities, and develop and share knowledge and responsibility (Guillermo, 1996).

COLLABORATIVE LEARNING APPROACH

Active learning is not a new concept in learning.
> *If you tell me, I'll listen.*
> *If you show me, I'll see.*
> *If I experience it, I'll learn*
>   Lao Tse, 420BC

Human beings learn better by doing but best in a collaborative environment. Tracey (1992) found that group collaborative learning (peer-to-peer interactions in conjunction with the teacher) can result in higher level reasoning strategies,

Figure 1: Learning models

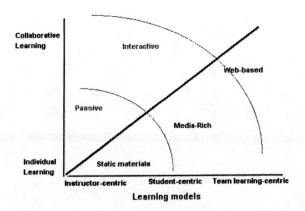

greater diversity of ideas, more critical thinking and increased creative response, compared to individual learning. The team learning centric model (see Figure 1) is therefore more suitable for training to support management objectives and the performance of an organization. It provides the opportunity for the development of effective teamwork, and interpersonal communication and listening skills. However, there are barriers to be considered.

THE BARRIERS TO COLLABORATIVE FLEXIBLE LEARNING

- *Bandwidth limitation*
  Broadband Internet services are now available, but the costs are often beyond what most students can afford. In many places the infrastructure does not support broadband services. Therefore, most systems are now designed specifically to work within a low bandwidth environment which means that there is more textual information with little sensory stimulated temporal enrichment. (Gallego, 1998)

- *Lack of feedback*
  Most current flexible learning environments rely solely on the web for the delivery of their courses. In this mode, an absence of feedback in the form of facial expressions and body languages between the learner and the educator may give rise to some misunderstanding (Pennell, 1996).

- *Campus lifestyle*
  Most people enjoy meeting new people and interacting with lecturers. Studying on campus enriches the life of a student and provides opportunities for the

development of social interactions and other life enrichment skills. The idea of a virtual campus will, however, deplete what is considered by many to be the best reason for going to a university.

- *Copyright and protection of unauthorized access*
  Developing an on-line learning package can be very expensive: obtaining copyright for all the materials and resources embedded within the package adds another strain to the slim budget of most academics (Inglis, Webster and Ling, 1999). Online learning packages need to be protected against hacking and copying. Although the technology to secure a web site is currently available, most institutions do not address the protection issue due to time or financial constraints.

- *No team based learning*
  Many on-line learning systems currently focus on flexibility of delivery and access and are often based on the student-centric learning module. Team-based learning factors are often neglected.

THE PROPOSED COLLABORATIVE FLEXIBLE LEARNING FRAMEWORK

The framework consists of the following components:

- *Flexible delivery of the course material and resources*
  Ideally, both on-line and off-line delivery media should be used. The course material should be delivered within an environment simulating traditional face to face teaching. Question and answer sessions should be provided.

- *Collaborative team learning*
  The environment should promote peer interaction, sharing of ideas and information, and team-based learning. It is aimed at providing a meaningful framework in which students can extend their knowledge, capacity and application of knowledge (Philip, 1994).

- *Learning packages development considerations*
  Bandwidth and related constraints should not limit the development of the learning packages. The packages should be supported by full multimedia enrichment to suit each student's learning style (see Table 1) and interactivity to promote *learning by doing*. Students should be able to learn through their preferred medium and by engaging with the same material in several media.

- *Course material and resource must be current and consistent.*
  The content of training materials must be accurate and consistent across different media as discrepancies in the material may result in trainees losing confi-

Table 1: Learning Styles

Learning style	Description	Multimedia Solution
Visual-Spatial	Drawing, jigsaw puzzles, reading maps and daydreaming. Learning is through drawing, verbal and physical imagery.	Hyperlinks, pop-up windows, audio and visual conferencing, texts with images and graphs.
Bodily-kinesthetic	Moving, making and touching things. Learning is through body language and physical activity.	Interactive space of images and 3D objects for writing, drawing, calculating, rearranging things can be introduced, for example, a Virtual Reality world can be used to simulate real world problems.
Musical	Sensitive to rhythm and sound. Learning is through lyrics, speaking rhythmically and tapping out the tempo. Tools like CDs, multimedia and radio would appropriate.	Teaching materials converted into lyrics and rhythms.
Interpersonal	These students learn best through interaction. Learning is through seminars and/or group activities.	E-mail, video-conferencing, chat-rooms to reach out to others.
Intrapersonal	This type of learner tends to shy away from others, but has strong will, confidence and opinions. Learning is through independent study and introspection.	Privacy in learning and progress is at learner's pace.
Logical-Mathematical	Think and reason conceptually, see patterns and relationships. Learning is through logic games, investigations and mysteries.	Concept modelling tools can be used to help students to learn and form concepts before they can deal with details.
Linguistic	Reading, playing word games or making poetry. Learning is through reading books or encouragement to say and see words.	Internet is virtually a huge repository of information. Web pages are more interesting than books and often more updated.

Adopted from: WestEd Home 1998 Jayne & Johnson 2000

dence in the program (Hawkins, 1997). Facilities must be provided to allow the materials to be corrected and distributed with minimal disruption. They should provide for easy updating of materials and resources.

- *Real world experience*
  Students learn better when they can see the real application of the knowledge that they are going to gain. The learning environment should therefore simulate a real world setting so the student can collaboratively tackle the real world problem using the information provided, the methodology instigated and the knowledge and skill gained. This scenario-based learning supports the Anchorage Instruction learning theories of Murphy, Jamieson and Webster (1998) in which an anchor or focus is created that generates interests and enables students to identify and define problems. Hence, students can pay attention to their perception of these problems.

- *Campus life*
  The flexible learning environment should not be seen as a potential replacement of the University campus. It should be used to enhance learning and encourage students to be self-directed and self-teaching. The teacher becomes a facilitator and spends more time in improving course content and contexts for better learning.

- *Minimizing changes to the course context and structures*
  After the implementation of a flexible delivery mode, changes to how the course is run should be minimized. All the useful learning components of the course must be retained.

- *Modularization of contents*
  A course built using modular design enables both teachers and the students to construct customized pathways through the content to match their learning requirements. Modularization has two advantages: it gives the learner just-in-time training (Gordon, 1997) and improves the retention rate as it conserves the bandwidth (Filipczak, 1996). Modularization also enables prerequisites to be incorporated in the learning process so a student would not be allowed to proceed from one module to the next if the latter relies on the acquisition of knowledge from earlier modules.

- *Secured access and student progress monitoring*
  No unauthorized access to the course materials and resources should be allowed. The progress of each student should be monitored automatically.

- *Courses should be available at affordable cost varied according to the resources that each student uses.*

A PROTOTYPE TO DEMONSTRATE THE FRAMEWORK

Figure 2 shows an implementation of a flexible system developed in line with the proposed framework. The subject unit is BUS5150/BUS4540 Project Management and is taught at the School of Business Systems, Faculty of Information Systems, Monash University, Melbourne, Australia

The course is taught at Master Degree level twice a year. The average class size is 180. The whole course comprises a 2-hour per week face to face lecture

Figure 2: An implementation of the proposed framework

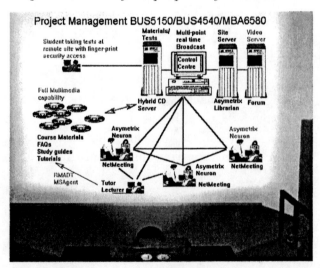

for 13 weeks and a 1-hour tutorial for 12 weeks. Most students are international, from Asia, and are studying Business Systems. They have Bachelor Degree from different disciplines.

The subject matter is project management. The contents are based on the recommendation of Project Management Body of Knowledge (PMBOK) of Project Management Institute (USA). The main aim of the course is to equip students with the skills, knowledge, methodology and techniques unique to project management and to prepare them to take on a role within a project team in their future careers. The main author of this paper who teaches the subject, combines over a decade of industrial experience as a project manager with eighteen years of academic research in Project Management. The focus of the subject is to clarify some of the myths about project management and keep students abreast of the latest developments in the field of project management.

The major assignment of the subject is team based and focused on a case study developed jointly between the team and the teacher/tutor. The process of project management is simulated over the duration of the project and problems/solution are created to demonstrate an understanding of the subject and the appropriate application of methodology and technique.

Project Management practitioners are invited as visiting lecturers during the course. Students in previous years have found these sessions both beneficial and stimulating.

The implementation consists of the following components:
- *Virtual Classroom*
  The web-based static course materials are support by a virtual classroom teaching (see Figure 3). The lessons are delivered using a hybrid CD-ROM ap-

Figure 3: Virtual Classroom

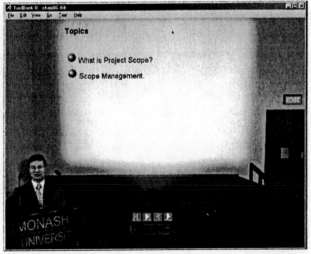

Figure 4: FAQ Module

proach wherein the parts of the course subject to frequent change are delivered transparently from the Web server. The video at the bottom left hand corner is real and synchronized with the PowerPoint style display but the classroom setting is artificially generated. The users are given total control to pause or replay the video, or to select any topic.

- *Frequently Asked Questions Module*
  This module provides the opportunity for students to clarify certain concepts or jargon that they find difficult to understand. The student types in the question and the teacher gives an answer verbally with textual response displayed within the bubble, as shown in Figure 4. Free text format entry is allowed and the best matched answer is retrieved from the database. The teacher (a MSAgent implementation) provides a lip-synchronized spoken response.

- *Web-based course management systems (CMS)*
  Asymetrix Librarian is a client-server course management system designed to provide centrally-control institution-wide learning activities including learner authentication, course delivery, collaboration and performance tracking. Librarian also enables the modularization of course materials. Rules can be set to determine how a student should progress from one level to another. Different modules can be selected to build courses to meet the needs from other schools. Librarian embraces industrial standards which allow quiz sessions (that were developed using professional authoring tools such as Asymetrix Instructor or Macromedia Authorware) to be automatically tracked and assessed (see Figure 5). The progression of each student through the course can be individually

Figure 5: Asymetrix Librarian

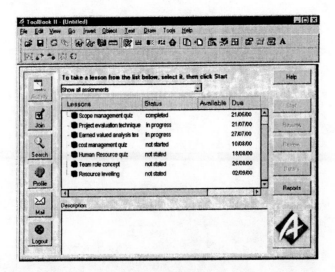

Figure 6: Collaborative environment

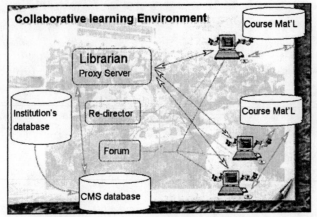

tracked and reported, including how much time a student spends on each page. Senior staff can use the output reports from Librarian to measure the effectiveness of the learning package.

Asymetrix Librarian is a database driven proxy server. It centrally controls student access while allowing stored course materials to deliver on-demand to locally enrolled students (see Figure 6).

- *Collaborative learning environment*
  The environment contains two modules: the Allaire Forum (see Figure 6) and Microsoft NetMeeting video conferencing system. The tutor/teacher can monitor the message tracks with each assignment group and offer helps when nec-

Figure 7: Video-on-demand

essary. A Microsoft Site server facilitates the control of the point-to-point tutor/teacher to student consulting sessions and multi-points conferencing between the assignment team members.

NetMeeting's application sharing (collaborative writing using Words), white board (electronic sketchpad) and chat system enable collaborative discussions and hence, the sharing of ideas and knowledge.

- *On-demand video streaming and live broadcasting*
  Streaming video is a technology that enables a video to start playing on the web while it is being downloaded. Products from Real Network are used to facilitate web- based video-on-demand and live broadcasting.
  Video-on-demand sessions are used for the delivery of new lecture materials created after the term has started. It can also be used for the delivery of materials to replace existing topics on the CD-ROM. It can be used as the medium to deliver materials on topics that are useful for other courses. An example of a video-on-demand lecture is shown in Figure 7. The format of the on-demand lecture is identical to that on the CD-ROM. A small low-quality streaming video appears at the bottom left hand corner over a full-sized matching background. The video is synchronized to the PowerPoint style texts using RealText technology and Synchronized Multimedia Integration Language (SMIL) language.

Visiting lecturers use the live-broadcast sessions for broadcasting their presentations.

- *Fast updating of course materials and resources using server-pushed technology*
When the course CD-ROM is used on a computer that has Internet access, the course web server checks the content on the CD-ROM with that on the server. If there are differences, the server downloads the new contents to the hard disk of the client machine. The course CD-ROM, the web server and the client machine work collaboratively to ensure all data are up-to-date. The lecturer can use this facility to replace any section of the course when needed.

- *Automated self-paced tutorial session to provide software skill*
Students use Microsoft Project to plan, monitor progress and help better decision-making to address the variations to the original plan of the assignment case project.
The multimedia-mediated tutorial system provides step-by-step interactive guidance on the learning of Microsoft Project. Video and voice-over, help learners to understand the relationships between the input to and output from Microsoft Project.

- *Smart card and Finger print device*
Finger-print devices are used to allow students at remote locations to sit for the competence tests at a nearby designated examination centre such as a community library The finger-print device can be sent to the examination centre when required and the only thing the library staff has to do is to ensure that only one person is at the computer station. Each student requiring remote authentication is issued with one smart card on enrolment and the fingerprint of the student is stored on the smart card.

VALIDATION OF THE IMPLEMENTATION AGAINST THE FRAMEWORK

The implementation adopted a hybrid CD-ROM approach for the delivery of the course to reduce the network bandwidth requirement. The rich data on the CD-ROM provides the sensory enrichments. The web connection, together with the server push technology, ensures that the contents can be kept up-to-date. Any inconsistency existing amongst the course materials can be replaced as soon as it is identified, using the same technology. The course materials can be delivered on the CD-ROM and Internet or both.

The virtual classroom on the CD-ROM and the web stimulates a real lecture environment, but in this class, the students have full control of the progression of the lecture. Students receives non-verbal cues from the lecturer and complex concepts can be explained using video, animations or bitmaps synchronized to voice–over. The FAQ module provides the questions-and-answers session. Students can now ask questions without worrying about whether others think they are stupid.

The proxy server of the Librarian (the web based course management system) authenticates students and prevents unauthorized access. Intellectual property rights are therefore protected. Competency tests involving multiple-choice, fill-in-the-blank, arrange-objects can be administered, tracked and accessed automatically by the Librarian.

The Allaire forum, together with the Microsoft NetMeeting, provides the collaborative learning environment. Members of the assignment teams can communicate amongst themselves while their messages can be automatically captured and tracked and used later for student evaluation purposes. The video conferencing enables tutors or lecturers to receive feedback from the students in the form of facial expressions and body language. This also provides the chance to meet new people and encourages interaction with fellow students. Team-based learning is therefore facilitated by this implementation. Under the collaborative environment, students can jointly establish the project case study, formulate the plan for the project, simulate the various parameters of the project and learn how to manage a project by actually doing it as if they are in the real world.

Tutorial sessions and lectures conducted by invited industrial practitioners are part of the implementation.

The course is developed in a modularization format. Librarian allows a course administrator to specify the path a student should go through and to set rules to ensure that a prerequisite module be completed before progression to the next module.

CONCLUSION

Interactive course packages provide learners with stimulating features and opportunity for active learning. The growth of the Internet and related multimedia technologies provides new possibilities for educators. Flexible learning, in terms of time, place, curriculum, pace and cost increases the success of learning and teaching. Low cost tools are now available for building collaborative environments within which students are encouraged to learn by doing.

This paper describes a framework used to guide the development of a team-based flexible learning environment and proves that such an environment can be built using available technology.

This particular environment, however, is not a model on which a virtual campus should be built: the authors believe that campus life is an integral part of the learning process. Students can come to the lab to watch the virtual classroom lecture at their own pace and at a time that suits them. They can choose to use the video conference facilities to interact with the tutors and lectures, or meet them face to face. The role of the lecturer can be transformed to one of facilitator. The lecturer can spend more time interacting with students, advising them on their simulated real life projects and improving course materials.

The Asymetrix Librarian chosen for this project is an enterprise-strength collaborative learning facilitation system and therefore, the cost may be beyond the budget of an average school. However, it could become feasible if the package were purchased at the institutional level.

Finally, it has been found that the cost of the technologies, when compared to that of course material development, is relatively low.

REFERENCE:

Bielenberg, D. R. & Carpenter-Smith, T. (1997). Efficacy of story in multimedia training, *Journal of Network and computer Applications*, 220, 151-159.

Filipczak, B. (1996). Chunking CBT, *Training, 33*, (9) 28.

Gallego, G.(1998). *The State of the Art in WBT*, Available at http://www.gracespace.com/weblearn/tlnotes.htm.

Gordon, J. (1997). Infonuggets: The bite-sized future of corporate training?, *Training, 34*, (7), 26-33.

Guillermo, E. P. (1996). *The Importance of The World Wide Web in Education K-12* Available at http://www.geocities.com/Athens/5461/paper_1.html.

Hawkins, D. T. (1997). Web-based training for online retrieval: An idea whose time is Coming, *Online, 21*, (93), 68-69.

Inglis A., Webster, L and Ling, P (1999). Costing Flexible Learning, Centre for Higher Education Development, Monash University.

Jayne, B. C. & Johnson E. C. (Access on 2.2.2000). *Pedagogy: A Primer on Education Theory for Technical Professional*, Available http://www.mircosoft.com/education/planning/online/wpPOP.doc.

Lotus Corporation (1997). White paper: *Distributed Learning* Available on-line at: http://www.lotus.com.

Louey, O. (1999). *Hybrid CD-ROM strategies*, a Honours thesis, Monash University

Murphy, D., Jamieson, P. and Webster, L. (1998). *What is Flexible Learning?* Centre for Higher Education Development, Monash University.

Pennell, R. (1996). *Managing Online Learning* , Available at http://elmo.scu.edu.au/sponsored/ausweb/ausweb/educn/pennell/paper.html.

Philip, C. G. (1994) *Distance Learning: A Different Time, a Different Place* Available at http://www.contarct.kent.edu/change/articles/julaug94.html.

PMI (1999). *Project Management Body of knowledge (PMBOK)*, Project Management Institute, USA.

Reid, J. E. (Access on 2.2.2000). *What Every student Should Know About Online Learning*, Available at http://illinois.online.uillinois.edu/online/course1/redi.htm.

Tracey, W. (1992). *Designing training and development systems* USA American Management Association.

WestEd Home (1998). *Learning Styles* , Available at http://www.wested.org/tie/dlrn/learning.html.

Chapter 12

Information Technology, Core Competencies, and Sustained Competitive Advantage

Terry Anthony Byrd
Auburn University, USA

The value of information technology (IT) in today's organizations is constantly debated. Researchers and practitioners have examined organizations to try to discover causal links between competitive advantage and IT. This paper presents and details a model that depicts a possible connection between competitive advantage and IT. Furthermore, this paper attempts to show how one major component of the overall IT resources, the IT infrastructure, might yield sustained competitive advantage for an organization. More precisely, IT infrastructure flexibility is examined as an enabler of "core competencies" that have been closely related to sustained competitive advantage in the research literature. The core competencies enabled by IT that are the focus of this study are mass customization and time-to-market. By showing that IT infrastructure flexibility acts as an enabler of these competencies, the relationship to sustained competitive advantage is demonstrated.

INTRODUCTION

A fiercely competitive business environment is an omnipresent reality in many commercial industries today. Forces such as global competition, ever changing consumer attitudes, rapidly decreasing cycles of technological innovations, social and cultural upheavals, and instantaneous access to

Previously Published in the *Information Resource Management Journal, vol.14, no.2,* Copyright © 2001, Idea Group Publishing.

widespread information have been catalysts of this competitive climate. These competitive pressures have prompted business organizations in virtually every industry to institute radical organizational initiatives and mandates to do battle among themselves. In recent years, senior management in large and small organizations has tried many different maneuvers such as total quality management (Choi and Behling, 1997), reengineering (Hammer, 1990; Hammer and Champy, 1993), downsizing (Robbins and Pearce II, 1992), rightsizing (Zeffane and Mayo, 1994), and flatten organizational structures (Daft and Lewin, 1993; Heydebrand, 1989) to stay competitive or to gain a sustained competitive advantage.

Many researchers and practitioners have advocated using information technology (IT) as a source of competitive advantage (Benjamin, Rockart, and Scott Morton, 1984; Clemons, 1986, 1991; Feeny, 1988; King, Grover, and Hufnagel, 1989; Neo, 1988; Parsons, 1983; Porter and Millar, 1985). Companies, such as Wal-Mart, American Airlines, and Baxter International, have been cited as corporations that gained sustained competitive advantage from IT. This paper investigates this concept of IT being an agent of competitive advantage and attempts to show how one major component of the overall IT resource, information systems (IS) infrastructure flexibility, might yield sustained competitive advantage for a firm. More precisely, IS infrastructure flexibility is examined through its relationships as an enabler of core competencies that have been closely linked to sustained competitive advantage in the management literature. The core competencies that are closed linked here with IS infrastructure flexibility are mass customization and time-to-market.

At one time, the competitive value of IT was thought to come from so-called strategic information systems (SISs) (Reich and Benbasat, 1990; Sabherwal and King, 1995; Sabherwal and Tsoumpas, 1993; Wiseman, 1988). SISs change the goals, operations, products, or environmental relationships of organizations to help them gain an advantage, at least temporarily, over other companies in their industry (Wiseman, 1988). During the 1980s and early 1990s, strategic systems like American Airlines' Sabre System (Hopper, 1990), Digital Equipment Corporation's XCON (Sviokla, 1990), Federal Express's tracking and sorting system (Stahl, 1995), and Baxter's International ASAP system (Scott, 1988) were popular. Many companies were desperately trying to develop their own SISs to win customers and market share.

However, some recent research evidence has cast doubt on the ability of SISs to sustain competitive advantage for their companies. Mata, Fuerst, and Barney (1995) reasoned that proprietary technologies like SISs are becoming increasingly difficult to keep proprietary. They noted that a wide variety of factors – workforce mobility, reverse engineering, and formal and informal technical communications – are present to disseminate detailed information about proprietary technology like SISs. Kettinger, Grover, Subashish, and Segars (1994) provided evidence that companies implementing SISs typically did not maintain their competitive advantage over time without other factors being present. In their study, they uncovered information that the preexistence of unique structural characteristics is an important determinant of SISs' outcomes, that is, whether they provide sustained competitive advantage or not. Neumann (1994) also rationalized that SISs need complementary assets to lead to sustained competitive advantage. Without such interrelated assets, he demonstrated that any technology can be easily imitated thus losing its competitive advantage.

In studying the research on the ability of SISs to maintain a competitive edge, one theme seems to permeate throughout. Focus always falls on the importance of the technical foundations of the firms implementing SISs. Capabilities like "unique structural characteristics" (Kettinger et al., 1994), "complementary assets" (Neumann, 1994), "managerial IT skills" (Mata et al., 1995), and "structural differences," (Clemons and Row, 1991) are nearly always used in connections with the ability of SISs to maintain competitive advantage. Kettinger and his colleagues (1994) discovered that one of these structural capabilities that seemed to make a difference was the technological platform, or infrastructure. Davenport and Linder (1994) also stated that the success of the few companies with SISs really was derived from long-term, well-planned investments in networks, databases, and applications, rather than ingenious individual applications. These networks, databases, and applications are components of an organizational IS infrastructure (Duncan, 1995). In light of all these discoveries, researchers now emphasize that the search for competitive advantage from IT has shifted from SISs to the strategic value of IS infrastructure (Davenport and Linder, 1994).

Researchers and practitioners alike have taken note of the potential value of an organization's IS infrastructure. In fact, the growing strategic value of the IS infrastructure is almost undeniable. IS infrastructure expenditures account for over 58 percent of an organization's IT budget, and the percentage is growing at 11 percent a year (Broadbent and Weill, 1997). Some even have called IS infrastructure the new competitive weapon and see it as being crucial in developing sustained competitive advantage (Boar, 1993, 1997; Davenport and Linder, 1994). Rockert, Earl and Ross (1996) reflect the ideal goals of an IT infrastructure in stating:

... an IS infrastructure of telecommunications, computers, software, and data that is integrated and interconnected so that all type of information can be expeditiously – and effortlessly, from the users viewpoint – routed through the network and redesigned processes. Because it involves fewer manual or complex computer-based interventions, a 'seamless' infrastructure is cheaper to operate than independent, divisional infrastructures. In addition, an effective infrastructure is a prerequisite for doing business globally, where the sharing of information and knowledge throughout the organization is increasingly vital.

From these statements, the strategic value of the IS infrastructure seems to be growing.

McKay and Brockway (1989) called IS infrastructure the enabling foundation of shared IT capabilities upon which the entire business depends. Weill (1993) also noted that IS infrastructure was a foundation for capability across business units or functional units. Davenport and Linder (1994) referred to IS infrastructure as that part of the organization's information capacity intended to be shared among all departments. They concluded that an IS infrastructure is a firm's institutionalized IT practice – the consistent foundation on which the specific business activities and computer applications are built. Congruent with these others, Duncan (1995) described IT infrastructure as a set of shared, tangible IT resources forming a foundation for business applications. The tangible IT resources composing an IS infrastructure are platform technology (hardware and operating systems), network and telecommunication technologies, data, and core software applications (Duncan, 1995).

As indicated by these statements, an IS infrastructure is the keystone for the development of business applications and the backbone for electronic communications in an organization. It also follows that the development of an IS infrastructure is arguably the most important aspect of managing IT resources in an organization. Based on the above definitions and descriptions from the literature, IS infrastructure in this study is defined in this paper as follows:

IS infrastructure is the shared, IT resources of hardware, software, communication technologies, data, and core applications that provide a unique technological foundation (1) for widespread communications interchanges across an organization and (2) for the design, development, implementation, and maintenance of present and future business applications.

Unique characteristics of an IS infrastructure determine the value of that infrastructure to an organization. Duncan (1995) wrote, "One firm's infrastructure may make strategic innovations in business processes feasible, while the characteristics of competitors' infrastructure may likewise cause their inability to imitate the innovation rapidly enough to mitigate the first mover's advantage. This set of characteristics has been loosely described as infrastructure 'flexibility' " (page 38). It is this characteristic of IS infrastructure that has captured much of the attention of researchers and practitioners. In fact, in most recent surveys featuring the issues most important to IT executives, the development of a flexible and responsive IS infrastructure, and related topics, are always at or near the top of the responses (Boar, 1997; Brancheau, Janz and Wetherbe, 1996; Niederman, Brancheau, and Wetherbe, 1991).

FLEXIBILITY

Flexibility is emerging as a key competitive priority in many organizational activities such as manufacturing (Gupta and Somers, 1992; Ramasesh and Jayakumar, 1991), high technology maneuvers (Evans, 1991), automation (Adler, 1988), and finance (Mason, 1986). Researchers also have heralded the competitive benefits of overall organizational flexibility (Aaker and Mascarenhas, 1984; De Leeuw and Volberda, 1996; Krijnen, 1979).

Flexibility in the management literature is defined as "the degree to which an organization possesses a variety of actual and potential procedures, and the rapidity by which it can implement these procedures to increase the control capability of the management and improve the controllability of the organization over its environment" (De Leeuw and Volberda, 1996, p. 131). Flexibility, therefore, gives an organization the ability to control outside environments effectively. For example, high flexibility corresponds to high managerial control of the organization with respect to the environment (De Leeuw and Volberda, 1996). The more control an organization has over its competitive environment, the better its competitive position. Control is any manner of directed influence. The environment is an external force that can dictate patterns in actions either through direct imposition or through implicitly preempting organizational choice.

Flexibility is related to terms like adaptability, versatility, agility, elasticity, and resiliency (Evans, 1991). Organizations with high flexibility in key areas should be able to respond very quickly to strategic moves by competitors (Boar, 1997). These organizations should also be adept at initiating strategic moves of their own in attempts to gain competitive advantage over their competitors. The research literature cited has acknowledged the importance of flexibility of key components of an organization. The implication of this literature is that flexibility of these key components is so very valuable in today's competitive environment. The IS infrastructure as discussed above is certainly one of the key components of an organization (Davenport and Linder, 1994; Duncan, 1995; Rockart, Earl, and Ross, 1996). Therefore, the investigation of IS infrastructure flexibility is assuredly a worthwhile study.

IS INFRASTRUCTURE FLEXIBILITY

Flexibility as it applies to IS infrastructure means the abilities of the infrastructure to support a wide variety of hardware, software, and other technologies that can be easily diffused into the overall technological platform, to distribute any type of information – data, text, voice, images, video – to anywhere inside of an organization and beyond, and to support the design, development, and implementation of a heterogeneity of business applications. These properties of an IS infrastructure help give management control over the external environment. For example, if an IS infrastructure supports a wide variety of hardware or software, the organization can more easily cope with changes in hardware or software industry standards. In the same way, if a technology platform can support the distribution of most types of data, new data like images and voice can more easily be distributed from one division of the company to another division.

The study of IS infrastructure is still in its infancy with only a few studies (e.g., Broadbent and Weill, 1997; Duncan, 1995; Weill, 1993). One of these has demonstrated one way to describe IS infrastructure flexibility more precisely with the qualities of *connectivity, compatibility,* and *modularity* (Duncan, 1995). Connectivity is the ability of any technology component to attach to any of the other components inside and outside the organizational environment. According to Keen (1991), connectivity – which he calls "reach" – "determines the locations the platform can link, from local workstations and computers within the same department to customers and suppliers domestically, to international locations, or ... to anyone, anywhere" (p. 39). Compatibility is the ability to share any type of information across any technology components. At one extreme of range, only simple text messages can be shared, while at the other extreme, any document, process, service, video, image, text, audio, or a combination of these can be used by any other system, regardless of manufacturer, make, or type.

Modularity is the ability to add, modify, and remove any software or hardware components of the infrastructure with ease and with no major overall effect. Modularity relates to the degree to which IT software, hardware, and data can be either seamlessly and effortlessly diffused into the infrastructure or easily supported by the infrastructure. It defines the options available to alter the configurations of hardware, software, telecommunications, and data. Issues surrounding the concept of modularity are portability, scalability, interoperability and openness.

An organization with high connectivity, compatibility, and modularity is viewed as having high IS infrastructure flexibility. A company using technologies with high connectivity, compatibility, and modularity, i.e, high flexibility, has the potential to quickly move its IS infrastructure to match many different changes in directions of the strategy and structure of the organization. In the competitive environment of today, such agility or versatility is almost a necessity to defend against rival firms.

Tapscott and Caston (1993) argued persuasively that a technology paradigm shift has enabled organizations to begin reinventing themselves around the characteristics of the post-industrial firm that features flexible IT as a primary component. They stated that IS compatibility helps break down organizational walls, empowers employees, and makes data, information, and knowledge in the organization readily available. Second, Tapscott and Caston (1993) affirmed that IS connectivity enables seamless and transparent organizations, those that are independent of time and space. IS modularity allows the seemingly contradictory achievement of integration yet independence of organizational components, businesses, and modules (Tapscott and Caston, 1993). Tapscott and Caston (1993) also noted that IS modularity allows the integration of data, text, voice, image, and other types of information into multimedia systems to create user-friendly multimedia systems.

SUSTAINED COMPETITIVE ADVANTAGE

Practitioners of strategic management in organizations are constantly on the lookout for resources that can bring their firms competitive advantage. Porter (1980, 1985) popularized the concept of competitive advantage. Porter said that competitive advantage grows from the value a firm is able to create for its buyers that exceeds the firm's cost of creating the product or service (Porter, 1985). Day and Wensley (1988) emphasized that a complete definition of competitive advantage must describe not only the state of the advantage but also how that advantage was gained. They wrote that competitive advantage consists of positional and performance superiority (outcomes of competitive advantage) as a result of relative (to the competition) superiority in the skills and resources a business deploys. Positional superiority pertains to how well a company has placed itself in the marketplace so as to have a competitive advantage over others in the industry. Performance superiority refers to the higher returns of a corporation on its assets relative to competitors.

Sustained competitive advantage flows from organizational capabilities and resources that are rare, valuable, non-substitutable, and imperfectly imitable (e.g., Barney, 1986, 1991; Lado and Wilson, 1994). Sustained competitive advantage is obtained by firms implementing strategies that exploit their internal strengths, through responding to environmental opportunities, while neutralizing external threats and avoiding internal weaknesses (Barney, 1991). It is argued below that mass customization and speed-to-market have been shown in the literature to be enabler of sustained competitive advantage. In turn, IS infrastructure flexibility is shown to be related to sustained competitive advantage by acting as an enabler of both mass customization and speed-to-market (See Figure 1).

Figure 1: A Model Relating Information Technology Infrastructure to Sustained Competitive Advantage through Core Competencies

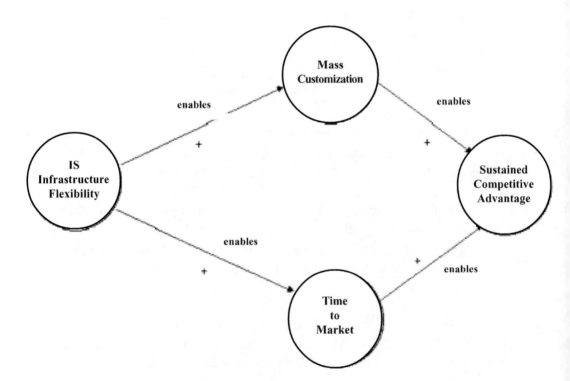

MASS CUSTOMIZATION AND COMPETITIVE ADVANTAGE.

Customization refers to manufacturing a product or producing a service in response to a particular customer's needs, and mass customization relates to doing it in a cost-effective way. Pine, Peppers, and Rogers (1995) said mass customization "calls for a customer-centered orientation in production and delivery processes requiring the company to collaborate with individual customers to design each one's desired product or service, which is then constructed from a base of pre-engineered modules that can be assembled in a myriad of ways" (p. 105). Mass customization requires a dynamic network of relatively autonomous operating units. The key to the process is that different operating units or modules do not come together in the same sequence every time a product is produced or a service delivered (Pine, Victor, and Boynton, 1993). Each customer's wants and needs dictate the combination of how and when the modules interact to make the desired product or provide the preferred services. Therefore, mass customization allows businesses to offer products and services to a wide variety of customers and meet changing product demands through service or product variety and innovation - all without an increase in costs (Boynton, Victor, and Pine, 1993).

Mass customization has been referred to as "customer of one" marketing (Marion and Kay, 1997), "market of one" (Foley, 1997), "one to one marketing" (Peppers and Rogers 1998), and "high variety strategy" (Kahn, 1998), among other things. The value of mass customization to organizations has been demonstrated in the literature (Boynton, Victor, and Pine, 1993; Gilmore and Pine, 1997; Marion and Kay, 1997; Peppers and Rogers, 1998; Pine, 1993; Pine, Peppers, and Rogers, 1995; Pine, Victor, and Boynton, 1993). Marion and Kay (1997) discovered, in their examination of companies using mass customization with a build-to-order strategy, that these corporations increased revenues, improved customer service and satisfaction, eased competitive pressures, and made the overall process more efficient. Pine, Peppers, and Rogers (1995) observed through case studies that the combination of mass customization and elicitation of customer wants and needs led to a learning relationship between company and customer. They reported on a number of examples where customers locked in with companies through the companies' abilities to collect information on these customers wants and needs and their capability to fulfill these wants and needs very quickly through mass customization. For example, Ross Controls, a 70-year-old manufacturer of pneumatic valves and air controls systems, uses this approach.

Through what is called the ROSS/FLEX process, Ross learns about its customers' needs, collaborates with them to come up with design precisely tailored to help them meet those needs, and quickly and efficiently makes the customized products (Pine, Peppers and Rogers, 1995). The ROSS/FLEX system has boosted revenues by 15% over the past four years. Ross plans through this customized approach to gain customers for life. It seems to be working, as many of its customers refuse to move to any other makers of pneumatic valves. Pine, Peppers, and Rogers (1995) tell the story of one such customer:

> Knight Industries, a supplier of ergonomic material-handling equipment, gives Ross 100% of its custom business and about 70% of its standard (catalog) business. When a competitor tried to woo Knight way, its president, James Zaguroli, Jr., responded, 'Why would I switch to you? You're already five product generations behind where I am with Ross?' (p. 107)

Ross uses its mass customization capabilities to lock customers in by providing superior service in comparison with its competitors.

Dell Computer Corporation is another example of a company that has used mass customization to gain a sustained competitive edge in its industry (Magretta, 1998). Dell, unlike most of its major competitors, sells directly to customers and builds products to order. Customers can call or go to Dell's Internet site and customize their computers from an array of choices of computer components and software. This direct model gives Dell certain advantages in its industry. The direct model allows Dell to collect a wide variety of information about its customers and, thus, enables Dell to better respond to the needs of its customers. For example, because of the close relationships with its customers, Dell was able to pioneer such service innovations as loading a customer's customized software on its computers during production, placing the customer's asset tags on personal computers as they are being manufactured, and developing easy to open and use computer cases. Dell is also able to keep inventory down very low compared to competitors like Compaq. Dell has an industry low inventory of eight to ten days while Compaq and IBM have inventory of at least four weeks or more. This low inventory permits Dell to react very quickly to offer new products and services as they hit the market in the fast-paced computer industry. These and other customization practices have given Dell a competitive advantage that has been difficult for its competitors to overcome.

Companies as diverse as Corning, Westpac, Bally, Citibank's CPG, and Asea Brown Boveri have used mass customization to their advantage. Mass customization allows a customer-centered orientation to production and delivery of services, requiring each corporation to cooperate with individual customers to design each one's specialized product or service, which is then built from a base of pre-engineered modules that can be assembled in almost unlimited ways (Pine, Peppers, and Rogers, 1995).

IS INFRASTRUCTURE FLEXIBILITY AND MASS CUSTOMIZATION

Pine (1996) reported that it takes a highly integrated IS infrastructure to support mass customization. He included among the IS infrastructure design tools, flexible switches and networks, common customer views with image processing and shared databases, computer integrated manufacturing, and workflow management and coordination software. Such an IS infrastructure automates linkages between processes and relationships between people. For mass customization to succeed in a company, Kahn (1998) claimed that organizations needed more flexible databases, flexible networks, and flexible CAD/CAM systems in their IS infrastructures.

A classic example of how an adaptive IS infrastructure enables and supports mass customization is reported in Boynton, Victor, and Pine (1993). They described how Westpac, a South Pacific financial services conglomerate that had previously dominated banking in its marketplace, moved to more flexible technologies to institute a new strategy of product differentiation. Westpac decided to overhaul its entire IS infrastructure and create a completely new systems development and operational environment. This new environment was called "CS90" (Core System for the 1990s) and was constructed to allow "Westpac to consolidate everything it knows about the processes and expertise required to create new financial products into a set of highly flexible software modules. The result would be a flexible and advanced software engineering that would combine different bits of knowledge quickly and at low cost, in response to changing product and service demands" (Boynton, Victor, and Pine 1993, p. 48). The competitive design goals included compatibility to easily mix and match software modules to satisfy customer demands, responsiveness that is the result of highly connected and integrated computer systems, and modularity so that software modules can be reused and recombined across changing products and services. Westpac is now able to fight off niche competitors that might have eroded its market share. With CS90, Westpac can match the cost of niche products while still offering a comprehensive portfolio of financial products and services.

Dell Computer Corporation has used its flexible infrastructure to support its mass customization strategy. The flexible infrastructure at Dell enables coordination across company boundaries to achieve new levels of efficiency and productivity (Magretta, 1998). The flexible infrastructure allows for just-in-time deliveries from a host of suppliers, a highly adaptive manufacturing facility, and the establishment of great relationships with customers. For example, Dell's manufacturing facility makes possible the production of hundreds of different computer combinations to satisfy the customized orders of its customers at costs that are the lowest among its major competitors. Additionally, the infrastructure allows Dell's best customers to access internal support information online in the same way as Dell's own technical-support teams do, saving time and money on both sides. These customers also have access to their own purchasing and technical information about the specific computer configurations they buy from Dell through customized intranet sites that are components in its overall IS infrastructure (Magretta, 1998).

Pine, Victor, and Boynton (1993) outlined four keys to coordinating process modules for mass customization. These were (1) instantaneous linkages, (2) costless links, (3) seamless links, and (4) frictionless links. For each one of these keys, a flexible IS infrastructure plays a major role in making it possible. For example, these authors noted that mass customizers like Dell Computer, Hewlett-Packard, ATandT, and LSI Logic use special flexible IS infrastructures that are so critical to their "instantaneous" product delivery processes as to be almost impossible without it. "Costless" linkage systems must add as little as possible to the cost beyond the initial investment to create them. USAA uses a company-wide database that allows any employee to access all corporate information about any customer he comes into contact with.

The concept of seamless links is seen with the concept of case managers in organizations like IBM Credit Corporation and USAA (Hammer, 1990). Case managers in each organization use flexible and adaptive IS infrastructures that combine shared databases, integrated computer networks, and expert systems to manage customer sales, concerns, and problems. Once these companies had a specialist in each step in business processes like approving credit to a customer. For example, in the past, a credit application being evaluated in IBM Credit Corporation would have travel through several departments and involved a relatively large number of people (Hammer, 1990). A case manager can now handle all steps in the process because of the powerful and flexible IT at his disposal.

Pine, Victor, and Boynton (1993) found the rapid foundation of frictionless teams was an advantage to mass customization. They stated that "the instant teams must be frictionless from the moment of creation, so information and communications technologies are mandatory for achieving this attribute. These technologies are necessary to find the right people, to define and create boundaries for their collective task, and to allow them to work together immediately without the benefit of ever having met" (p. 115).

From the discussion here, it seems like an adaptive, integrated IS infrastructure is omnipresent in organizations where mass customization is prevalent. From these observations, it seems that a flexible IS infrastructure may be a prerequisite for mass customization in corporations.

TIME-TO-MARKET AND COMPETITIVE ADVANTAGE

Time competition can be divided into at least two different categories. One is the so-called "time-to-market" and the other is delivery performance. Time-to-market refers to the elapsed time between product definition and product availability (Vessey, 1991). Delivery performance pertains to the ability to deliver a customized product within a shorter elapsed time than can competitors in the same market, and is usually measured in terms of delivery lead time (Handfield, 1993). This type of time competition is related to mass customization because lead time is especially critical in industries with customized products. In fact, a number of firms, including ATandT, General Electric, Hewlett-Packard, Northern Telecom, Toyota, and Seiko, have all taken advantage of shorter delivery times to give themselves a strategic advantage (Bower and Hout, 1988; Dumaine, 1989; Merrills, 1989; Stalk, 1988). Since this type of time competition is related to mass customization, the two are discussed together in this paper. Time-to-market competition is discussed in this section.

George Stalk (1988) was one of the first strategists to propose the idea that time is as much a strategic weapon as money, productivity, quality, and innovation. In his classic article in Harvard Business Review, Stalk (1988) presented several examples where Japanese competitors had bested their American counterparts through time-to-market strategies. He noted at the time:

- In projection television, Japanese producers can develop a new television in one-third the time required by U.S. manufacturers.
- In custom plastic injection molds, Japanese companies can develop the molds in one-third the time of U.S. competitors and at one-third the cost.
- In autos, Japanese companies can develop a new product in half the time as the U.S. and German competitors. (1988, p. 49).

In these and many other industries, the Japanese were able to win significant market share due to time-to-market of new products and services.

Vessey (1991, 1992) maintained that time-to-market has become "doubly important" because of the pervasive nature of change. All of this is an attempt to satisfy the seemingly endless appetite for new products in the marketplace. There are new products and services, improved products and services, new and improved products and services, extensions and expansions of products and services, and revisions and enhancements of products and services, all with the intent to keep a steady stream of new products coming to market (Vessey, 1991). Vessey (1992) also cited several examples of corporations benefiting strategically from time-to-market. Ford Motor Company was one such example. Vessey wrote this about Ford:

> Ford Motor Company created "Team Taurus" to develop the Taurus and Sable line of automobiles. Team members included designers, engineers, production specialists, and even customers (who were asked what they wanted in a car). The team addressed profitability and competitiveness in both the design stage and production cycle. In their effort to rationalize the car's mechanical components and the way in which it would be built, they replaced sequential engineering activities with simultaneous input from the diverse group. Before the first clay model was built, they knew how the car would be assembled. Under the previous system, manufacturing managers didn't see the cars to be built until eight or nine months before production stated. Their success is cited as a significant factor in the renewal of Ford Motor Company (1992, p. 72).

This example help to give insight into how new products are being created in modern organizations.

Material Handling Engineering (1992) reported that industry studies by the Boston Consulting Group show that companies that respond twice as fast to customer demands grow at 5 times the industry average with prices 20% higher. Stalk (1992) stated that as companies focus on time-to-market competition, within about 2 years they are experiencing reductions of wait time of about 60%, inventory reductions of 50% to 60%, and dramatic improvements in quality and labor and asset productivity. Handfield (1993), in gathering data from 35 managers in large global organizations, asserted that time has been recognized as a critical element of global competitiveness. He stated that companies like ATandT, General Electric, Hewlett Packard, Northern Telecom, Toyota, and Seiko have all recognized the importance of shorter product development and delivery in providing a strategic advantage. In consumer goods, an empirical study showed that the second firm to enter a market did only 71 percent as well as the innovator, and the third firm did only 58 percent as well (Urban, Carter, Gaskin, and Zofia, 1986). Robertson

(1988), in a study of pioneer advantages in industrial markets, found that market pioneers tend to achieve substantially higher market shares, the early follower can expect to do only 76 percent as well as the market pioneer, and the late entrant only 51 percent as well as the pioneer. Although disadvantages for companies that are first to market have been cited, it is generally accepted that innovators gain strategic advantage from being first (Robertson, 1993; Vessey, 1991).

IS INFRASTRUCTURE FLEXIBILITY AND TIME-TO-MARKET

The revolutionary rise in the capability and flexibility of IT has fundamentally altered the product and service design process, lessening inefficiencies and enabling new levels of performance (Hull, Collins, and Liker, 1996). Flexible IT, such as computer-aided design and computer-aided manufacturing, has allowed better links between design and manufacturing and brought about more manufacturing friendly product designs. Flexible IT has also enhanced the capability of organizations to more rapidly respond to the changes in product design resulting in faster product development and reduced costs (Hull, Collins, and Liker, 1996; Vessey, 1992).

Hull, Collins, and Liker (1996) explored the effects of flexible IS infrastructure on two concurrent engineering practices. Concurrent engineering is important to time-to-market because it bring together multiple functions in decision making on product design so that downstream issues such as manufacturability, marketability, serviceability, and total life cycle problems, are anticipated at early steps (Clark, Chew, and Fujimoto, 1992; Hartley, 1992; Susman and Dean, 1992). Anything to facilitate concurrent engineering should also promote time-to-market. Two core concurrent engineering practices are early simultaneous influence (ESI) and in-process design controls (IDC). ESI refers to the participation of multiple, upstream, and downstream functions in initial stages of the product design process. Hull, Collins and Liker noted: "...high levels of early involvement increase opportunities for evaluating varied design alternatives and selecting ones which may reduce the risks of costly, late stage problems" (1996, p. 134). IDC refers to common design methodologies and protocols employed by the participants (Hull, Collins, and Liker, 1996). IDC emphasizes in-process inspection instead of relying on final inspections much like in process quality control.

Hull, Collins, and Liker (1996) surveyed manufacturing engineering from 74 Fortune 500 companies to try to determine if the combination of flexible IT, ESI, and IDC would lead to improvement in product development performance. Using statistical tests on the data from these companies, they found that flexible IT has a significant effect on both ESI and IDC. They found that the greater the use of flexible IT, the greater the positive effects of ESI on product development performance. In addition, they found, in the same way, that the greater the use of flexible IT, the greater the positive effects of IDC on product development performance. In both cases, flexible IT played a vital role in helping cross-functional teams of engineers achieve higher levels of performance.

The above study gives evidence that a flexible IS infrastructure is critical to the success of time-to-market initiatives. There is also other evidence that flexible IT enables a time-to-market competency. Vessey (1992) noted that "time to market, with its inherent product and process design, is a function of speed of information which must be shared by engineering and manufacturing" (p. 72). Because of this requirement, he declared that integrating enterprise-wide IT was a necessity in the ability for all team members to know what was occurring throughout the design process. He surmised that ancillary and immediate benefits could accrue from the elimination of redundant information and an integration of disparate data sources. Flexible IT, Vessey concluded, was important in establishing a seamless flow of information to all team members.

A case featuring Nissan also shows the importance of a flexible IS infrastructure for time-to-market. Nissan has built an intelligent system, known as Intelligent Body Assembly System (IBAS), to link production facilities around the world, making it a highly proactive assembly system (*Material Handling Engineering*, 1992). A key component of this system is a worldwide network based on production process data from each department within system. The system supports concurrent engineering, which is the central component of the Nissan production. The system makes it possible for Nissan to begin production preparations of new types of vehicles immediately at their manufacturing plants in any country and gives Nissan a competitive advantage. Again, as with the core competency of mass customization, a flexible IS infrastructure seems to enhance the core competency of speed-to-market in organizations.

IS INFRASTRUCTURE FLEXIBILITY AND SUSTAINED COMPETITIVE ADVANTAGE

The link between IS infrastructure and a sustained competitive advantage has been hypothesized through the discussions in this paper. IS infrastructure is firmly established as an enabler of two competencies that are shown to be closely related to sustained competitive advantage in organizations. Strong links between IS infrastructure flexibility and sustained competitive advantage have not been firmly established in the research literature. This paper has been a start in the quest to better understand how a flexible IS infrastructure might be a causal agent for sustained competitive advantage. The evidence presented in this paper suggests that a flexible IS infrastructure enables certain core competencies that, in turn, are closely aligned with sustained competitive advantage in organizations.

The two core competencies presented in this paper are not meant to be comprehensive. They are held up as examples of how a flexible IS infrastructure enables core competencies in an organization to give sustained competitive advantage. Other core competencies that could have been examined include organizational learning and knowledge management. These and others are left for other research studies. However, the value of a flexible IS infrastructure has been clearly indicated. Further research on the relationships between IS infrastructure, core competencies, and sustained competitive advantage is definitely needed.

CONCLUSION

The investment in IT by modern organizations continues to skyrocket (BusinessWeek, 1993; 1997). The expenditures on IT in many organizations exceed the spending on all other capital stock (BusinessWeek, 1997). With investments of this magnitude, it becomes absolutely necessary to wring as much value from IT as possible. Researchers and practitioners had once focused on the value of so-called "strategic information systems" as the "Holy Grail" of IT. These systems were seen as valuable in bringing competitive advantage to the companies that adopted them. However, later evidence cast doubt that these SISs alone would yield sustained competitive advantage.

More recently, researchers and practitioners have started to turn to IS infrastructure as a possible source of sustained competitive advantage. This paper has provided evidence of the value of the primary characteristic of an IS infrastructure, its flexibility. This paper has linked the concept of IS infrastructure flexibility as being an enabler with certain core competencies that have been empirically related to sustained competitive advantage in the research literature and in practice. By enabling these competencies, the value of IT, specifically the IS infrastructure, should be recognized.

The stakes are high when investing in IT; therefore, the returns must be high. The challenges presented by the this paper linking IS infrastructure flexibility to sustained competitive advantage through competencies like mass customization and time-to-market is to move forward to empirically examining these assertions. If the model hypothesized here can be firmly established, researchers must then turn their attentions to discovering the strategies that best accommodate using an adaptive IS infrastructure as an enabler of core competencies.

REFERENCES

Aaker, D.A. and Mascarenhas, B. (1984). The need for strategic flexibility. *Journal of Business Strategy*, 5(2), 74-82.

Adler, P.S. (1988). Managing flexible automation. *California Management Review* 30(3), 34-56.

Barney, J.B. (1986). Organizational culture: Can it be a source of sustained competitive advantage? *Academy of Management Review* 11, 656-665.

Barney, J.B. (1991). Firm resources and sustained competitive advantage. *Journal of Management* 17, 99-120.

Benjamin, R.I, Rockart, J.F., and Scott Morton, M.S. (1984). Information technology: A strategic opportunity. *Sloan Management Review*, 25(3), 3-10.

Boar, B. (1993). *Implementing client/server computing: A strategic perspective*. New York: McGraw-Hill.

Boar, B. (1997). *Strategic thinking for information technology: How to build the IT organizations for the information age*. New York: John Wiley and Sons, Inc.

Bower, J.L. and Hout, T.M. (1988). Fast cycle capability for competitive power. *Harvard Business Review* November-December, 110-118.

Boynton, A.C., Victor, B. and Pine, B.J. II. (1993). New competitive strategies: Challenges to organizations and information technology. *IBM Systems Journal* 32(1), 40-64.

Brancheau J.C., Janz, B.D., and Wetherbe, J.C. (1996). Key issues in information systems management: 1994-95 SIM Delphi results. *MIS Quarterly* 20(2), 225-242.

Broadbent, M. and Weill, P. (1997). Management by maxim: How business and IT managers can create IT infrastructures. *Sloan Management Review* 38(3), 77-92.

BusinessWeek, (1993). The technology payoff. 3323, 57-61, 64, 68.

BusinessWeek, (1997). The new business cycle. 3520, 58-61, 64-65, 68.

Choi, T.Y. and Behling, O.C. (1997). Top managers and TQM success: One more look after all these years. *Academy of Management Executive* 11(1), 37-47.

Clark, K.B., Chew, W.B. and Fujimoto, T. (1992). *Product development process.* Boston, MA: Harvard Business School.

Clemons, E.K. (1986). Information systems for sustainable competitive advantage. *Information and Management* 11(3), 131-136.

Clemons, E.K. (1991). Competition and strategic value of information technology. *Journal of Management Information Systems* 7(2), 5-8.

Clemons, E.K. and Row, M. (1991). Sustaining IT advantage: The role of structural differences. *MIS Quarterly* 15(3), 275-292.

Daft, R.L. and Lewin, A.Y. (1993). Where are the theories for the 'new' organizational forms? An editorial essay. *Organization Science* 4(4), i-vi.

Davenport, T.H. and Linder, J. (1994). Information management infrastructure: The new competitive weapon. In *Proceedings of the 27th Annual Hawaii International Conference on Systems Sciences*, IEEE, 27, 885-899.

Day, G.S. and Wensley, R. (1988). Assessing advantage: A framework for diagnosing competitive advantage. *Journal of Marketing* 52(2), 1-20.

De Leeuw, A.C.J. and Volberda, H.W. (1996). On the concept of flexibility: A dual control perspective. *Omega* 24(2), 121-139.

Dumaine, B. (1989). How managers can succeed through speed. *Fortune* February 13, 54-59.

Duncan, N.B. (1995). Capturing flexibility of information technology infrastructure: A study of resource characteristics and their measure. *Journal of Management Information Systems* 12(2), 37-57.

Evans, J.S. (1991). Strategic flexibility for high technology manoeuvres: A conceptual framework. *Journal of Management Studies* 28(1), 69-89.

Feeny, D. (1988). Creating and sustaining competitive advantage with IT. In M. Earl (ed.): *Information Management: The Strategic Dimension*, Oxford, U.K.: Oxford University Press.

Foley, J. (1997). Market of one: Ready, aim, sell! *Informationweek* 618, 34-44.

Gilmore J.H. and Pine, B.J. (1997). The four faces of mass customization. *Harvard Business Review*, January-February 75(1).

Gupta, Y.P. and Somers, T.M. (1992). The measurement of manufacturing flexibility. *European Journal of Operational Research* 60, 166-182.

Hammer, M. (1990). Reengineering work: Don't automate obliterate. *Harvard Business Review* 68(4), 104-112.

Hammer, M. and Champy, J. (1993). *Reengineering the corporation: A manifesto for business.* New York: Harper Business.

Handfield, R.B. (1993). The role of materials management in developing time-based competition. *International Journal of Purchasing and Materials Management* 29(1), 2-7.

Hartley, J.R. (1992). *Concurrent engineering: Shortening lead times, raising quality, and lowering costs*. Cambridge, MA: Productivity Press.

Heydebrand, W. (1989). New organizational forms. *Work and Occupations* 16, 323-357.

Hopper, M.D. (1990). Rattling SABRE – New ways to compete on information. *Harvard Business Review* 68(3), 118-25.

Hull, F.M., Collins, P.D., and Liker, J.K. (1996). Composite forms of organization as a strategy for concurrent engineering effectiveness. *IEEE Transactions on Engineering Management* 43(2), 133-141.

Kahn, B.E. (1998). Dynamic relationships with customers: High variety strategies. *Academy of Marketing Science Journal*, 26(1): 45-53.

Keen, P. (1991). *Shaping the future: Business design through information technology*, Boston, MA: Harvard School Press.

Kettinger, W.J., Grover, V., Subashish, G. and Segars, A.H. (1994). Strategic information systems revisited: A study in sustainability and performance. *MIS Quarterly* 18(1), 31-58.

King, W.R., Grover, V. and Hufnagel, E.H. (1989). Using information and information technology for sustainable competitive advantage: Some empirical evidence. *Information and Management* 17, 87-93.

Krijnen, H.G. (1979). The flexible firm. *Long Range Planning* 12, 63-75.

Lado, A.A. and Wilson, M.C (1994). Human resource systems and sustained competitive advantage: A competency-based perspective. *Academy of Management Review* 19(4), 699-727.

Magretta, J. (1998). The power of virtual integration: An interview with Dell Computer's Michael Dell. *Harvard Business Review* 76(2), 73-84.

Marion, L. and Kay, E. (1997). Customer of one: The next market paradigm. *Software Magazine* 17(13), 38-50.

Mason, S.P. (1986). Valuing financial flexibility. in B.M. Friedman (ed.): *Financing Corporate Capital Formation,* Chicago, IL: University of Chicago Press.

Mata, F.J., Fuerst, W.L. and Barney, J.B. (1995). Information technology and sustained competitive advantage: A resource-based analysis. *MIS Quarterly* 19(4), 487-505.

Material Handling Engineering. (1992). Compressing time-to-market: Today's competitive edge. 47(4), IM2.

McKay, D.T. and Brockway, D.W. (1989). Building IT infrastructure for the 1990s. *Stage by Stage* 9(3), 1-11.

Merrills, R. (1989). How Northern Telecom competes on time. *Harvard Business Review* 67(4), 108-114.

Neo, B.S. (1988). Factors facilitating the use of information technology for competitive advantage: An exploratory study. *Information and Management* 15, 191-201.

Neumann, S. (1994). *Strategic information systems: Competition through information technologies.* New York: Macmillan College Publishing Company.

Niederman, F., Brancheau, J.C., and Wetherbe, J.C. (1991). Information systems management issues in the 1990s *MIS Quarterly* 15(4), 474-499.

Parsons, G.L. (1983). Information technology: A new competitive weapon. *Sloan Management Review* 25, 3-14.

Peppers, D. and Rogers, M. (1998). Better business – one customer at a time. *Journal of Quality and Participation* 21(2), 30-37.

Pine, B.J. (1993). *Mass customization: The new frontier in business competition.* Boston, MA: Harvard Business School Press.

Pine, B.J. (1996). Serve each customer efficiently and uniquely. *Network Transformation* January, 1-5.

Pine, B.J., Peppers, D. and Rogers, M. (1995). Do you want to keep your customers forever? *Harvard Business Review* 73, 103-114.

Pine, B.J., Victor, B. and Boynton, A.C. (1993). Making mass customization work. *Harvard Business Review* 71, 108-119.

Porter, M.E. (1980). *Competitive strategy: Techniques for analyzing industries and competitors,* New York: Free Press.

Porter, M.E. (1985). *Competitive advantage: Creating and sustaining superior performance.* New York: Free Press.

Porter, M.E. and Millar, V.E. (1985). How information gives you competitive advantage. *Harvard Business Review* 63, 149-160.

Ramasesh, R. and Jayakumar, M. (1991). Measurement of manufacturing flexibility: A value-based approach. *Journal of Operations Management* 10(4), 446-468.

Reich, B.H. and Benbasat, I. (1990). An empirical investigation of factors influencing the success of customer-oriented strategic systems. *Information Systems Research* 1(3), 25-347.

Robbins, D.K. and Pearce II, J.A. (1992). Turnaround: Retrenchment and Recovery. *Strategic Management Journal* 13(4), 287-310.

Robertson, W.S. (1988). Sources of market pioneer advantages: The case of industrial good industries. *Journal of Marketing Research* 25, 87-94.

Robertson, T.S. (1993). How to reduce market penetration cycle times. *Sloan Management Journal* 35(1), 87-96 .

Rockart, J.F., Earl, M.J., and Ross, J.W. (1996). Eight imperatives for the new IT organization. *Sloan Management Review* 38(1), 43-54.

Sabherwal R. and King. W.R. (1995). An empirical taxonomy of the decision-making processes concerning strategic applications of information systems. *Journal of Management Information Systems* 11(4), 177-214.

Sabherwal, R. and Tsoumpas, P. (1993). The development of strategic information systems: Some case studies and research proposals. *European Journal of Information Systems* 2(4), 240-259.

Scott, S. (1988). ASAP express: Toward all-vendor systems. *Computers in Healthcare* 9(10), 38-40.

Stahl, S. (1995). Information is part of the package. *InformationWeek* 596, 206-208.

Stalk, G. (1988). Time – The next source of competitive advantage. *Harvard Business Review* 66(4), 41-52.

Stalk, G. (1992). Time-based competition and beyond: Competing on capabilities. *Planning Review* 20(5), 27-30.

Susman, G.I. and Dean, J.W. (1992). Development of a model for predicting design for manufacturablity effectiveness. In *Integrating design and manufacturing for competitive advantage*, (Susman, G.I., Ed.), 207-227. New York: Oxford University Press.

Sviokla, J.J. (1990). An examination of the impact of expert systems on the firm: The case of XCON. *MIS Quarterly* 14(2), 127-140.

Tapscott, D. and Caston, A. (1993). *Paradigm shift: The new promise of information technology.* New York: McGraw-Hill.

Urban, G.L., Carter, T., Gaskin, S. and Zofia, M. (1986). Market share rewards to pioneering brands: An empirical analysis and strategic implications. *Management Science* 32(6), 645-660.

Vessey, J.T. (1991). The new competitors: They think in terms of speed-to-market. *Academy of Management Executive* 5(2), 23- 34.

Vessey, J.T. (1992). The new competitors: They think in terms of speed to market. *Production and Inventory Management Journal* 33(1), 71-75.

Weill, P. (1993). The role and value of information technology infrastructure: Some empirical observations. in R. Banker, R. Kauffman, and M.A. Mahmood (eds.): *Strategic information technology management: Perspectives on organizational growth and competitive advantage,* Middleton, PA: Idea Group Publishing, 547-572..

Wiseman, C. (1988). *Strategic information systems.* Homewood, IL: Irwin.

Zeffane, R. and Mayo, G. (1994). Rightsizing: The strategic human resource management challenge of the 1990s. *Management Decision* 32(9), 5-9.

Chapter 13

Fitting EMS to Organisations

Carlos J. Costa
Departamento de Ciências e Tecnologias de Informação
ISCTE, Lisboa

Manuela Aparício
Lusocredito - Sociedade de Estudos e Contabilidade, Lda

A major purpose of an electronic meeting system (EMS) is recording data, which allows the production of an immediate and unbiased report. But reports produced by commercial EMSs have some weaknesses that make difficult the organisational integration of meeting results. In order to contribute to the solution of this problem, it was developed a new system supported in the concept of communication genre and genre system. A prototype was implemented and used in corporate environment. Preliminary results from its application showed that this approach contribute to a better fit to organisational needs than the traditional EMS.

INTRODUCTION

The concept of genre had its genesis in the literature. In that context, a literature genre considers a category of literary works that, having the same fundamental purpose, will present similar structure and will obey to similar norms. Its systematic study started with Plato, in the Republic, and Aristotle, in the Poetic, that sought to typify the literary works according to its common characteristics. During centuries, this concept was used either as mere form of organising the literature either as a way of imposing rules to the literary creation. Consequently, it originated so much strong oppositions as staunch defenders. This concept passed then for other areas of the artistic creation, like the movies and the television. More recently, it was incorporated in the organisational context (Yates and Orlikowski, 1992).

Previously Published in *Managing Information Technology in a Global Economy*, edited by Mehdi Khosrow-Pour, Copyright © 2001, Idea Group Publishing.

A major purpose of an electronic meeting system (EMS) is to record data, allowing the production of an immediate and unbiased report. But those reports have some characteristics that can be seen as weaknesses in the perspective of the organisational integration of meeting results. It means that its characteristics make difficult the flow of information from the meeting to the rest of the organisation.

- Those reports are a digital replica of a printed reports, it means that some of the features supplied by multimedia are not presented in those meeting reports.
- Most of the reports are even longer than the printed ones, being even more difficult to "read" either by humans or by machines.
- Those reports are not adjusted to a specific target (specific process, department, agent or system).
- The meeting reports are not integrated with context or support data. It means that there are a great quantity of information related to a meeting that typically does not appeared in the final meeting report.

In order to answer those and contribute to the answer the problem of organisational integration of meeting results it is presented here a solution based in the concept of communication genre and genre systems. After a brief literature review related to the communication genres, the solution is here presented and prototype produced is also described, as well as its use in an organisational context.

LITERATURE REVIEW

Genres of organisational communication are socially recognised types of communicative actions that are habitually enacted by members of a community to perform particular social purposes (Yates and Orlikowski, 1992).

Linked to the concept of genre are concepts like repertoire of genres and genre systems. In fact, the set of genres routinely enacted by a particular community form what can be called a repertoire of genres. On the other hand, genre system is a complex web of interrelated genres where each participant makes a recognisable act or move in some recognisable genre, which them may be followed by a certain range of appropriate generic responses by others (Baserman, 1995).

Communication genre proved to be a very useful concept in the analysis of organisation communication. (Orlikowski and Yates, 1994; Yates and Orlikowski, 1992). In fact, it was used in several organisational areas with the purpose of making the diagnosis of communication. It was used with the purpose of analysing groupware (Orlikowski and Yates, 1998), in the analysis of Internet documents (Crowston and Williams, 1997) or in the analysis of meetings (Yoshioka, Yates, and Orlikowski, 2000)

The use of genre was complemented with concepts like decomposition and specialisation, in order to create more integrated frameworks to analyse organisational communication. (Yoshioka and Herman, 1999).

The emphasis has been put in the analysis, but this concept may also play an important role in the production of new or improved artefacts. For example, it was used to redesign documents supported by electronic document management systems (Tyrväinen and Päivärinta, 1999). In this context, it was verified that organisational document genres and genre systems should be systematically re-think in collaboration with information systems specialists, organisation designers and domain experts. Some authors also used the concept of genre to produce better WebPages and network applications (Shepherd and Watters, 1999). Some authors also propose genre as the principal object of design for new media (Agre, 1998).

The concept of communication genre is widely used and by many media (Agre, 1998), this is a reason because there are a number of competing definitions of genre, and discussions about what actually constitutes a genre.

Miller (1984) defines genre as "typified rhetorical actions based in recurrent situations". It means that a communication genre implies not a single document or other communication artefact but a stream of them. It implies a community of users, composed of a particular sort of audience and a particular sort of activities, as well as a relationship between the producer and consumer of the material in question (Agre, 1995).

Swales (1990) emphasises the role of communicative purpose. In this context, a collection of communicative events becomes a genre due to a shared set of communicative purposes. These purposes are recognised by the discourse community owning the genre. A discourse community is a group of people linked together by occupation, working premises, special interests or with some set of shared knowledge, possessions and behaviour.

Miller (1984) suggested that genre may be defined at different levels in different cultures in different times, depending on how the recurrence of rhetorical situations is viewed. For example, the business letter may be a genre at one point in time, and at an another moment be more general and be transformed in a kind of super-genre assembling discourses. Yates and Orlikowskib (1992) propose the notion of sub-genres. For example, the positive recommendation letter would be a sub-genre of the recommendation letter.

Bhatia regards sales promotional letters and job application letters as belonging to the same genre, the promotional genre. This is due to the similar purpose of these letters. A promotional letters and job applications are aiming to obtain a specific response from its readers (to buy the products or to call the applicant for an interview). However, sales promotion letters and job application letters are two well-established names of different types of letters in the discourse communities where they are used. This situation is may be the result of Bhatia mistakenly equating communicative purpose with the linguistic notion of communicative function. At this point, some authors make confusion between speech acts and genre purposes, neglecting the role of the community of users as true definers of communication genres.

While some authors emphasise the importance of the form others emphasise the purpose, there are also other authors that propose additional concepts to characterise genres, like functionality (Shepherd and Watters, 1999). According to those authors, the use of this concept helps not only understand the influence of the Internet as new medium, but it also helps to use genre effectively in the design of computer and network-based applications.

Based in this important perception, it was developed a system based in the concept of communication genres and genre system.

Figure 1: Interaction between users and genre

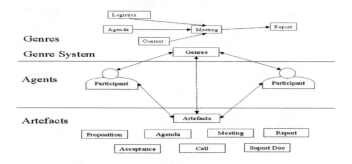

USING GENRES TO SUPPORT MEETINGS

Based in the concepts of genre and genre system, it is proposed here a meeting support system. A repertoire of genre systems embedded in the system is used to help the participants of a meeting session. In the meeting process, the interaction between agents through genres is processed in the way that is described in the following figure, where the interaction between users and genres is made through artefacts, like proposition letters, acceptance memos, calls, meeting agendas or meeting sessions.

Using a genre is just a phase in the genre life cycle. In fact, the communication genre life cycle can be decomposed in creation, choice and use. This last phase can be decomposed in artefact production and artefact use.

Creation of genres

The genre creation is a social process that may take a long time. Typically, the artefact is produced with a purpose and is composed of a set of components. By producing several artefacts, sometimes there is the need of classifying them, consequently, genres are created.

Associated with a community of users, a repertoire of communication genres may be identified. As noticed by Agre (1998), any kind of life involves the routine use of several genres. For example, tourism involves guidebooks, menus, street signs, timetables, roadmaps, phrase books, photos and postcard notes back home.

Choice of a communication genre

The choice of a communication genre depends on the situation. Typically, associated to each situation there is a set of communication genres that compose a genre system. Like in the tourism example, there is a system of genres, composed with a set of genres. Each genre is enacted according to a pre-defined order but some events may also contribute to change this order. In an annual general meeting (AGM) of an enterprise, a meeting agenda has the same structure most of the times, the same support and context documents (profit and lost accounts, balance sheet, management report and auditor report) and the same expected results (approval of the financial statements and instructions to the accountancy). But some genres may be enacted according to the approval, or not, of the financial statements. If there is profit or losses, the resulting genre produced may also be different. Therefore, in a particular meeting there is a specific communication genre associated with it, but according to decisions taken during the meeting session, or some external factors, other genres may be used.

Using a communication genre

The use of a communication genre consists in the production of an artefact (e.g., book, software or leaflet) based in the genre template and also in the use of the artefact (reading or listening). In fact, in opposition to literature genres where there is a clear differentiation between producers (e.g., novel writer) and consumers (novel reader) of the artefacts (book) which are the support of the genre (novel), in the organisational communication everybody may be producer and consumer of memos, meetings or reports.

SYSTEM DESIGN

Based in the concept of communication genre it was created a software system to support the meeting process. This system was implemented in the web (with HTML, Javascritp and Perl). The processes, which are supported by the system, are:
- Analysis process, where it is made the identification of the repertoire of genre and genre systems. This process is related to the genre creation phase in the genre life cycle.

Figure 2: Class Diagram

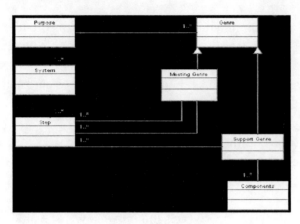

- Planning process, where it is produced the plan of the meeting, by choosing communication genres and genre systems among the repertoire of genres. This process corresponds broadly to the choice of communication genre in the genre life cycle.
- Meeting session process, where the meeting is performed. In this process genres are used.

In order to understand the system it is presented the data structure that supports the analysis process as well as what was called the "genre system mechanism". Finally it is described when users and specially facilitators choose the communication genres and genre systems.

In this analysis process, it is made the identification of possible organisational situations in which users identified what genres they expect to use. In this process the community of users is asked to participate in the identification of the repertoire of genres and genre systems. They may also participate in the process of change of genres and genre system repertoire if needed. This information is stored in order that in the future all this information could be easily changed or used. The system produced to support the phase meeting of analysis process is beard a database structure based in the class diagram presented in Figure 2.

After using a functionality that supports the analysis process, users have a repertoire of genre and genre systems that can be used in a specific situation. It means that by having all this information stored in a database, there is a repertoire of communication genres and a genre system, ready to be used in the meeting planning process. Here, the concept of communication genre is supported mainly in forms, help menus and context description. With all this elements, artefacts are produced. Among those artefacts there are agenda, agenda items, meeting sessions, decisions or outcome statements

Figure 3: "System mechanism"

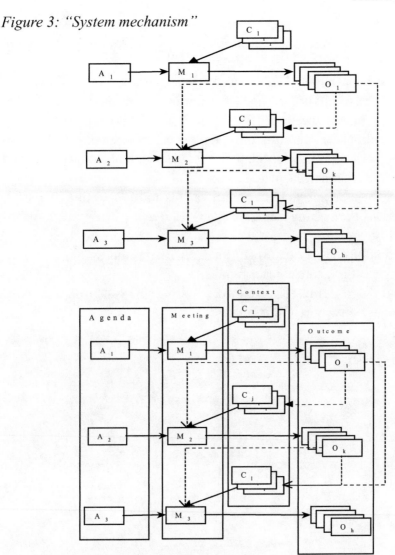

The "system mechanisms" is the structure of the genre system linked to a specific meeting session or repertoire of meeting sessions. As long as the "system mechanism" is nuclear in the implementation of the genre system, it is broadly described in the following paragraphs.

The system mechanism used in the system is presented in Figure 3. The agenda item (A_1) is used to plan the meeting issue or meeting decision (M_1). To support this meeting issue there is additional information (C_1 to C_{j-1}). As result of the meeting process, one or all of the expected results may be produced. Possible results are O_1 to O_{k-1}. Results produced may be incorporated in the next meeting issue (M_2) or included in the support data (C_1, C_j, C_1, etc.).

O_1 to O_{k-1} includes all the possible results produced in meeting issue M_1. It includes the most likely results if M_1 is decided, the most likely results if M_1 is not decide and the less likely but possible results.

Those possible results are defined when the analysis process is performed. Then, the expected results are defined when the issue is planned (A_1) and more strictly defined during the meeting (M_1).

After describing the data structure and the "system mechanism," it is also important to describe how, and specially when, the communication genres and genre systems are chosen in the meeting process.

Having as basis a repertoire of genre systems and a repertoire of genres, users and specially the meeting facilitator chooses the genres in several moments:
- during logistics process the most adequate meeting systems are chosen;
- agenda definition consists in the identification of a meeting system as well as each communication genre for each moment;
- some times the agenda must be redefined, so the meeting system or each one of the communication genres may be changed;

Figure 4: Meeting Genre System Repertoire

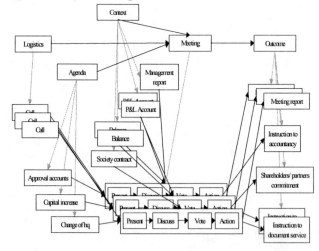

- decisions taken during meeting, more specific outcome genre are defined, as well as context genres;
- even after the meeting and according to type of decisions, some outcome genres may be changed.

In conclusion, the system developed supports the analysis process, meeting planning process and meeting session process. In the analyse process, users identify the repertoire of communication genres they use or need to use in a meeting process and then store (through a HTML interface) all this information in a data-

Figure 5: Implementation of an AGM genre system (a schema)

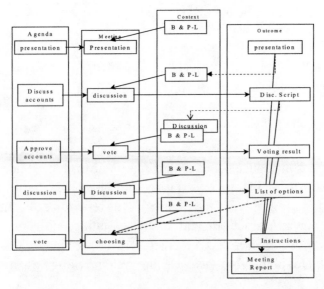

Figure 6: Implementation of an AGM genre system (a prototype)

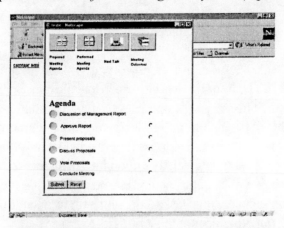

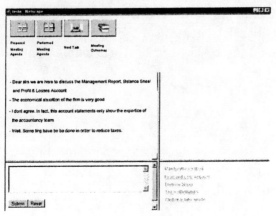

base (Figure 2). In the meeting planning process, the facilitator (or the group of participants leaded by the facilitator) chooses the adequate communication genres to plan a meeting. In the prototype developed, this process consists in the production of HTML forms and Perl script. Behind this, an important tool was the "system mechanism" already described. Finally, during the meeting session, participants are supported by the system to produce results.

EXAMPLE

The system described before was used in a small accounting firm, with the purpose of supporting annual general meetings (AGMs) and extraordinary general meetings (EGMs). In this context it was produced the repertoire of genres and genre systems presented in the Figure 4. This repertoire of genres was obtained by interviewing accountants and also by consulting legislation.

For illustrative purposes, it is presented here the meeting for financial statement approval. This is already a specific genre system belonging to a repertoire of genre systems

This genre system is chosen when, in the first quarter of the year, financial statements of the last economic year must be approved. Then, based in this information, it was created a system architecture (Figure 5).

Then it was produced a prototype that implements this AGM genre system (Figure 6). As it was mentioned, this prototype was developed in HTML, Javascript and PERL. The figure shows the screen that the participants use during the meeting session. This screen is composed of an agenda, a set of tools to support the actual task (decision) and links to support documents (profit and losses account, balance sheet) and help/comments. It also may show images of the other participants, a feature especially important in a distributed environment. The facilitator screen is a more sophisticated one because he has the possibility of leading the group by locking some tasks (e.g., items of the agenda), changing the agenda, or handing out other documents.

Deducing from statements, several decisions may change the initial genre system. Supposing that financial statements are not approved. In those circumstances other kind of decisions must be taken, instead of deciding what to do with profits.

PRELIMINARY RESULTS

At this moment, a formal evaluation of the system developed was not performed yet. The system was implemented in a small accounting firm to support the process of production reports by the annual general meetings (AGMs) and extraordinary general meetings (AGMs). Through the use of the system some observations where already collected.

It was found that performance of the server and databases employed were modest, what made the process slow and the interaction between users was affected. But, because of the existence of a clear agenda that everybody could follow it was noticed that participants did not spend time in accessory subjects. It was also noticed that results produced were much clear to the accountants, as long as in addition to the meeting report it was produced a specific document to the accountancy.

By comparing this system with some commercial EMS already used by the participants it was found that this one was more adjusted to the specific situation but less flexible. In fact, the production of the repertoire of genres is a process that takes some time.

The use of HTML and Javascript for the interface with users was also an advantage because it was possible to make little changes very easily. Those changes on the interface were made according to the needs or preferences of the users, in order to facilitate the introduction of the system. Some of the changes were the following: changes in colours, the use of the trademark of the client or the use of an additional window or frame.

This preliminary evaluation consisted in the reporting of user opinion about the system. At this moment it is possible to classify opinions according to some categories: performance of the system, flexibility, perception of fitness to the activity, participants' interface, ease of understanding results and ease of converting results to the other processes.

CONCLUSIONS

Electronic meeting systems have some weaknesses that make difficult the organisational integration of results produced during the meeting. In order to deal with this problem, it was developed a new system supported in the concept of communication genres and genre systems.

This system supports (1) the identification of a repertoire of communication genres and genre systems; (2) the planning of a meeting session by choosing specific genre systems; and (3) the use of a specific genre system in the meeting session and post-meeting phase of the meeting process.

A prototype was implemented and used in a corporate environment. This system proved to be more adjusted to specific situations, but less flexible than commercial electronic meeting systems (EMS). In fact, this system can better fit in the needs of the organisation than other EMS also tested in the same organisation. But, the process of analysis needed to identify and produce or enlarge the repertoire of genres or genre systems takes a longer time compared to the meeting planning process in others electronic meeting systems.

REFERENCES

Agre, P. (1998). Designing genres for new media: Social, economic, and political contexts, in S. Jones (ed.), *CyberSociety 2.0: revisiting CMC and community*; Sage.

Bazerman, C. (1995). Systems of genres and the enactment of social intentions, in A. Freedman and P. Medway (eds.), *Genre and the new rhetoric*; London: Taylor and Francis.

Bhatia, V. K. (1993). *Analyzing genre: Language use in professional settings*; London: Longman.

Crowston K. and Williams, M. (1997). Reproduced and emergent genres of communication on the World-Wide Web, in *Thirtieth Hawaii International Conference on Systems Science* (HICSS–30), Maui, HI.

Miller, C. R. (1984). Genre as social action, *Quarterly Journal of Speech*, 70, pp. 151-167.

Orlikowski, W. and Yates, J. (1994). Genre repertoire: the structuring of communicative practice in organizations, *Administrative Science Quarterly, 39*, pp. 547-574.

Orlikowski, W. and Yates, J. (1998). Genre systems: structuring Interaction through communicative norms, *CCS WP 205 Sloan MIT WP 4030*, July.

Shepherd, M. and Watters, C. (1999). The functionality attribute of cybergenres; in *Thirtieth Second Hawaii International Conference on Systems Science* (HICSS–32), Maui, HI.

Swales, J. M. (1990). *Genre analysis: English in academic and research settings*; Cambridge: Cambridge University Press.

Tyrväinen, P. and Päivärinta, T. (1999). On rethinking organizational document genres for electronic document management, in *Thirtieth Second Hawaii International Conference on Systems Science* (HICSS–32), Maui, HI.

Yates, J. and Orlikowski, W. (1992). Genre of organizational communication: A structurational approach to studying communication and media, *Academy of Management Review*, 17 pp- 299-326.

Yoshioka, T. and Herman, G. (1999). Genre taxonomy: a knowledge repository of communicative action, *CCS WP209*, October.

Yoshioka T., Yates, J. and Orlikowski, W. (2000). Community-based interpretative schemes: exploring the use of cyber meetings within a global organization, *CCS WP213*.

Chapter 14

Ad Hoc Virtual Teams: A Multidisciplinary Framework and a Research Agenda

Guy Paré, Ph.D. & Line Dubé, Ph.D.
École des Hautes Études Commerciales de Montréal, Canada

INTRODUCTION

Virtual arrangements are proposed as a way for organizations to face the challenges of the upcoming century and to operate both efficiently and innovatively (Bleecker, 1994; Jarvenpaa & Ives, 1994). Information and communication technologies (ICT) serve as powerful enablers of virtual organizing in the form of various intra- and inter-firm arrangements (Knoll & Jarvenpaa, 1995). Among other emerging arrangements, virtual teams, both within and across organizations, are relatively recent phenomena brought about in part by the emergence of technologies such as electronic mail, Internet, groupware and videoconferencing (Barnatt, 1995; Iacono & Weisband, 1997; Lipnack & Stamps, 1997). The reluctance of many workers to relocate for a new job, the global nature of the marketplace, the need to complete projects as quickly as possible, and the need to tap the best brains no matter where they may be, are all examples of drivers of virtual teams within and across organizations (Geber, 1995; Duarte & Snyder, 1999; Lipnack & Stamps, 1997).

According to some researchers and practitioners, virtual teams are a benefit as well as a necessity for companies, and are bound to become more prevalent (Bozman & Ellis, 1993; Gorton & Motwani, 1996; Lipnack & Stamps, 1997). Anecdotes concerning the success of virtual arrangements have received considerable attention in the popular press. This literature typically claims that ICT form the basic foundation for the creation and management of virtual teams or organiza-

Previously Published in *Challenges of Information Technology Management in the 21st Century*, edited by Mehdi Khosrow-Pour, Copyright © 2000, Idea Group Publishing.

tions (Barnatt, 1995; Henry & Hartzler, 1998; Jarvenpaa & Ives, 1994). Despite widespread interest in virtual models and their importance for both the professional and scientific communities, this topic has been largely overlooked by business scholars. To date, studies on virtual arrangements have focused mainly on the concept of telecommuting (e.g., Gray, 1995; Nilles, 1994) and most articles have been anecdotal in nature. Given the lack of empirical evidence in this area, there is a pressing need for *rigorous conceptual work* to examine virtual team functioning and success.

As a preliminary step toward *theory building*, this chapter contributes a conceptual framework for future research on virtual teams. Our endeavor is in line with the recommendation of McGrath & Hollingshead (1994) to the effect that studies on groups and technology should be planned using a comprehensive framework. As presented in detail later, our framework builds upon and integrates the various constructs and variables of complementary research frameworks and models from the fields of organizational behavior and small group dynamics, project management and management information systems. The resulting integrative framework provides a useful guide for the development of a research agenda on virtual teams.

But who are these teams? A virtual team, like any other team, is a group of people who interact through interdependent tasks guided by a common purpose. Unlike conventional teams, a virtual team works across space, time, and organizational boundaries, with links strengthened by webs of communication technologies (Lipnack & Stamps, 1997). In other words, virtual teams are globally distributed teams, i.e., teams in which personnel, resources and work may be dispersed over multiple, geographically separate work sites. Further, they may be intact workgroups that work together indefinitely (permanent team) or they may be groups brought together for a finite time to tackle a specific project (ad hoc team). The comprehensive framework developed in this chapter focuses on ad hoc virtual teams.

LITERATURE REVIEW

As a preliminary step towards theory development, we find it is useful to build a conceptual framework of the research problem at hand. The framework should consider the full panoply of variables that are potentially relevant to the functioning and effectiveness of ad hoc virtual teams, and should place them in functional relation to one another.

A small group dynamics perspective

Small groups, work groups and, more recently, teams have been studied extensively by social scientists (e.g., Hare, 1992; McGrath, 1964; Shaw, 1976).

Building on the work of McGrath (1964), Gladstein (1984) conducted an extensive literature review on small group behavior, and integrated the research findings into a general, widely-accepted model of group behavior (see Figure 1). We posit this model makes some interesting and key contributions to the study of virtual teams. First, the model considers several levels of analysis, all of which should be included in future empirical research on virtual teams. Most important are the group level and organizational level factors. Group level factors include group composition variables (e.g., skills, heterogeneity, and organizational and job tenures) and group structure variables (e.g., operating norms, specific roles, and size) while organizational level factors include elements such as available resources (e.g., training and technical support) and organizational structure (e.g., reward for performance and supervision). All of these variables are likely to influence virtual team effectiveness both directly and indirectly through their impacts on group processes and dynamics. For instance, many ad hoc virtual teams have formal value statements that members agree to uphold when they join the team (e.g., commitment, individual accountability). Teams frequently devise a set of operating norms based on the team's values (Henry & Hartzler, 1998). These could include things such as meeting deadlines, attendance at teleconferences, and expectations around communications. Once the agreements are clear and in place, they enhance the development of a common language, increasing at once group process behaviors. Second, Gladstein's framework clarify the key construct of group processes which refers to two broad categories of group behaviors, namely, maintenance behaviors and task behaviors (Gladstein, 1984). Maintenance be-

Figure 1: General model of group behavior (adapted from Gladstein, 1984)

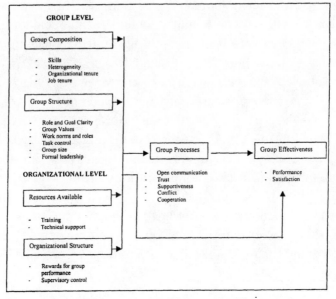

haviors are required to build and maintain group synergy and momentum (e.g., open communications, level of collaboration and participation, level of conflict, level of trust), while task behaviors are those needed to solve problems that prevent the group's objectives from being achieved (e.g., information processing, consensus generating, decision making).

Other contextual issues of importance are the precise relationships and roles of each member in a virtual team. Here, Gorton & Motwani (1996) proposed three organizational models that can influence virtual team structure. The models in question are cooperative (all members share overall project management responsibilities), delegation (a supervisor assumes overall management but delegates specific responsibilities), and consultative (specific tasks are sub-contracted to outside experts). Further research could provide a deeper understanding of these interaction models, their implications for group process behaviors and project management strategies and their ultimate influence on virtual team effectiveness. It also appears important to investigate the effects of technological support on the degree of structure (how standardized and stable) and the type of structure (how formal) of group processes in the context of distributed work groups.

A project management perspective

Project management professionals and researchers have contributed for several years to our understanding of the factors influencing project success (Cleland & King, 1998; Kerzner, 1997). One of the key frameworks in this field is that developed and promoted by the Project Management Institute (PMI), namely the Project Management Body of Knowledge (PMBOK, 1987).

This framework provides several key insights for the study of virtual teams in organizations. First, in line with the small group literature, it posits that any given project evolves in a larger system (an organization, a network or a society) and has to be managed with due consideration for the structures, cultures, and expectations of that larger environment. Second, the project management life cycle posits that most projects generally go through four phases, namely, conception, development, implementation, and termination (see Figure 2). Each phase has its own challenges and hence its own set of activities and strategies. For instance, at the conception stage, goals and objectives of the proposed project will be clearly defined and stated and the overall feasibility of the project will be assessed. This initial stage is particularly critical for virtual teams since when team members are in remote locations, alignment and commitment are more difficult to generate. Virtual team leaders must then find effective ways to deal with this major challenge. During the implementation phase, coordination and communication are of utmost importance. The control of every aspect - budget, time, quality, stakeholder satisfaction (including team members) – represents the project leader's major con-

Figure 2: The project management life cycle (from the PMI PMBOK Standards Committee, 1987)

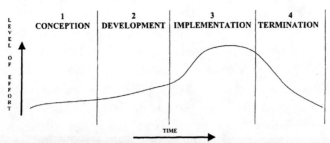

cern. Creating an elaborate formal and informal communication approach that replaces face-to-face interaction; finding the spark of energy and excitement that bounds team members and creating conditions for risk-taking and commitment represent key challenges for virtual team leaders at this stage of the project life cycle. In this light, the PMBOK framework provides guidelines on how knowledge areas such as time and cost management, quality management and human resource management should be addressed. It also offers a series of tools and techniques such as work breakdown structure, PERT/CPM network, GANTT chart, and responsibility assignment matrix to be used at each phase of the project life cycle. Future research should then explore how these guidelines, tools and techniques could be applied in a virtual life cycle environment.

A collaborative technology and group perspective

The literature typically claims that ICT constitute the basic foundation for creating and managing virtual teams (Geber, 1995; Jarvenpaa & Ives, 1994; Lipnack & Stamps, 1997). Information systems and small group behavior researchers have conceptualized the relationship between technological support and group effectiveness as involving several factors (e.g., Hiltz & Turoff, 1978; Kraemer & Pinsonneault, 1990; McGrath & Hollingshead, 1994).

In their seminal book entitled *The Network Nation*, Hiltz & Turroff (1978) were among the first to study groups interacting via computers, and some of their central ideas are echoed in the key frameworks reviewed below. As a first example, they described the impact of computer mediation on the group discussion and decision-making process, an issue central to the study of virtual teams. In this line of research, Kraemer & Pinsonneault (1990) developed a framework from the literature of organization behavior and group psychology and applied it to the literature of Group Decision Support Systems and Group Communication Support Systems. The broad theoretical notion states that technological support facilitates group process by enhancing group capabilities, removing barriers to group interaction, improving the group in its task, and building or reinforcing the social value of the group to its members through successful task performance.

Another key contribution of this framework lies in its group process variables. In the context of virtual teams, decision characteristics refer to the ways in which decisions are made by such groups (Kraemer & Pinsonneault, 1990). This include the depth of analysis, the degree of participation of the team members, the degree of consensus reached in making a decision, and the time it takes to reach a decision. As another example, communication characteristics refer to the clarification efforts made by team members in trying to understand the problem to be solved, the task to be performed and the decision to be made, as well as the nature of the information exchange between team members and the degree of task-oriented communication between team members. Finally, interpersonal characteristics include the degree of cooperation in the virtual team and the degree to which certain team members dominate the group processes. As discussed later, all these characteristics are fundamental to our understanding of virtual team functioning and hence should be considered by researchers.

In *Groups Interacting with Technology*, McGrath & Hollingshead (1994) posit that "the impact of technology depends on the time and space distribution of group's work, the nature and quality of the tasks in which they are engaged, and the degree to which various portions of the group's work are pre-structured, as well as on various characteristics of the group, its members, and its context". (p.94). To summarize their conceptual view, the authors present a framework (see Figure 3) which construes the research problem in terms of a sequence of variables.

The first set of variables comprises input factors that form the basic constituents of work groups in context, namely member attributes (cognitive, affective, demographic), team attributes (e.g., heterogeneity, degree of status hierarchy), variables related to task/ project/ purposes, variables related to technological support (hardware and software properties), and variables in the group's physical, social and temporal context (e.g., cultural norms, deadlines, weekends). In addition to these basic classes of input variables, other variables sets lie at the intersection of each pair of classes. For instance, some variables are a joint function of group members and technology – for example, computer experience and attitudes - rather than a property of either one independently.

Figure 3: A framework for studying the impact of technology on groups (adapted from McGrath & Hollingshead, 1994)

INPUT FACTORS	PROCESS VARIABLES	OUTCOME FACTORS
• Member attributes	• Participation	• Task effectiveness
• Group attributes	• Information processing	• User reactions
• Task/Project/Purpose	• Consensus generating	• Member relations
• Technological support	• Normative regulation	
• Context factors		

Separately and in combination, all the variables are potential contributors to the shaping of group interaction processes, namely communication, trust, cooperation, information processing (sharing, redundancy, integrative complexity), consensus generating (amount and intensity of disagreement, conformity pressures) and normative regulation (expressions of commitment, satisfaction and solidarity). In turn, these group processes form an important basis for the shaping of project outcomes.

AN INTEGRATIVE FRAMEWORK AND A RESEARCH AGENDA

The ultimate intent of this paper is to offer an integrative research framework that will guide future empirical work on ad hoc virtual teams. This framework, presented in Figure 4, incorporates the main key constructs and variables discussed in the preceding section, namely project context, project management strategies, information and communication technologies, team dynamics and processes, and project success. Each component of the research framework is described below, along with a series of relevant issues and research questions for future empirical work.

Project Context

As emphasized in Gladstein's (1984) framework, work groups, and more specifically multi-cultural work groups, evolve in a broader societal or environmental system that cannot be ignored (see also Hare, 1992; Schwartzman, 1986). For instance, the culture of a society in terms of work norms and values (e.g., priority

Figure 4: A comprehensive framework for the study of virtual teams in organizations

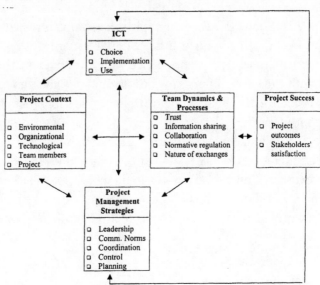

of work in individual life, working hours) and technology adoption behaviors, to name but a few, are likely to influence the functioning and effectiveness of cross-cultural dispersed teams (Duarte & Snyder, 1999).

Teams also evolve in an organizational context that cannot be neglected (Bleecker, 1994; Duarte & Snyder, 1999). In virtual projects, ICT shift the locus of knowledge and power in the organization (Bleecker, 1994; Davidow & Malone, 1992; Gray, 1995). Consequently, organizational politics, resistance, inertia and other change problems are likely to be more pronounced in virtual arrangements such as virtual teams (Applegate, Cash, & Mills, 1988; Jarvenpaa & Ives, 1994). Besides the political dimension, the organizational climate and culture may also influence ICT choices and implementation strategies, and affect team members' attitudes toward and acceptance of computer systems (Duarte & Snyder, 1999). Interestingly, the inclusion of organizational culture should help researchers understand how the norms, values and assumptions held by an organization's members about issues such as remote work and information sharing may impede or enable the successful implementation of virtual teams (Applegate *et al.*, 1996). Finally, previous organizational experiences of failure with technologies and/or the structure of existing resources and commitment (e.g., hardware or software) are likely to constrain ICT adoption and implementation choices. Such organizational considerations are critical at this stage of theory development and hence need to be investigated in future empirical research on virtual teams.

Team members' characteristics, such as skills and expertise, job tenure, spoken language(s), self-motivation, and ability to work in groups, have been connected to group processes and outcomes (Gladstein, 1984; Kerzner, 1997). The size of the team and the extent of the team members' shared work experience are other examples of variables that have been found to have a major influence on communication patterns, level of trust, and project leadership and coordination (Kerzner, 1997; Shaw, 1976). Geographic dispersion is also likely to influence ICT adoption choices as well as project management strategies (as discussed below). Team members' prior experience with ICT appears to be crucial, since it is likely to influence their attitudes towards technology and the acquisition of computer skills which, in turn, may influence training and support implementation decisions. Importantly, the task performed by the group (e.g., system development, building construction, magazine editing and publishing) also plays an important role in determining the extent of group effectiveness and project outcomes. Therefore, future research on virtual teams should therefore consider the nature, complexity, and uncertainty of the task performed by the group and its influence on ICT choices, project management strategies and, ultimately, group processes.

Project Management Strategies

The complex, usually uncertain, and highly interdependent nature of different project tasks, together with the geographical, temporal, structural, and cultural gaps fundamental to distributed teams, makes the management of virtual projects a relatively complex undertaking. Even the experienced project manager finds himself immersed in unknown territories. Two key project management issues in the context of dispersed teams are likely to be project leadership and maintaining synergy and communication. If leadership is necessary for co-located groups to be efficient (Kerzner, 1997) it is likely to be even more vital in the context of virtual teams. Indeed, a clear definition of the desired outcomes of the team's work is critical. All teams need a vision, a mission and objectives with individual account-ability to the team's work. When teams are dispersed, it is easier to lose sight of the goal and ultimate desired outcomes. Team leaders shall find means to accomplish this with dispersed members. In this light, it is often argued that starting with a face-to-face meeting at the kick-off of a new project is a necessary investment, and gives people a chance to establish relationship, trust, and collaboration. Such hypothesis could be investigated through a laboratory or field experiment.

But perhaps the greatest challenge to a virtual team is how to keep the synergy and creativity flowing with day-to-day interaction (Henry & Hartzler, 1998). Communication is the vehicle for creating the synergy, keeping the team together, and moving forward. How does a project leader build an effective information and communication system, one that makes information easily accessible, fosters open communications, and documents the issues raised and the decisions made? Such system should consider the potential for miscommunication in a virtual context as well as the diversity and cross-cultural differences, the need for informal interaction, and the characteristics of existing ICT. In short, project management strategies are likely to differ in virtual teams and researchers should help managers to identify and clarify the strategies that will increase the chances of success in such context.

Information and Communication Technologies

For virtual teams, the conditions under which they communicate across space and time boundaries are intimately connected to the nature of the information technology they use and its level of interactivity. Virtual teams have access to a wide array of media and are able to choose among them for specific purposes (McGrath & Hollingshead, 1994). For instance, each member of a virtual team must be able to send information to and receive information from one or more other members of the team. The ICT that fulfill this initial function include videoconfencing, teleconferencing, voice messaging systems, fax machines, electronic mail systems, Internet, corporate intranet and groupware technologies. As another example, individual group members must also be able to send messages to and/or receive messages from a number of extra-group information databases (e.g., sales records, evaluation results, production data, newspaper files). The ICT serving this second function include systems for accessing information from databases and other information archives, and for selecting, processing, and presenting that information.

How well a given group using a given technology will fulfill its intended purposes depends not only on the intended functions of the technology and its other features (newness, diversity, complexity and user-friendliness), but also on the specific history of the group, together with its task and its circumstances. From this standpoint, there are a number of issues that we regard as critical for future research on virtual teams. For instance, some information systems researchers have argued that much of the impact of a given new technology on a given organization or group arises not from the features of the technology itself, but from the organizational policies and practices that constitute the context within which the technology is implemented (e.g., Kling & Iacono, 1989). Researchers could then consider how a given technology is brought into and put to use within a particular virtual group in order to understand its effects on the team's functioning and, ultimately, on project outcomes.

Team Dynamics and Processes

As shown in Figure 4, team dynamics and processes are colored by the characteristics of the context in which the virtual project takes place, the way ICT are implemented and used and by the appropriateness of the project management strategies adopted. Distributed work groups are likely to raise specific issues such as group communication, trust, cooperation, and information processing (Gorton & Motwani, 1996; Henry & Hartzler, 1998). For instance, it is assumed that trust, arising from competency, must be present if virtual teams are to work smoothly, and that it is more difficult to build this trust from a distance and in cross-functional teams created for a finite period of time to complete a project (Fallows, 1994). Furthermore, it appears important to investigate the effects of technological support on group process variables. For instance, some people report that conflict on dispersed teams is minimized because the anonymity of the technological methods of communication leads to a lack of hierarchical status and domination by those with more forceful personalities (Henry & Hartzler, 1998). Key issues like these could be investigated through a series of field and/or laboratory studies.

Project Success

While the relationship between team processes and project success is not as clear as social scientists would like it to be, all group performance models posit that the two constructs are interrelated (Goodman et al., 1986). Following Baker et al. (1988), we propose to assess success in terms of both project outcomes and stakeholder satisfaction. On the one hand, project outcome criteria include the extent to which the project was completed on time and within budget and complied with technical performance specifications, and the extent to which the product developed (e.g., information system, magazine) meets the initial objectives (Kerzner, 1997). On the other hand, stakeholder satisfaction includes the satisfaction of key people from the parent organization, the client organization, and the project team. The satisfaction of project team members is often dismissed, but is nevertheless very important. In a context where virtual team functioning is under scrutiny in organizations, criteria such as the extent to which team members were affected by the process of working from a distance – the level of stress they experienced due to confusion, technological problems, overtime, and conflict, their level of motivation and new learning, and the extent to which emerging problems were addressed and satisfactorily resolved - are very important. We argue that a multi-dimensional view of project success such as that proposed by Baker *et al.* (1988) is most appropriate, and hence should be adopted in empirical research on virtual teams.

CONCLUDING REMARKS

The integrative research framework presented in this paper suggests that the success of virtual teams depends on a myriad of conditions and factors. How well a given virtual team with multiple communication technologies will fulfill its intended purposes depends not only on the functions the technological system is intended to serve and its other features, but also on the attributes of the team and its members, the type of task being performed, the contextual conditions under which team members are working, and the interaction of group, task, technology and context.

There are several benefits associated with the adoption of this framework by researchers. For example, the framework will help make sense of occurrences, ensure that important issues are not overlooked, provide a set of key constructs and variables to be investigated, and guide the interpretations and focus of researchers. Moreover, it provides a consistent, shareable, knowledge-based approach for the study of virtual teams and allows researchers from different fields to test ideas and improve practical knowledge on the planning of research into virtual teams. In conclusion, we hope the comprehensive framework and the research agenda developed in this paper will provide useful information and some direction for future research to advance our understanding of virtual teams in organizations.

REFERENCES

Applegate, L., Cash, J., & Mills, D. Q. (1988). Les ordinateurs font sauter les organigrammes. *Harvard L'Expansion*, 58, 33-43.

Applegate, L. M., DeSanctis, G., & Jackson, B. (1996). Technology, teams, and organizations: Implementing groupware at Texaco. http://www.hbs.harvard.edu /mis/multimedia/link/stexaco.html, May 19th.

Baker, B. N., Murphy, D. C., & Fisher, D. (1988). Factors affecting project success. In D. I. Cleland & W. R. King (Eds.), *Project Management Handbook* (2nd ed.) (pp. 902-919). New York: Van Nostrand Reinhold.

Barnatt, C. (1995). Office space, cyberspace and virtual organization. *Journal of General Management*, 20(4), 78-91.

Bleecker, S. E. (1994, March/April). The virtual organization. *The Futurist*, 9-14.

Bozman, J. S., & Ellis, B. (1993). Looking forward to office 2001. *Computerworld*. 27(2), 28.

Cleland, D. I., & King, W. R. (1988). *Project Management Handbook* (2nd ed.). New York: Van Nostrand Reinhold.

Davidow, W. H., & Melone, M. S. (1992). *The virtual corporation*. Harper Business.

Duarte, D.L. & Snyder, N.T. (1999). *Mastering Virtual Teams*. San Francisco: Jossey-Bass Publishers.

Fallows, J. (1994, May 16th). The information revolution: New strains for Europe, America and Asia. *International Herald Tribune*.

Geber, B. (1995). Virtual teams. *Training,* 32(4), 36-40.

Gladstein, D. (1984). Groups in context: A model of task group effectiveness. *Administrative Science Quarterly*, 29(4), 499-517.

Goodman and Associates (Eds.), *Designing Effective Work Groups*, (pp.120-167). San Francisco: Jossey-Bass.

Gorton, I. & Motwani, S. (1996). Issues in co-operative software engineering using globally distributed teams. *Information and Software Technology*, 38, 647-655.

Gray, P. (1995, August). The virtual workplace. *OR/MS Today*, 22-26.

Hare, A. P. (1992). *Groups, Teams, and Social Interaction: Theories and Applications*. New York: Praeger.

Henry, J. E., & Hartzler, M. (1998). *Tools for Virtual Teams: A Team Fitness Companion*. Milwaukee, WI: ASQ Quality Press.

Hiltz, S. R., & Turroff, M. (1978). *The Network Nation: Human Communication via Computer.* Reading, MA: Addison-Wesley.

Iacono, C. S., & Weisband, S. (1997). Developing Trust in Virtual Teams. *Proceedings of the 30th Annual Hawaii International Conference on Systems Science.*

Jarvenpaa, S. L., & Ives, B. (1994). The Global Network Organization of the Future: Information Management Opportunities and Challenges. *Journal of Management Information Systems*, 10(4), 25-57.

Kerzner, H. (1997). *Project Management : A Systems Approach to Planning, Scheduling, and Controlling* (6th ed.). New York: John Wiley.

Kling, R., & Iacono, S. (1989). The Institutional Character of Computerized Information Systems, *Office, Technology & People*, 5(1), 7-28.

Knoll, K., & Jarvenpaa, S. L. (1995). Learning to work in distributed global teams. *Proceedings of the 28th Annual Hawaii International Conference on Systems Science*, 92-101.

Kraemer, K. L., & Pinsonneault, A. (1990). Technology and Groups: Assessments of the empirical research. In J. Galegher, R. E. Kraut, & C. Egido (Eds.), *Intellectual Teamwork, Social and Technological Foundations of Cooperative Work,* (pp.373-405). Hillsdale, NJ: Lawrence Erlbaum Associates.

Lipnack, J., & Stamps, J. (1997). *Virtual teams: Reaching across space, time, and organization with technology.* John Wiley & Sons.

McGrath, J. E. (1964). *Social psychology: A Brief Introduction.* New York: Holt, Rinehart & Winston.

McGrath, J. E., & Hollingshead, A. B. (1994). *Groups Interacting with Technology.* Thousand Oaks, CA: Sage Publications.

Nilles, J. M. (1994). *Making Telecommuting Happen: A guide for Telemanagers and Telecommuters.* New York: Van Nostrand Reinhold.

PMBOK Standards Committee (1987). *Project Management Body of Knowledge (PMBOK) of the Project Management Institute.* Newtown Square, PA: Project Management Institute.

Schwartzman, H. B. (1986). Research on work group effectiveness: An anthropological critique. In P. S. Goodman and Associates (Eds.), *Designing Effective Work Groups,* (pp.237-276). San Francisco: Jossey-Bass.

Shaw, M. E. (1976). *Group Dynamics: The Psychology of Small Group Behavior.* New York: McGraw-Hill.

Chapter 15

Overcoming Barriers in the Planning of a Virtual Library: Recognising Organisational and Cultural Change Agents

Ardis Hanson, MLS
The Louis de la Parte Florida Mental Health Institute
University of South Florida, USA

INTRODUCTION

The University of South Florida (USF) Libraries consist of five separate entities, two located at regional campuses in St. Petersburg and Sarasota and three libraries located on the main campus in Tampa. These libraries operate in a collegial, cooperative way yet each operates independently of the others. This arrangement allows the individual missions of each of the Libraries to be met while ensuring collaboration and cooperation. The many initiatives within and among the USF Libraries depend upon a reliable and advanced networked infrastructure and on staff, facility and financial decisions focussed on true programmatic cooperation. This paper addresses the interaction between the USF Libraries in defining and realising institutional commitment to its virtual library plan.

The USF Virtual Libraries Planning Committee first convened in September 1995. At that meeting, the committee was charged with the task of preparing a proposal for a university-wide virtual library. The committee was comprised of eight librarians, seven representing the USF Libraries and the eighth from Florida Gulf Coast University who provided an "outsider" view of the process. The three USF campuses serve a variety of clientele, ranging from a large undergraduate and graduate research library, an undergraduate and graduate regional campus library, a unique undergraduate college regional campus library, an academic health sciences library, and a mental health research facility library. Because of the significant geographic distance between several of the participating libraries, weekly conference calls were conducted to communicate individual and group progress relating to the project. Information was distributed to the group via electronic mail.

In order to improve the process of developing the plan, a number of factors were examined. The first was the commitment to recognise problems involved in the process and to undertake actions to either prevent them or address them. The USF librarians had a strong commitment to the success of this project despite the legacies of past library relationships. Project outcome is shown to depend upon the behaviour and resources available during the development process and these depend upon the level of commitment (Lytinen & Hirschheim, 1987). Additional factors included the possibility of budgetary constraints, top-management's technological non-sophistication, and the reluctance to draw up a very detailed operating plan — the idea being to recommend a series of actions to implement in the creation of the virtual library. Finally, barriers on systems implementation included hesitation in accepting a system (Kiely, 1990), lack of standard formats (Ewusi-Mensah & Przasnyski, 1991), and unrealistic priorities and expectations (Konsyuki & McFarlan, 1990) from the parties involved. These barriers are particularly true in the design of a virtual library where resource and technical standards are still under development.

THE ASSIGNMENTS

As the process of developing the plan began, the Virtual Library Planning Committee (VLPC) distributed four assignments. The first assignment, a shared literature review, was an on-going process throughout the ten-month project. The literature review included a search for relevant workshops or conferences and the monitoring of a variety of listservs. Most of the library literature dealt with technical matters; little addressed the social or organisational ramifications within an interpersonal context.

The second assignment was the design of a survey instrument and the selection of peer institutions to receive the survey. The survey examined specific details on electronic collections and services, the status of cataloguing electronic resources, hardware available, staffing, and fiscal support. The group worked via electronic mail on the design of the survey. The survey was sent to fifteen peer institutions with a total of eight responses. The USF Libraries were included in the survey.

The third assignment was the use of focus groups to determine the needs of an ethnically diverse, urban population. User groups surveyed included USF teaching and research faculty and staff, USF libraries faculty and staff, graduate and undergraduate students, the Academic Computing Committee, and the Systems Administrators Group. The breakout of the USF Libraries faculty and staff was one tactic for building commitment to the project in its design phases. Seeking employee input and participation is believed to aid in commitment to projects since it instills a sense of ownership of the goals and objectives being pursued (Manz, Bastien, Hostager, & Shapiro, 1989).

The fourth assignment was a formal presentation to the Library Directors' Group. Resource requests included institutional support for attendance at conferences and an allotment for the purchase of pertinent works. It is a well-documented fact that commitment influences the behaviour of individuals and their interaction within a team. Without commitment from administration, the belief of the individual and/or the team in the relevance of the project wavers or they become indifferent to the project. In fact, an organisational commitment to the project and a commitment to change are key factors in determining the success of a project (Pascale, Millemann, & Gioja, 1997).

ORGANISATIONAL CHANGE

The VLPC was convinced that organisational changes in technology, services, and governance would have to be dealt with in the implementation of a virtual library. Three key concepts identified were successful leadership, human resources, and organisational structure. Within each of those three concepts is the ability to show flexibility and rapid response to change (Higher Education Information Resources Alliance, 1992-1995) - qualifications necessary for staff to work effectively in a rapidly changing environment.

The successful implementation of a virtual library at the University would be based upon the commitment of each of the libraries (administration, faculty, and staff) and the commitment of the University to this project. Since open discussion of barriers is an effective strategy for implementation and adaptation of change (Beer & Eisenstat, 1996), the VLPC examined each of the libraries with a critical eye. Positive and problematic areas and staff were identified and examined resulting in solutions or actions.

Seven problems were identified. These were: 1) the geographic locations of the USF Libraries, 2) the lack of parity in equipment and technologies among the libraries, 3) budget issues, 4) ownership by staff across all the USF Libraries, 5) difficulty in selling this as a USF Libraries project, not just as one library's project, 6) unrealistic expectations by management and staff, and 7) resistance by staff and/or management.

Problems identified as undesirable situations but impossible to correct were noted but not much time was spent on them. The group was more interested in devising answers or actions to potentially correctable problems.

INTEGRATING THE LITERATURE WITH ACTIONS

To promote ownership of the virtual library plan among the libraries' administration, faculty, and staff, the VLPC devised "actions" for each of the areas under design within the virtual library. Samples of the inclusive language used throughout the document and the establishment of multi-type working groups follow. The first excerpt from the USF Libraries *Blueprint* deals with the organisation of the various work groups needed to implement the virtual library concept. Successful team-based organizational arrangements coalesce where teams are able to cross both organisational and physical boundaries (McGarry, 1994; Engardio et al.,1994; Cohen, Ledford, & Spreitzer 1996; Saltzer, 1992; Schein, 1996).

At institutions that have successfully implemented a virtual library, work groups and task forces were developed to review workflow, policies and procedures, overlap, and to create implementation plans to effect organisational change and major projects driven by the new technologies (Conway, 1994). Some emerging virtual libraries have created multi-disciplinary teams across academic disciplines and support services to implement their plans (Anderson, 1995). Other successful plans have been comprised of large groups who use phased plans covering a number of years (State University of New York, 1992; Birmingham, Drabenstott, Warner, & Willis, 1994). Based upon these case studies, the VLPC determined that

> "A well-planned project group composition is crucial to each project group's success.... Composition for each of these groups will be individually tailored but should have the same basic features: representation from each library, representation from multiple departments, and a representative of the oversight committee."(p.23).

The VLPC believed that alternative organization design principles which replace individual job design with task design (e.g., task forces and teams) and replace "one best way" with choices in both the organizational and technological solutions (Kolodny, Liu, Stymne, & Denis, 1996) were the best way to handle the enormity of the proposed design process. Such solutions can cope with more complexity and unpredictability when people in the teams are multi-skilled and delegated more autonomy and responsibility (Cohen, Ledford, & Spreitzer, 1996; Emery, 1976; Schrage, 1990; De Gennaro ,1990; Mohrman & Cummings, 1989).

The second selection from the *Blueprint* deals with the coming culture shift and the organisational change within each of the libraries. It acknowledges the past technological, and subsequent staffing, changes over the past five years.

> "Library faculty and staff need to be assured of their importance and value within the new organizational structure. A strong, well-defined and equitably funded staff development program needs to be put in place.

Staffing levels must be reviewed to accommodate changing work functions, for example, the consequences of access to versus ownership of materials. This process needs to be proactive rather than reactive which will avoid unnecessary stress and morale problems." (p.24).

The VLPC wanted to acknowledge that the process of change would also impact the operations of a complex library system. It is inevitable that the implementation of a virtual library would cause significant changes within each department across the libraries and campuses. However, the VLPC felt that real ownership would come about only with a commitment from management to 1) educate and train staff in the new technologies and procedures, 2) manage the change process as openly and honestly as possible, and 3) disseminate information as openly and widely as possible. Each one of these commitments is essential to the change process (Tennant, 1995; Argyris, 1990).

The coming of a virtual library will significantly impact the culture of libraries. Schein (1992) defines culture as the set of shared, taken-for-granted implicit assumptions that a group holds and that determines how it perceives, thinks about, and reacts to its various environments. Policies, procedures, and behaviour are a visible manifestation of these assumptions that most members of a culture never question or examine. The members of a culture may not even be aware of their own culture until they encounter a different one.

Cultural models are as much an issue in libraries as in corporations and other areas when organisational change occurs (Langan-Fox, 1997). The cultural constructs by which the various types of librarians and other staff view the world must be considered in the redesign of any organisation. As indicated above, we know very little about the working conditions and institutional and organizational practices that will make digital libraries most usable by library faculty, and staff (Kling & Elliot, 1994). Emerging cultural models for virtual libraries include a focal technology, its immediate users, and various inter-relationships with other groups and organizations in which the technology is developed, adopted, and used (Kling, 1987).

The members of the VLPC tried to envision how library culture would change as technology and a growing reliance on "virtual" materials and services increased. Specific service points and their job functions were analysed. This excerpt from the *Blueprint* acknowledges the importance of recognising and managing the change process as well as emphasising the need for staff development.

"Much of this report's cited literature discusses change at the technological level. Catalogers will develop bibliographic records using SGML hyperlinks, collection development librarians will select internet sources, reference librarians will provide online reference services, interlibrary loan will make the shift to end user electronic document delivery, re-

serves will shift to an electronic full-text format, and the library administration will move towards a networked paper-less society. This process
of change will require creativity, a more global point of view, flexibility,
and adaptability. These will be the qualities of highly valued staff. ...
Staff will need to understand not only their own role within the organization, but also the structure of other departments and the relationships
between departments." (p.26)

Priority actions included a more global understanding of library processes,
cross training and shifting staff between departments, continuous training to remain current with technology, and time for staff to develop projects and procedures across departmental boundaries.

The VLPC also wanted to ensure that the recommended actions be a long-
term commitment by the libraries' administrations (upper- and middle-manage-
ment) to their staff (Kunze, 1994; State University of New York, 1992). Strategies to continue the change process, identified on both an individual and administrative level for professional development, included funding for each library faculty
member and staff to conferences, training and cross-training sessions on current
library operations for staff both inside and outside the involved departments,
utilisation of campus training programs, ongoing evaluation program to ensure that
training is available for new technologies, workflow, and responsibilities, creation
of a new technologies committee whose members are responsible for training their
department, and up-to-date documentation on policies and procedures.

Inter-institutional collaboration is difficult to define and implement, and even
more difficult to implement well (Stewart ,1996). When successful, it has the ability to transform significant elements of the way academia conducts its activities.
The VLPC believed that four additional infrastructure elements - attention to continuing planning, process, people, and administrative elements- were essential to
the project. This becomes even more important with a conscious commitment to
maintaining tradition while implementing a virtual workplace (Allcorn, 1997).

"The most single important factor for the success of such a system is a
vision that is meaningful to the directors, their faculty, and staff... one
that is shared by the directors and strenuously advocated within their
individual institutional settings. ...The Library Directors need to have
the ability to foster an environment which supports the innovations in
technology and services without fear of losing their autonomy or institutional authority. This environment, collegial and collaborative in nature,
should encourage more inter-institutional activities and decision-making
processes." (p.20)

The VLPC tried to place the implementation of the virtual library within the
larger context of the University of South Florida. The role of the USF libraries is to

establish an atmosphere and a process that promote the integration of new technologies with each other within the mission and core values of the University, i.e., the support of scholarship and the development and continuance of a sophisticated and individualised learning environment. The key to this scholarly environment is the development of organisational, instructional, and informational infrastructures that capitalise on the technology and reinforce the values and the identities of the institution (Higher Education Information Resources Alliance, 1992-1995). Critical technical challenges in the Libraries' *Blueprint* included parity in networking, workstation, and desktop requirements; a single, uncomplicated point of access for the USF Libraries' electronic resources; standard, staff-utilized software packages; measurable information applications that are scalable, efficient, and interoperable; multiple simultaneous access with minimal down/lag time; technologies and services that are user-friendly and provide privacy, security, stability, mobility, and ubiquity.

Many of the colleges and/or departments had invested in voice, data, and image networks; institutional information systems; personal computers and workstations for students, staff, and faculty; and strategic plans for information and computing technologies. For the Virtual Library Project to be successful, it would need to extend these technologies and plans and support future technologies used at the university.

The Virtual Libraries Committee also identified three additional issues of importance that are especially relevant to libraries and their user communities -- content, access, and support. All three issues identified are extremely dependent upon funding. Money buys research resources (content), telecommunications infrastructure (access) necessary to deliver the content and pays staff to run the infrastructure (support). A quick look at trends in higher education indicates that 1) traditional funding sources are flat or decreasing (Battin 1989); 2) public and state mandates call for more accountability in the spending of state dollars; and 3) consumer expectations demand more sophisticated services and greater access to data. The USF Libraries needed to develop funding mechanisms that transcended the efforts of the individual USF libraries.

SUMMARY

The real evolution in libraries is about communication, not automation. The essential catalyst for change must be in how our cooperative efforts are communicated both internally and externally, especially in the development of new systems. The VLPC was a "community-in-practice." This type of work group evolves from three characteristics: 1) valuation of work roles (Bourdieu, 1977), 2) the degree of participation in "peripheral" learning permitted under working conditions such as conferences, workshops, and networking opportunities (Lave & Wenger, 1991) and 3) opportunities for participation in innovative implementations (Brown & Duguid, 1991).

All participants of the group were professional librarians, each with different areas of expertise, years of experience, levels of knowledge, and pride in their abilities. All were learning, not only abstract knowledge from the extensive reading required, but how to be a member of the "community." Learners, according to Brown and Duguid, occur through practice. "The central issue in learning is *becoming* a practitioner not learning about *practice*" (p.48, original emphasis).

Conference participants hear the stories of others involved in project design and/or implementation. They learn the languages used within the larger community, what are acceptable practices, new and emerging technologies and standards, and how to communicate needs and knowledge to a larger group as well as to members of their work environment.

Last, they were all participants in an innovative implementation - a virtual library. While knowledge is often thought to be the property of individuals, a great deal of knowledge is both produced and held collectively. Such knowledge is readily generated when people work together in tightly knit groups. As such work and such communities are a common feature of organizations, organizational knowledge is inevitably heavily social in character (Lave & Wenger 1993; Brown & Duguid, 1991).

This chapter demonstrates the importance of commitment in the design of a virtual library plan within a multi-library, multi-campus environment. The committee members established a good working relationship with each other and were united by a strong desire to make the virtual library plan a reality. The members of the committee discussed issues more openly as the group progressed toward the writing of the document and the analysis of the focus groups. Such candidness promoted a high level of cooperation between all the committee members, despite disagreements, and helped maintain the level of commitment to the group and the project development.

The workgroup practices were fluid and ignored many of the traditional assumptions about librarianship, librarians, and libraries. Teleconferencing was used extensively as was e-mail and editing through the use of a common HTML page. There was an intentional sharing of information and educating the members of the group to facilitate discussion. This allowed them to work, learn, and innovate together.

This chapter examined the various levels of commitment necessary for each of the major stakeholders in the project implementation, from staff to management to the University. It briefly described some of the problems encountered and the perseverance of the Virtual Library Planning Committee in the development of the virtual library document.

What are the implications for future research? Can a commitment from a small group be an effective, ongoing catalyst for change in a large, multi-institutional academic library setting? Can this group process be replicated to create a larger community-in-practice across the libraries? And finally, what actions can library administrations take to ensure this kind of commitment within their own libraries?

REFERENCES

Allcorn, S. (1997). Parallel virtual organizations: managing and working the virtual workplace. *Administration & Society, 29*(4), 412-440.

Anderson, G. (1995). MIT: the distributed library initiative: collaboration, vision, prototyping. *Publications of Essen University Library, 18*, 61-89.

Argyris, C. (1990). *Overcoming organizational defenses: facilitating organizational learning.* Wellesley, MA: Allyn and Bacon.

Battin, P. (1989). New ways of thinking about financing information services. In Hawkins, B. L. (ed.). *Organizing and managing information resources on campus*. McKinney, TX: Academic Computing Publications

Birmingham, W. P., Drabenstott, K. M., Frost, C. O., Warner, A. J. & Willis, K. (1994) The University of Michigan Digital Library: This is not your father's library. http://www.csdl.tamu.edu/DL94/ paper/umdl.html (6 Apr. 1997).

Bourdieu, P. (1977). *Outline of a theory of practice*. Cambridge, NY: Cambridge University Press.

Brown, J. S. & Duguid, P. (1991). Organizational learning and communities-in-practice: Toward a unified view of working, learning, and innovation. *Organization Science, 2*(1), 40-57.

Cohen, S. G., Ledford, G. E., & Spreitzer, G. M. (1996). A predictive model of self-managing work team effectiveness. (Special Issue: Organizational Change in Corporate Settings). *Human Relations, 49*(5), 643-677.

Conway, P. (1994). Digitizing Preservation, *Library Journal, 119*(Feb.1), 42-45

De Gennaro, R. (1990). Technology and Access: the research library in transition. In H.C. Clark (ed.). *Organizing a research agenda: information studies for the '90s*. Halifax, Nova Scotia: Dalhousie University.

Emery, F. E. (1977). *Futures we are in*. Leiden: Martinus Nihoff.

Engardio, P. (1994). High tech jobs all over the map. *Business Week: Special 1994 Bonus Issue, 21st Century Capitalism, 3399*(Nov. 18),112-115,118,119.

Ewusi-Mensah, K., Przasnyski, Z. H. (1991). On Information Systems Project Abandonment: An Exploratory Study of Organizational Practices, *MIS Quarterly, 15*(1), 67-86.

Higher Education Information Resources Alliance. (1992-1995). HEIRAlliance Executive Strategies Series. http://cause-www.colorado.edu/collab/heira.html (2 Feb. 1996).

Higher Education Information Resources Alliance. (1992-1995). HEIRAlliance Executive Strategies Series #6: What presidents need to know about evaluating institutional information resources. http://causewww.colorado.edu/collab/ heirapapers/hei1060.html (2 Feb. 1996).

Kiely, T. (1990). The two faces of EDI, *CIO, 4*(1), 80-91.

Kling, R. (1987). Defining the Boundaries of Computing Across Complex Organizations. In R. Boland & R. Hirschheim (eds). *Critical Issues in Information Systems*. New York: John-Wiley.

Kling, R. & Elliot, M. (1994). Digital Library Design for Usability. http:// csdl.tamu.edu/DL94/paper/kling.html (11 Nov 1998).

Kolodny, H., Liu, M., Stymne, B., & Denis, H. (1996). New technology and the emerging organizational paradigm. *Human Relations 49*(12), 457(31)

Konsyuki, B. R. & McFarlan, F.W. (1990). Information partnerships: shared data, shared scale, *Harvard Business Review, 68*(5), 114-120.

Kunze, J. A. Functional Requirements for Internet Resource Locators (IETF URI Working Group Internet-Draft, 27 July 1994), [[section]]4, "Resource Access and Availability" <URL:ftp://ds.internic.net/internet-drafts/ draft-ietf-uri-rl-fun-req-01.txt>.

Langan-Fox, J. (1997). Images of a culture in transition: personal constructs of organizational stability and change. *Journal of Occupational and Organizational Psychology, 70*(3), 273-294.

Lave, J. & Wenger, E. (1991). *Situated learning: legitimate peripheral participation*. Cambridge: Cambridge University Press.

Lytinen, K. & R. Hirschheim. (1987). Information systems failures: a survey and classification of the empirical literature. In *Oxford Surveys in Information Technology* (v.4), P.I. Zorkoczy (ed.) Oxford: Oxford University Press.

Manz, C.C., D.T. Bastien, T.J. Hostager, & G.L. Shapiro. (1989). Leadership and innovation: a longitudinal process view. In A.H. Van den Ven, H. L. Angle, & M.S. Poole (eds). *Research on the management of innovation*. New York: Ballinger/Harper & Row.

McGarry, D. (1994). Playing on both the home and away teams. *Business Quarterly, 59*(2), 81-88.

Mohrman, S. A., & Cummings, T. G. (1989). *Self-Designing Organizations: Learning How To Create High Performance*. Reading, Massachusetts: Addison-Wesley.

Pascale, R., Millemann, M., Gioja, L. (1997). Changing the way we change (organizational change). *Harvard Business Review, 75*(6),126-140.

Saltzer, J. (1992). Technology, Networks, and the Library of the Year 2000, In A. Bensoussan & J.-P. Verjus (eds*). Future Tendencies in Computer Science, Control, and Applied Mathematics, Lecture Notes in Computer Science 653*. New York: Springer-Verlag.

Schein, E. H. 1996. Culture: the missing concept in organization studies. (40th Anniversary Issue) *Administrative Science Quarterly, 41*(2), 229-241.

Schrage, M. (1990). *Shared minds*. New York: Random House.

State University of New York (1992). Strategic Directions, 1992-1997: A plan for the University at Stony Brook Libraries. [ERIC document ED377 841].

State University of New York (1992). Strategic Directions, 1992-1997: A plan for the University at Stony Brook Libraries. [ERIC document ED377 841], 16-19.

Stewart, T. A. 1996. The invisible key to success (communities of practice). *Fortune, 134*(3),173-176.

Tennant, R. (1995). The virtual library foundation: staff training and support, *Information Technologies and Libraries, 14*, 46-49.

Virtual Library Planning Committee (1996). The USF Virtual Library: a blueprint for development [final document]. Tampa, Florida: University of South Florida.

Chapter 16

The Wicked Relationship Between Organisations and Information Technology

Gill Mallalieu, Clare Harvey and Colin Hardy
University of Sunderland

The concept of the "wicked problem" is useful in coming to terms with any studies, which involve people, organisations and information technology. It helps to define the shortcomings of traditional positivist approaches in areas which display social complexity. This paper describes how the relationship between an organisation's business processes and its legacy IT systems is considered under the RAMESES project as a wicked problem. The way in which this conceptualisation has led the authors to adopt the grounded theory methodology is discussed. The particular, detailed method undertaken within this framework is outlined; some results presented and conclusions about the success of the approach are drawn.

The relationships between people, organisations and IT (information technology) present a complex range of factors to be disentangled. Our approach has been to find a way to conceptualise this complexity which would give us a way of defining our problem and formulating a solution. The concept of the "wicked problem" (Churchman, 1967) has been particularly helpful to us and is further described in Section 2. It provides a mechanism by which the relationship between people, organisations and IT can be unravelled. The concept of the "wicked problem" does not lead the researcher to attempt to reduce the problem to isolated variables, and a series of steps to be followed

Previously Published in the *Journal of End User Computing, vol.11, no.4*, Copyright © 1999, Idea Group Publishing.

sequentially. Instead, it advocates a pragmatic oscillation between problem and solution, so that our understanding of each of them evolves concurrently.

The project in which this conceptualisation was tested out was the RAMESES project (further described in Section 3). The overall objective of this project is "to provide a strategic model for the risk assessment of legacy software systems within SMEs (Small-to-Medium Enterprises) considering business process change." Thus the relationship between the organisation, the way its staff carried out its processes and their legacy IT systems was at the centre of our concerns.

In order to allow our problem definition and our solution to evolve together, we chose grounded theory (Strauss & Corbin, 1997) as our methodology and populated that with a method which helped us to focus on both the problem area and solutions at the same time. This paper describes how the broad conceptualisation of the problem led to a detailed method to address it and the results available to date.

THE PROBLEM OF ORGANISATIONS
Wicked Problems

The term wicked problem was used by Rittel and Webber (1984) in a design context and Budgen (1993) picked out the four characteristics most relevant to the process of software design. These are also those most relevant to the more general study of information systems in organisations and are as follows:

- **There is no definitive formulation of a wicked problem.** A wicked problem cannot be reduced to a series of steps that need to be followed in order to reach a solution. Any series of steps so designed will address only part of the problem. By following a series of steps one may not even arrive at a partial solution, the process may actually make the problem worse.

- **Wicked problems have no stopping rule.** Wicked problems are dynamic. One may derive a solution, which appears to solve the problem at one point in time, but that solution will in itself affect the problem. People will react to the solution that they are given and the problem will evolve in new and unexpected ways. Often the scenario, which is nominally designated as the solution, is only acknowledged as such because time and/or money have run out on the problem. Concepts such as "structuration" (Giddens, 1984) are important for tackling wicked problems. They acknowledge that the way in which people interact with the structures within which they operate acts upon the structures themselves to change them.

- **Solutions to wicked problems are not true or false, but good or bad.** Because the way to tackle the problem is not reducible to a series of steps the solution will never be a neat fit. The notion of a *good* or *bad* solution has a subjective tenor to it. That is because it is subjective. A solution can only be evaluated in the light of what one wished to achieve, not in any absolute sense.

- **Every wicked problem can be considered to be a symptom of another problem.** Because of the interconnectedness of things, one's investigation into a wicked problem might reveal deeper underlying causes, or simply other factors at the same level, which are embedded in different issues. What is a "good solution" to the problem must be judged entirely on the basis of what the researcher was expected and empowered to achieve, not on the basis of completeness or finality.

'Solving' Wicked Problems

Both Conklin & Weil (1998) and Budgen (1993) refer to the waterfall model of software design (Royce, 1970) as having some elements which are useful in the solution of wicked problems and some elements which are not. The fact that the waterfall model implies a simple progression from one stage to the next in the process of designing software is unrealistic in the case of wicked problems. It is highly unlikely that a wicked problem could be grasped or understood from the start in order to allow a simple progression to the design of a solution. Concessions to the complexity of real life (and to what Budgen (1993) calls "the wickedness of problems") are the multiple feedback loops that move back up the waterfall. They introduce the notion of going back and reformulating the problem.

Conklin & Weil (1998) describe the behaviour of designers in the MCC Elevator study. Their study showed that designers did not, in fact work in a linear progression from analysis of the problem to formulation of a solution. These processes were not two sequential stages, but were different activities between which the designer oscillated. Analysis was carried out in order to assess the feasibility of possible solutions. The solutions that were available to some extent guided the analysis that was possible.

In terms of the traditional waterfall model, this manner of oscillating between analysis and design might be considered at best pragmatic, and at worst disorganised. However, in light of the characteristics of wicked problems (described above), this is the only sensible approach. Therefore, a method that insisted that analysis be complete before work may start on the design of a solution would be doomed in the arena of wicked problems. Such a problem needs to be scoped in terms of the time and budget allowed for its solution, the kind of solution expected, and the subject or area which is to be addressed by the solution (e.g. communication, over-competitive behaviour, or competition culture). Therefore, the problem space will be determined by the solution space. In the words of Conklin & Weil (1998): "You don't understand the problem until you have developed a solution."

Why organisations are wicked

Organisations are "wicked" in a number of different ways. Positivist science tends to look at an area of study, identify variables, isolate them and study each in isolation, and then model the way in which these act together. In this way, hypotheses are accumulated and are articulated as a theory. In the study of organisations, it is possible to identify the variables that bear upon a particular situation, and often to have some feel for their relative importance, but to isolate them is not meaningful. To decontextualise a process or an operator in order to study them, is to take away their meaning or *raison d'être*. Positivist scientists feel that an experiment should be "controlled": i.e. all extraneous factors should be removed, in order to better observe the working of the variable under study. By contrast, many interpretivists believe that there is no such thing as an extraneous factor. If you try to remove some of the factors that operate on a situation, then you are removing context and meaning. It can be seen then that any problem with a social element will ramify greatly (Shurville *et al.*, 1997) thus making it wicked. Just as the interconnection of variables is endless, so are the implications of any change or posited solution.

If you isolate a variable, you remove it from its context. For instance, during the RAMESES project (see section 3), the authors have been studying the relationship between an organisation's legacy systems and its business processes to see whether the fit was good or whether there were areas of risk. It is possible to isolate this relationship in the following way. One could model the way in which the process works according to the appropriate manager, and then using the same technique, show the way in which the software related to that business process works, and then compare the two mappings. This would allow an analysis of fit or lack of it, however many important factors have been excluded. Both managers and the staff who operate the computer system may have different expectations of it from those that it was designed to deliver. A study of the business process and the computer system as they operate will reveal a different pattern from the ideal ones modelled above. Such a study will reveal shortcuts, extra activities, and clever solutions to problems, even abuses. Both the way in which the business process is carried out, and the way in which the computer system is being used will be affected by company culture, by the degree of unionisation and demarcation, by the education and flexibility of the staff, and by whether the company is buoyant and profitable or defensive and unprofitable. The geographical locus on a site or between sites will have an effect. The wider context of the organisation may have a huge influence: for instance, where a particular computer system may have a role in the supply chain. A particularly important supplier or customer may have dictated its use with no reference to the organisation's business processes. Above all, the **history** of both the computer system and also the business process will have an effect: e.g. resentments may still endure following poor practice in technology transfer or in change management.

Beyond this lies a mirroring layer of complexity. This is the layer of the researchers' own attitudes, shaped by their background, their history of experiences and their personality. In some ways this is not open to study by the researcher since they are inside the situation and cannot see the whole of it. Positivist scientists favour objectivity - the putting aside of the researcher's own views and values in order to establish objective truths. Interpretive social scientists feel this is impossible (Winch 1958), as being inside the situation, the researcher cannot even identify all those factors that need to be filtered out. In fact, the most fundamental and influential factors may be those, which the researcher is least able to see because they are so much a part of them. Interpretive social scientists recommend instead reflexivity. They acknowledge that a researcher's findings will be influenced by their own values and outlook, and instead promote the idea that the researcher should explore and acknowledge them. The self-knowledge will still be imperfect because the researcher is too close to the subject, but at least contemplation is encouraged with the notion of reflexivity.

What has been portrayed so far is a very indeterminate situation. It bears little resemblance to the neat isolation of variables and the extraction of objective truths favoured by positivist natural scientists. However, there are two important anchors in this complexity. One is that there is always some information about an organisation which is empirical: this is often the kind of information which is present on the annual report about number of employees, annual turnover and profit, and also demographic information about the qualifications, age and sex of staff. This kind of information is a good basis for benchmarking and comparison among companies. The other anchor is the kind of information that one needs to know about the company; i.e., what is the researcher's intention in studying the company. If the researcher knows what kind of problem they are interested in, or alternatively, what kind of solution they can offer then they are better able to see which variables are in the foreground and which fall into the background behind them. In this, as in the other features, organisations present situations that conform to the definition of a wicked problem.

THE RAMESES WICKED PROBLEM
The RAMESES Wicked Problem Described

The issues reported in this paper have been identified as a result of detailed case study analysis of four small organisations in Northeast England. The core business activity of the companies revolves around manufacturing and/or distribution. Although their software systems are important as a support mechanism, the primary business focus is not in software, its development or maintenance. These organisations are being studied as part of an on-going project, RAMESES (Risk Assessment Model: Evaluation Strategy for Existing Systems). In the RAMESES project, the factors that affect the fit between business processes and legacy systems are being defined and categorised. These factors are being used to populate an evolving risk assessment method to aid small businesses in understanding the range of risks facing them when they consider change (of business process or IT) typically in the context of their component-based systems. The project has adopted a wide definition of legacy systems in that legacy systems are considered to be "existing systems components that will impact upon potential changes." To this end the boundary of study may include hardware, software, comms ware and peopleware.

To study this area of risk is indeed a wicked problem. The ramifications of change in a business process are far wider than just the relationship with legacy software systems, and vice versa. The change itself may be a symptom of a threatening economic climate, or of a trend for needlessly scrapping old software systems. Change in a legacy system or in a business process may have ramifications in some of the following social and technical areas:

- employee satisfaction • staff training • degree of integration of the computer-based systems • degree of integration of legacy systems in business processes • personnel profiles •   technology transfer issues • skills base of the technical staff • configuration management procedures • standards operated • quality systems used • service issues • communication between technical and end-user personnel • data independence • labour relations

Therefore, to fully analyse the effects of any change before undertaking it is not possible. However, in recognising that we were dealing with a wicked problem, we were able to find a way to approach it.

Initiating a Solution to the RAMESES Wicked Problem

The focus of the RAMESES project, (and indeed of the EPSRC's software engineering for business process change programme that funded it) is the relationship between legacy systems and business process change. Thus, our solution is given a precise context. The derivation of the solution is circumscribed both in terms of time and of money (two researchers for a total of three years - part one and part two). The form of solution promised by the project is a tool, which allows a manager or consultant within an SME to assess the risk involved in changing either a business process or a legacy IT system. All those factors which may be drawn into this wicked problem (and are listed in the subsection above) are thus of importance only in so far as they influence the relationship between business process change and legacy software systems and have no importance in their own right. To contextualise the issues both a foreground and background have been sketched in. Furthermore, the other factors in this wicked problem are given a role by the way in which the authors have chosen to conceptualise the relationship between business process change and legacy systems: which is in terms of **risk**. A broad gap or disharmony in the relationship between a business process and its supporting legacy software systems is seen to represent a large risk, and therefore, an opportunity for change.

We have identified this complex shifting environment as a wicked problem. The investigation of wicked problems calls for techniques and methods beyond the scope of the positivist scientific tradition. To this end, the RAMESES project has called upon the social sciences for support in developing a framework more suited to the multi-dimensionality of organisational understanding. Interpretive methods have been employed to substantiate the empirical findings of the case studies, while this is not new within the realms of systems research the application of critical theories, and an acknowledgement of the contribution of both quantitative and qualitative methods, has improved the viability of the method which is under development. The breakdown of the organisational arena into a number of determinate and indeterminate viewpoints offers an appropriate means of summary. This level of abstraction allows the complexity to be deconstructed in order that a grasp may be gained on the boundaries of the problem domain.

THE METHODOLOGICAL APPROACH TO THE RAMESES WICKED PROBLEM
Grounded Theory

The research method chosen for the RAMESES project was grounded theory. This methodology was developed by Glaser and Strauss (1967) and allows for the emergence of theory from an empirical investigation. The framework under which this occurs encourages a constant iteration between the collection and analysis of empirical data, and reflection on literary sources. This exploratory and inductive approach becomes increasingly pertinent within complex or "wicked" situations where it is difficult firstly to isolate variables and secondly to measure the cause and effect relationships between them. Grounded theory requires (perhaps optimistically) that a study should be undertaken without preconceptions, in order that a preconceived conceptual description is avoided. The framework of operation allows the use of many different techniques for the collection of data. However, the keynote of these techniques is that they be based upon observation rather than action and experimentation. This approach matches the research problem of investigation in that it is situated within an environment (small organisations) which, to a large extent, has not been examined by the information systems field. In using grounded theory, we can explore the concept of business process and IT change without imposing the generalisations gleaned from research focused on large-scale corporations. Understanding the specific needs of small businesses is the key to the development of the method, which is the focus of the RAMESES project. This research methodology also allows for the exploration of a complex and multi-faceted environment, this being an important aspect of any 'real world' scenario. Therefore, in summary, the choice of grounded theory for this work was based on the research method being: inductive; qualitative; flexible in terms of research techniques that can be used; suitable for the time frame of the project; investigative not prescriptive. And not reliant, in the first instance, on previously reported IS research. Using grounded theory led us to undertake fieldwork and to collect information from organisations as the necessary precursor to deriving theories.

The Context of the Case Study Organisations

The RAMESES fieldwork was conducted at three manufacturing organisations and at one organisation in the retail and distribution sector in the Northeast of England. Each of the manufacturing companies is termed a "job shop" in that its manufacturing activity revolves around made-to-order, low volume, high value products. Companies in this sector tend to encounter problems as soon as they attempt to procure, and use, standard off-the-shelf packages that are aimed at the manufacturing industry. The main reason being that in such packages manufacturing is viewed as a batch environment, producing high volume, low cost products. The detailed IT audit that was carried out in each company established that the structure of their sociotechnical legacy system consisted of a number of loosely coupled components. These components ranged from off-the-shelf packages to customized systems. Typical examples of these components are a Manufacturing Requirements

Planning (MRPII) system, accounts software and office support software that is used to create company specific applications.

Company A is a manufacturing company with around 50 employees, working in the area of commercial drive products. Company B is a manufacturing company with around 70 employees, working in the area of prefabricated components. Company C is a retail distribution company with around 80 employees. Company D is a manufacturing company with around 100 employees, supplying components and services to the global defence industry. The senior management at each of these organisations had recognised that their legacy system was not effectively supporting their business requirements. This analysis was precipitated in each case, not by a review of their software, for quality or suitability, but by a management initiated business change. The reasons for these planned changes were varied. Company A was being brought into a larger consortium and, to effectively work within this larger grouping, they needed to assess the interfaces that would exist between themselves and other consortium members. Company B had relocated to new premises following a merger with a sister company and needed to ensure compatibility in work processes and IT support in the new environment. Company C had undertaken formal business process reengineering of the organisation along the lines recommended by Hammer and Champy (1993). Company D was subject to less radical changes but the directors were planning ahead for a change in management structure.

None of these organisations had set out with the purpose of reviewing their IT systems. However, as they began their business process changes it became obvious to them that what they wished to do was, in certain instances, impeded by their use of software. For instance, Company C had experienced business process reengineering exercises, which had been carried out by internal teams supported by consultants. In the first instance, the company had realigned its activities and personnel to match the identified core business processes. When our fieldwork began, they had identified a mismatch between their unaltered software systems and their now processually-defined structure.

THE RESEARCH METHOD USED IN THE RAMESES PROJECT
The Rationale for the Method

The RAMESES project is aimed at producing a tool, which allows risk assessment within SMEs of changes to business processes or to IT systems. This solution therefore requires that the problem be analysed in such a way as to shed light on the organisation, its IT and the way in which people use it. This approach is aligned with a sociotechnical systems (Mumford & Beekman, 1994) approach, which seeks to integrate the social, the technical, and the organisational aspects of an open system.

In this scenario, an environment is investigated from these three perspectives, the social, the technical and the system, we have aligned this to broadly read that:

- the *social* perspective is equivalent to people factors,
- the *technical* issues relate to the information system,
- the *system* relates to issues of the organisation as a whole

From gathering this data a rich understanding of the organisation begins to emerge. However, it was then necessary to decide on the viewpoints from which to gather the information as a wicked problem is a deeply tangled and enmeshed entity. There are an infinite number of viewpoints on the problem both from the outside and from the inside of the problem. It is necessary to derive precise criteria for deciding where the viewpoints for one's study of the problem are. In this study, it was known that the area for study was the relationship between legacy systems and business processes. It was assumed by the authors that the relationship between legacy systems and business processes is always supposed to be close. As described earlier, many factors may affect this relationship. However, the focus for the research is that the closeness or lack of it in a relationship will be manifested in a gap or lack of it. A large gap in the relationship between the legacy system and the business process is indicative of an area of high risk. A large gap may imply a lack of data integrity, work having to be redone, processing bottlenecks or muddled responsibilities. Therefore, it was necessary to choose viewpoints on the RAMESES wicked problem which would detect a gap. Both a business process and a computerised software system may be seen as a sequence of events. Both are characterised by the fact that the way that events are designed to occur is not the way that they actually occur when the system/process is in use. The way they are supposed to occur should leave very little gap between the two, but the way they actually occur will reveal the gap. Therefore, the following viewpoints for study were chosen:

- The functional view, which expands the top-level knowledge of the organisation.
- the process view describes a business process from the receipt of an enquiry to a paid invoice,
- The cellular view is a bottom-up approach, which seeks to explain how the process actually happens.

This understanding encompasses organisational type, managerial culture and strategy, issues of power and information, all in all this involves a

Figure 1: Model Showing Linkages Between Perspectives

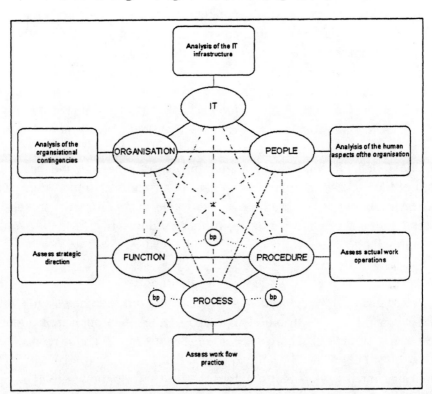

plethora of facts and fantasies. From the issues that have been emerging during the case studies, a generic view of the scenario has been assembled. This has been used to produce an evolving model of the linkages between the different factors in the problem-solution space. Figure 1 shows this model, relating the organisational viewpoints to the perspectives accorded by the socio-technical systems approach (Mumford & Beekman, 1994).

By understanding the problem and the solution from the aspects denoted within the diagram, a more holistic account can emerge.

Research Techniques

The systematic analysis of the organisations is dependent upon a variety of research techniques. Individual situations of investigations may require different forms of study. The key practices used in this project are observation, informal and formal interviewing, documentation review, system and process audits. These approaches offer a degree of triangulation within the data collection process by approaching the problem arena from differing perspectives. Within the first phase of the research, the chosen method of data collection is a combination of semi-structured interview backed by process mapping. At any stage within the collection process the data gathered may be analysed to provide a systematic categorisation of the findings. Categorisation requires the identification of characteristics within the data and the identification of relationships between those categories. Having identified the characteristics and pertinent relationships between them the next essential step in terms of informing the method is to allocate weightings to the results.

The outcome from this level of investigation is a 'rich' understanding of the interactions between the business process that we are investigating, the people responsible for the implementation of those processes and the relationship of the process and people in regard to any information system, which exists in support of that process. The generic qualities of process and interactions emerging from this deep understanding will inform the evolution of our method.

Interviewing Protocols

The protocol we devised was to tape record our interviews and enhance the data with the construction of maps of the functional area under the manager's command. There were no objections raised to our recording the interviews: however, it became apparent that the greatest difficulty in tape recording interviews is that much of the best information is relayed to the interviewer after the official interview has been terminated. While the tape recorder is running, the interviewee is focused on the task in hand. However, when the business of the interview is concluded most interviewees continue to talk informally about their work and the company. Much of this information is extremely valuable in terms of a rich understanding of the company culture. However, the fact that it is off the record means that it would be, perhaps, unethical to divulge it in written appraisals of the task. This information can therefore be used only to inform the researcher, for instance, as how to best approach people, or to have awareness of political situations that may be sensitive. The ability to make the most of an interview opportunity depends upon the reflexivity of the researcher in reading the situation. Alienating interviewees by appearing unsympathetic or by holding a controversial opinion can seriously impede the process of data extraction.

Mapping the Scene

The interviews were reinforced with construction of maps, which laid out the role of managerial functions; this enabled a more thorough understanding of the data being collated. By mapping the area being studied, the interviewee could improve upon the understanding of the interviewer and

Figure 2: Quality Map from Technical Director

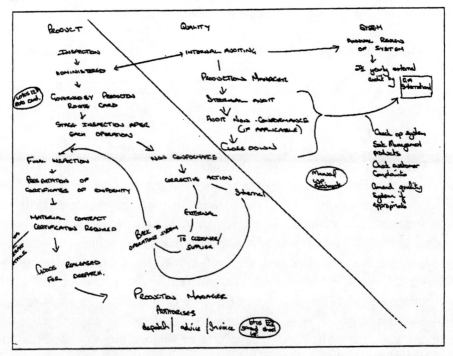

Figure 3: Transcribed "Rich Map" of the Technical Director's Quality Processes

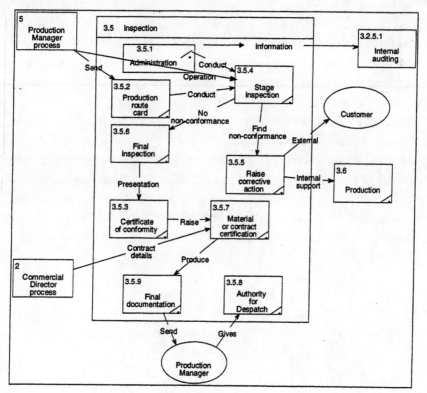

further clarify points of confusion. The more complicated the function, the more relevant the role of the mapping became. The hand-drawn maps have been duplicated within this paper in their original format to avoid a further level of interpretation. The maps (for example, see Figure 2) were hand drawn during the interview then analysed using a SSADM tool (see Figure 3). Although this was an interpretative process, care was taken to ensure the meaning of the data was not altered.

Transcripts and Emerging Themes

Another key task in the research process was the transcription of the interview data. Full transcripts were made of the interviews, which were then subject to analysis. From the analysis of the transcripts themes were identified as being pertinent when they reoccurred in the data. Transcripts were analysed for emergent issues and previous academic work on the subject was sought. This iteration between data and theory is a feature of research conducted within a grounded theory framework and reinforces the rigour that such interpretative studies require. From the emergent themes, two key sets of information emerged. Firstly, information which is specifically related to the company under investigation. These sets of themes identify the areas of concern or interest that are context dependent. The second set of themes are those which are of a more generic nature and progress the advancement of the RAMESES method.

EXAMPLES FROM THE CASE STUDIES

The initial data collection process consisted of 35 interviews with various managerial and support staff from the four case study organisations. The interviews ranged from around 20 minutes to one hour depending upon the complexity of the interviewees' position. To illustrate the means, by which we collected information and our subsequent analysis of it, extracts from the case studies have been included. In the initial meetings with the companies' general managers, we gained information about the size of the company, its area of business and its expectations of the research. We also offered information on what we would hope to achieve and the amount of time that we would spend on data collection. Arrangements were also made for the next meetings at which time we could commence with the collection of data.

Setting the Scene

The preliminary meetings took the form of an "informal chat" with the project's sponsor in each company. We talked in general about the company and the sort of information we required for analysis. We did not preempt the results of this meeting by setting a formal agenda, our approach was to talk to the key stakeholder of the project within the company and find the issues that he considered to be pertinent, using his knowledge of the company to direct the research. (In each case, the sponsor was a "he.") However, we did enter each meeting with the express purpose of setting future dates. In Company A, this meeting lasted, for example, about 30 minutes. The technical director explained in general terms the structure of the company, a company "who's who" and his understanding of the research project and what he thought it would offer them. We set the date for another more formal interview where we intended to map the functions that he oversaw and to identify the people who also had a managerial role. This meeting set the agenda for the first round of formal interviews. We had an idea of the company structure and the duties that the technical director undertook. It was obvious from this description of his role that his duties were varied and widespread throughout the company and that we would have to devise a method that would enable us to disentangle the complexities of his role. This resulted in the interviewing protocols described below.

After this first round of interviews, more formal sessions followed. The protocol for these had been adopted from previous studies and found to be suitable. This was to tape record our interviews and enhance the data with the construction of maps of the functional area under the manager's command. No objections were raised to the recording of the interviews although, as ever, some of the most pertinent information was spoken once the tape recorder had been switched off.

The Formal Interviewing Process

The first of the formal interviews was with each company's technical director. He had been instrumental in the formation of the company and possessed the engineering expertise on which the business was founded.

To explore his viewpoint, we used a combination of qualitative research techniques. Our focus was a semi-structured interview: we entered the interview with a description of the type of information that we needed for analysis, as we interviewed a 'rich' diagrammatic map (see Figure 2) of the functional viewpoint was drawn.

A typical question asked was "Could you describe your role, the tasks you undertake and especially how they link to the other departments?" The initial information we received was a list of the other directors, managers and key workers in the administrative roles. This was a valuable piece of information, as it gave a structured picture of the key company staff (although much of this information could have been taken from the company handbook, which had been written by the technical director). Although we had been given a copy of the quality manual that included this information, the addition of personal descriptions of the task and the person who carried it out was useful and enlightening information. In Company A, all of the information was presented by the technical director in a very formal and structured fashion: it was tempting to attribute that to his engineering background, as this structured and hierarchical view was not given by all of the interviewees.

The technical director was involved in a key position in many of the company's functional areas, which made it difficult in some ways to disentangle his roles. He had written the quality manuals of the company for the British quality standard, ISO 9000 accreditation and was also the key quality controller. During the interview, we drew a large map of the function that was being described (this is shown in figure 2)

Onto the drawing of the function, the individual processes that were supported by some sort of IT were clearly marked. We marked the location of IT support at this functional level, and further supported that investigation with a round of technical interviews to firmly map the IT system and its impact upon the organisation.

The technical director had developed his own technical support tools to assist in performing rough calculations when conducting estimates. He entered the various design parameters into a BASIC program that he had written, which then performed the various calculations. The outputs of this program were entered into an estimating package that had been purchased from the USA (this was a Maths CAD package which incorporated an interactive screen). The results from this were then entered into another self-written program to conduct further calculations. In total he used four programs for one quotation, and had to retype the outputs of each previous program as inputs to the next. It was apparent that the use of the computer was as an automation of the manual process, and did not use the computer to inform more advanced processes. The software had been developed in-house, and it was his attempt to put years of experience in performing the calculations in software terms.

Other management tools were integrated as part of the Lotus suite, these were used for support and to provide him with the information he required to carry out his managerial functions. The original computer software contained an accounts system. Over time, the system was improved with the addition of a word processing package and CAD software, as well as the "little bits" that enabled him to do various other jobs within the department. The technical director described the system as "piecemeal." It was currently useful just for the elements that he did, although he did consider that his tasks would be aided by some form of integration, perhaps development of an integrated package on the network. He was the only person able to use his personal packages; these are used for the design procedures, including quotations (he currently processes all the technical quotes). He wants to make this more interactive or perhaps user- friendly, so that anyone could handle it.

The Rich Maps

After the combination of a functional interview (to gather information about the technical director's role) and the technical interview (to establish the support offered to that role by the company's IT system) the information was transferred from the large hand drawn maps to a modelling tool. The translation process itself was a very interesting one, for the researchers had to be aware and alert to the temptation to restructure and influence the data that had been gathered from the interviewees. Our aim was to transcribe the view as expressed by the technical director but to put it into a format that was more amenable to analysis at a later date. The rich maps that were drawn of the processes were translated into digital format using an SSADM tool. Using the tool allowed us to construct diagrams in a standard format, from the information given regardless of the form of the initial rich maps. Figure 1 shows an example of such a transcription for the Technical Director.

Rich maps were constructed during each formal interview with the top-level management of the company these were then transcribed into the standard format. This meant that using the individual section maps (which were each, initially, very different in character) an overall picture of the organisation was developed. The use of the tool was advantageous during the subsequent analysis of the data. A colour-coded approach has been used so that, although there was a standard format to the organisational/IT support maps, the sections could still be identified. This colour coding enhanced the clarity of the picture developed and as a result, the initial stage of data collection and analysis identified two major areas of concern for the company. Although the tool gave us a good representation, it was not flexible enough to incorporate all of the information that we needed to present and the methodology of SSADM was somewhat at variance with our overall aims. Using the tool, the tendency was to force the information given in interview into structured and hierarchical formats, which was not necessarily how it had been presented. It took restraint from the researchers not to impose the limitations of the tool upon the data that had been collected. The data we gathered represented a complex and varied environment which was through the eyes of its owners and while we could perhaps see structure which lay beneath the data, the integrity of the viewpoint which we were analysing required that our understanding was secondary to the interviewees. The maps of each director's functional areas were compiled to create an organisational mapping. This mapping gives an overview of the company, its key figures, main processes and highlights some areas of concern.

Transcripts and Emerging Themes

From the initial interviews several themes emerged from both a context dependent and generic perspective. For example, within this case study was related to issues of data. Much of the data within this organisation was transferred by manual reentry; this issue was relayed in several of the interviews and so became the focus of 'focused' coding where data issues were sought from subsequent transcripts. Issues relating to the handling of data have informed the development of the RAMESES method in that it is one of the means by which the state of existing systems may be categorised.

Identification of Areas of Concern

The first concern identified was that the technical director carries too many sets of responsibilities, which is a risk to the company if any events occur that mean his knowledge is no longer available to them. The second concern is that there is an overall lack of recognition from the directors of the role of efficiency: this is evidenced by the lack of acknowledgement of the role that job costing played within the organisation's procedures. The General Manager had already highlighted these issues as being of strategic importance and saw the organisational map as a support for his objectives.

The second phase of the organisation revolved around a specific business process within case study A. Once the initial functional analysis was completed the second stage was to follow a business process from enquiry in to payment of an order completed. Understanding the business process involved a 'walk through' one of the business processes identified by the company. The managing director and researcher followed the trail of an enquiry, by collecting all relevant documentation, and discussing with each employee involved what tasks they undertook to fulfil the order. This information was then plotted onto the organisational map drawn from the first round of interviews. The objective here was to seek points of complexity, bottlenecks or smooth processes from the comparison of the two sets of data. This analysis again raised the issue of the complexity surrounding the technical director's function, as he became a bottleneck for progress as so much work had revolved around his contribution.

Phase three was to study in-depth the issues raised by the first two investigations although in this particular study it would have been politically difficult to carry out the required work due to the seniority of the person involved.

OUR RESULTS

The results of the project have focused on using the data gathered and the issues that the analysis raised to identify the most pertinent and useful aspects of organisational analysis. Taking the three perspectives of the sociotechnical system as a starting point has lead to the development of ontology, which seeks to represent all three of these aspects. This ontology has identified issues relating to organisation, business process and IT system as being the key to sociotechnical understanding. The Method framework, which has developed as a result of the research, has a matrix of information as its tool for undertaking risk analysis.

In the first stage of the method data is collected in a factual manner relating to the type of organisation which is being studied, the way in which their business processes vary from generic processes, and the sort of IT which is in support of those processes. In the second stage, in-depth data is gathered from the perspectives that have been identified as pertinent from the identification of the problem boundary. As organisation's problems or needs are generally 'wicked' then setting the solution space is imperative to identifying the issues which require attention. The third stage takes both sets of data and by comparative means seeks to weigh up the risk of any proposed change. This method framework is laid out in the following diagram.

Using the RAMESES Method of Risk Assessment

The adoption of the RAMESES tool for informing strategic decisions can be seen in a variety of ways:

- That a one-time run through of the tool will aid in a specific problem situation.
- That the tool may offer a route by which problems may be identified then assessed
- That the adoption of the tool may be undertaken with a view to long term commitment to organisational improvement.

For this third option, the use of the tool will still aid in the previously mentioned fashions, but will offer a further level of future analysis. It is in this scenario that the tool will offer the most effective information. At this level, a company will in the initial stages undertake to log all:

1. business processes
2. IT hardware
3. IT software
4. IT skills
5. organisational internal characteristics
6. external markers

Logging all of this information may seem in the first instance a tedious and complicated process. It may be that initially the tool requirements capture procedure may require assistance from professional analysts. The usefulness of analysts is, however, limited in the understanding they have of the company. External advisors must be considered as just that, the future usefulness of the tool will depend upon the in-depth knowledge of a company that is only understood from within. The elicitation of knowledge with regard to the external world is a different matter, as this position becomes clear by comparison and knowledge of benchmarking of some such similar technique is most appropriate with external aid. This is the macro/micro viewpoint of the organisation. (Walsham, 1997). The combination of all this information enables a complex and comprehensive portrait of the organisation to evolve. The evolution of the organisational portrait will require regular iterations. The

Figure 4: Diagram of RAMESES Method

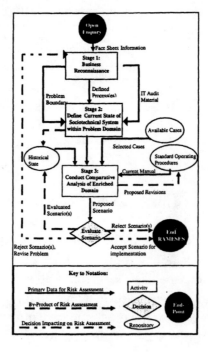

development of an organisational history in conjunction with an organisational memory will enable rigorous analysis of potential changes. The history of change will allow the organisation to learn more effectively the methods and techniques, which are most successful within their unique position. The case-based reasoning element of the tool which learns by the experience of consultants, business advisors and academics, as well as by other organisations will offer information that will be complemented and further tailored by the techniques from which the company has most benefited from in the past.

CONCLUSIONS

The Problem Shape Corresponds to the Solution Shape

At the start of the RAMESES project, it was not known which factors would prove relevant to the relationship between an organisation, its business processes and its IT. In that sense, the problem was not well defined. However, it was known that the solution which was the aim of the project was to provide a tool which would allow small-to-medium sized enterprises (or consultants working with them) to perform their own assessment of the risk involved in changing either a business process or a legacy IT system. They would have to get to know themselves in just the same way as we got to know the companies in our case study. The ways in which the tool would ask them to assess themselves and the questions it suggests they ask themselves are directly derived from the factors which assumed significance during the case studies. This is then a very clear case of interaction between solution and problem as advocated by the wicked problem literature (Rittel & Webber, 1984). The notion of assessing risk allowed us to focus on the problem, while the mechanism of a tool by which enterprises could assess themselves led us to draw out the factors that they needed in order to do this.

Viewpoints on an Organisation

An organisation may be examined from an infinite number of viewpoints, but where the researchers stand is determined by what they are looking for. In observing, interviewing and mapping, the researcher has always to consider that the questions are about something. This "aboutness" is a viewpoint. Grounded theory advocates a very open and inductive style, but each study must have its focuses, its "abouts" and its viewpoints. Our viewpoints were set to reveal the parallax and the gaps between business processes, IT processes, and the usage of both, because a gap was taken to represent a risk. As we were looking for risk, we stood in the best place to see it. To the furtherment of our aims, our solution space determined the problem space that we were prepared to look at. Had we not taken this teleological approach to the project, we would have found that it ramified too widely for analysis to have ever been concluded. Instead, our investigations have been undertaken with a consistent and useful perspective, and a highly usable tool is emerging.

ACKNOWLEDGEMENTS

The RAMESES (Risk Assessment Model: Evaluation Strategy for Existing Systems) is funded by the EPSRC, as part of its "Software Engineering for Business Process Change" programme. Further details about this work are accessible from the RAMESES web site (http://osiris.sunderland.ac.uk/rameses).

REFERENCES

Budgen, (1993). *Software Design*. Wokingham, England: Addison Wesley.

Churchman, C.W. (1967). Wicked Problems. *Management Science 14*, 141-142.

Conklin, E.J. & W. Weil (1998). Wicked Problems: Naming the Problems in Organisations. *3M Meeting Network:* http://www.mmmco.de/...work/readingroom/gdss_wicked.html, last accessed 6/7/98.

Giddens, A. (1984). *The Constitution of Society: An Outline of the Theory of Structuration.* Oxford, England: Polity Press.

Glaser, B. and Strauss, A. L. (1967). *The Discovery of Grounded Theory: Strategies for Qualitative Research.* Chicago: Aldine Publishing Co.

Hammer, M and Champy, J (1993). *Reengineering the Corporation: A Manifesto for Business Revolution.* London, England: Nicholas Brearley.

Mumford & Beckman (1994). *Tools for Change and Progress: A socio-technical approach to business re-engineering.* Netherlands: CSG Publications.

Rittel H.J. & Webber, M.M., (1984). *Planning problems are wicked problems. In Developments in Design Methodology.* Cross N., Ed, pp. 135-144. Chichester, England: Wiley.

Royce, W.W. (1970). *Managing the development of large software systems: Concepts and Techniques.* Proceedings of WESCON.

Shurville *et al.*, (1997). *A development methodology for composer: a computer support tool for academic writing in a second language.* In: Jakobs and Knorr (eds.) 1997, The production of scientific texts in the age of the computer,

Strauss & Corbin (1997). *Grounded Theory in Practice.* London: Sage.

Walsham, G. (1997). Micro-Studies and Macro-Theory. Bit97 Conference

Proceedings, CD-ROM, Cambridge, England.

Winch, P. (1958). *The Idea of a social Science: and its Relation to Philosophy.* London: Routledge & Kegan Paul.

Chapter 17

Inspecting Spam: Unsolicited Communications on the Internet

Ellen R. Foxman
Associate Professor, Bentley College, MA

William T. Schiano
Assistant Professor, Bentley College, MA

INTRODUCTION

Much coverage of the Internet focuses on undesirable, sometimes intrusive, communication, often referred to as "spam." Spam has been decried as antisocial, wasteful, and/or fraudulent, with individuals, organizations, and media reports widely advocating regulation or outright banning of the practice, yet no uniform definition exists. Participants in the electronic communication and commerce process generally operate on an "I know it when I see it" basis that is shaped by their personal experience and expectations.

This chapter begins with a brief history of this new medium, then defines spam within a typology of undesirable Internet communications. Conflicting definitions of spam are examined in light of their implications for suggested remedies. The paper concludes with recommendations on controlling spam for individuals, managers, and policy makers.

HISTORY OF ADVERTISING ON THE INTERNET

Advertising is "paid, non-personal communication about goods, services, etc., transmitted through the mass media by an identified sponsor" (Evans and Berman, 1997). Because of its reliance on mass media, advertising has been viewed as communication of a single message to a mass audience. Communication on the

Previously Published in *Challenges of Information Technology Management in the 21st Century*, edited by Mehdi Khosrow-Pour, Copyright © 2000, Idea Group Publishing.

Internet can take on many forms, not all of which can be fairly classified as a mass medium (Hoffman and Novak, 1995; Morris and Ogan, 1996).

If we accept the Internet as a mass communication medium, advertising on an *ad hoc* basis has occurred since the development of commercial service providers – prior to that, messages were not "paid." Early advertising was placed in specific mailing lists or newsgroups by subscribers. With the Internet's expanded reach and the development of the World Wide Web, businesses have recognized greater value in the medium, and the number and kinds of advertising have increased.

Company websites are developed and maintained as advertisements for company products and services, and increasingly for many other commercial purposes. Commercial websites can reduce marketing costs and improve relationships with customers (Peterson, Balasubramanian et al., 1997), but they are expensive to create and maintain, and consumers must seek them out.

Some businesses advertise directly to consumers via e-mail, or place advertisements in Usenet newsgroups. These "push" methods have several advantages: advertisers obtain extraordinary reach at a minimal cost, and can target specific consumer groups either by accessing subscriber profiles in a company like America OnLine (AOL), or by choosing newsgroups that relate to their offering.

E-mail or newsgroup advertising has some serious disadvantages that relate both to its "push" nature and to Internet culture. This type of advertising is similar to direct mail or telemarketing solicitation in that consumers view it negatively if they are not interested in the offering. Within Internet culture, such unsolicited commercial communications often provoke negative and even virulent attacks from those who receive them.

TYPES OF UNDESIRABLE INTERNET COMMUNICATION

A typology of undesirable Internet communications was derived from examination of academic research, trade, and technical articles and informal discussions with computer users and the authors' direct experience. The proposed classification, illustrated in Table 1, includes eight types of electronic communication: sales pitches, other persuasive messages, off-topic posts, flaming, flooding, denial of service, and at least in some cases, banner ads, and "push" technologies.

Other persuasive messages include messages that express political, religious, or other personal convictions. Unlike sales pitches, they "sell" ideas, not products or services. Off-topic posts are messages that violate appropriate content guidelines. These messages are often cross-posted or multi-posted (sent to multiple related or unrelated groups).

Table 1: Characteristics of Undesirable Internet Communications

Undesirable Communication Type	Communication Mode	Sender Personally Known by Recipient?	Selling Message?	Who Bears the Cost?	Values Congruence
Sales Pitches	e-mail or USENET	No	Yes	Recipient Group (USENET)	Possible
Other persuasive messages	e-mail or USENET	No	No	Recipient (e-mail) Group (USENET)	Possible
Off-topic posts	Usenet	No	Possible	Group (USENET)	Possible
Flaming	e-mail or Usenet	Possible	No	Recipient (e-mail) Group (USENET)	No
Flooding	e-mail or Usenet	Possible	No	Recipient's Host	No
Denial of service	e-mail or WWW	Possible	No	Recipient's Host	No
Banner ads	WWW	No	Yes	User	Possible
"push"	WWW	No	Possible	User	Possible

Flaming is the sending of inappropriately vehement, usually vitriolic, messages to a specific target. Flooding involves the deliberate sending of large numbers of messages to drown out all other communication. Denial of service attacks are a class of techniques used to overwhelm or otherwise disable a firm's internet connection.

While banner ads have become commonplace, many users still find them intrusive and objectionable. "Push" involves the ability of content providers to update new content to a user's web browser, and may exacerbate objections of Web page advertising.

Media Definitions of Spam

Like pornography (Jacobellis v. Ohio, 1964), people may not be sure how to define spam, but they are convinced they know it when they see it. To derive a more explicit definition of the practice, sixty-seven articles on spam from June 1994 to September 1997 were examined for definitions of spam. The majority of articles provided no definition, or defined it only parenthetically.

A few sources have developed explicit definitions of spam. The Hacker's Dictionary (Raymond, 1996) calls spam "unsolicited mass commercial communication on the Internet." A Business Week article (Himelstein, 1995) defines spamming as, "the practice of sending unwanted junk mail, usually product advertisements, to a large number of people via electronic mail or the Internet" (p.44). A few other definitions have been proposed, including:

"Spam refers to any unsolicited commercial e-mail whose content could be marketing drivel, pyramid schemes, or religious or political messages" (Murphy, 1997, p.4); and

"'Spamming' is the act of sending mass e-mails, often called electronic junk mail, which is not illegal, but is considered by many on-line purists to be contrary to proper Internet etiquette" (Wilen, 1996, p.1).

These definitions reveal a lack of consensus on what constitutes spam. If people cannot agree on the nature of spam it will be impossible to regulate (or ban) the practice effectively. Clearly, spam is unsolicited and involves sending copies of the same message to many individuals. Spam is also unwanted, although this tends to be implicit in most definitions.

There is less agreement on the content of spam. Most writers agree that spam is commercial: something is offered for sale, but many view spam more broadly, including advertising, and unsolicited religious or political messages. Some label anything unwanted as spam.

Spammers' Definitions Of Spam

Individuals who send, or facilitate sending, unsolicited commercial e-mail messages insist that such messages are simply advertising and therefore protected under the First Amendment (Murphy, 1997). Bulk e-mailers also view the Internet as a public good since its development was taxpayer funded.

"Spam King" Sanford Wallace, President of Cyber Promotions, Inc., vigorously defends his company's right to send unsolicited e-mail, claiming to have obtained the 1.3 million names on his mailing list from legitimate sources. Cyber Promotions survived hacker attacks, a deluge of bad publicity, and lawsuits, but was shut off in September 1997, along with two other spamming ISPs, by AGIS, its "upstream" service provider.

An Objective Measure of Spam

One objective, quantitative measure for Spam for Usenet postings is the Breidbart index (BI). For each identical message, count the number of newsgroups the message was posted to. Add the square roots of the counts for each instance of the message to get the index (Gimon, 1997). The accepted threshold for cancellation as of June 1997 was a BI of 20 over a 45 day period (Lewis 1997). Usenet spamming has increased since 1994 and many unmoderated newsgroups now contain more spams than on-topic messages (see Cancelmoose at http://www.cm.org).

Proposed Definition Of Spam

Based on the information discussed above, we define spam as "a single message transmitted unsolicited to multiple recipients; recipients do not personally know the sender, and they judge the message to be offensive." Note that under our definition, every one of the undesirable Internet communication types in Table 2 could be spam. The definition highlights the term's ambiguous meaning and may also in part explain hesitance to formulate an explicit definition of spam. What is spam to one recipient may be useful information to another.

SPAM HAPPENS...BUT WHY?

Lawyers Laurence Canter and Martha Siegel implemented the first large-scale spam in 1994, when they sent a message offering help with the Immigration and Naturalization Service's "green-card lottery" to thousands of Usenet newsgroups. Thousands of angry recipients sent nasty messages (flames) to NETCOM, Canter and Siegel's Internet service provider (ISP), causing the provider's machine to overload and crash. The ISP shut down Canter and Siegel's account rather than risk its ability to provide service to its other customers. Canter and Siegel spammed a few more times through other ISPs, then wrote a "how to" book on spamming (Canter, 1994).

Unlike direct mail or other types of advertising, out-of-pocket costs to businesses that choose to spam are extremely low, with a CPM (cost per thousand) approaching zero. Cyber Promotions Inc. charges $50/month to send unsolicited commercial e-mail messages to Cyber Promotion's list of 1.3 million Internet addresses. The following calculations give a cost estimate (Bovee, 1995):

CPM = [(cost of media unit) / (gross impressions)] X 1000
     = ($50/month) / (1,300,000) X 1000
     = $.04/month for each thousand messages

Note that this CPM is not the effective cost, that is, the cost per response or the cost per completed order. These cannot be calculated without some indication of the non-flame response rate to spam messages.

One advertisement for software that allows one to create and bulk deliver unsolicited e-mail ads contains testimonials that indicate purchase and/or response rates of 0.08% to 0.5% (Bray 1997). Applying a 0.5% response rate to the cost calculation above gives:

CPM = ($50/month) / (1,300,000 X .0005) X 1000
     = $76.92 / month for each thousand messages resulting in a completed

order. While this is much higher than the unadjusted CPM, it is still extraordinarily cheap.

Senders may incur other costs besides the direct cost of the ads in choosing to send unsolicited e-mail advertisements. First, they almost certainly face a large volume of e-mail complaints, which can result in service outages or denial of service by ISPs. Consumer complaints are also resulting in regulatory and legislative scrutiny, and the growing likelihood of controls on this type of advertising. Finally, consumers and other groups may sue, resulting in legal and/or settlement costs.

IMPACT ON RECIPIENTS

In large part because of the history of the Internet, many users feel they have a right to be free from commercial messages. This has led to a strong sense of violation by spam. There are also significant economic costs of spam for individuals. Users must download the spam from their ISP, paying for the telecommunications connection, and often for connect time to the ISP. Wading through and/or deleting spam also takes individual time and effort. Spam is particularly troublesome for disabled users who rely on computers and for whom manual filtering requires more time and effort (Hoffman, 1997). Recipient firms are forced to invest additional resources to handle the increased volume from spam.

Impact on ISPs

Some ISPs exist to provide spam capability. For most ISPs, however, spam presents problems on multiple fronts even though the processing overhead for spam e-mail does not pose a major problem (Nass, 1997). First, subscribers who receive spam may complain to the ISP, demanding that such messages be screened out from their mail, a difficult task. ISPs must also spend time answering questions and complaints.

Second, subscribers who send spam expose the ISP to a vituperative deluge of recipient complaints that may overwhelm the ISP's server. This results in interruption of service, not merely for the spammer, but also for all the other clients of the ISP. Finally, ISPs' addresses may be "hijacked" and used as return addresses in spam (Himelstein, 1995). In such cases, the ISP receives all the hate mail, and the spammer usually provides a fax number or street address for responses. Senders don't even bother to remove undeliverable addresses because the cost would exceed the costs incurred in using them.   ·

REMEDIES FOR SPAM

Spam can be addressed and managed, with varying degrees of success, by individuals, recipient firms, ISPs, trade organizations and public policy makers. The most basic remedy, norms against spam, may have reduced the growth of spam, but has proven insufficient. Appendix outlines the various remedies and responsible parties, along with each remedy's limits.

Individual

The most basic defense against e-mail spam for individuals is to stay off spammers' mailing lists. Consumers can alter the return address on their e-mail to prevent address "harvesting" for inclusion in e-mail advertising databases. Others maintain a separate account for sending e-mail whose address spammers will likely target, such as in USENET postings or web site registrations. This makes legitimate responses more difficult as a "reply" goes to a non-existent or unread account.

If individuals are unable to hide their addresses from spammers, they can try to filter spam out. Filtering software packages list undesired senders or key phrases. The filters must be constantly updated since spammers tailor messages and change their addresses frequently to get around filters. Users also face the risk of filtering out desired messages that share attributes of spam.

Users can complain about spam, but while the sending address can be tracked down, this process is time consuming and confusing. Net Services has created Spam Hater, a freeware package which will track down Spam e-mail authors and complain automatically. Complaints can also be lodged with ISPs through which the spammers connect.

Individuals' abhorrence of spam and the strong culture of the Internet has led to a variety of stronger vigilante-like responses. Actions have ranged from creation of the fairly benign Cancelmoose to flaming and blacklists, and have helped mitigate the growth rate of spam. These self-declared "net cops" are appreciated by many and self-regulate effectively. However, in an extreme example, angry recipients of spam sent by Jeff Slaton, a New Mexico "Spam King," retaliated by publishing his real name, employer, supervisor at work, home phone number, address, and Social Security number on the Internet, and encouraging other recipients to make Slaton's life miserable (Garfinkel 1996).

Recipient Firms and USENET Groups

Firms can also set filters on incoming mail, blocking specific addresses or domains or screening mail content for key spam identifiers. While they face the same challenges described above, firms do have the advantage of checking for multiple instances of the same messages as an additional indicator of spam. Such content-based filtering requires inspecting the body of e-mail messages. While inspecting employee e-mail is legal in the United States, many firms prefer to respect employee privacy.

Internet mail need not have a valid return address. Most spammers use "spamoflage," placing the address or phone number for ordering the product in the body of the message and providing an invalid return address. Some recipients refuse to deliver mail that does not have a valid return address.

Some USENET groups are moderated by volunteers who screen out spam and other undesirable messages. This creates a lag in the appearance of messages and requires a major investment in busy groups. There is also a risk that modera-

tors will be biased in their screening. Some groups have also encouraged participants to post with a label specific to the group. Readers can then ignore any
message without such a label. This requires all users understand the convention,
and does not prevent marginally sophisticated spammers from adding such labels
to their messages.

ISPs

ISPs have responded to spam-related problems in a variety of ways. Subscribers who spam are warned and/or denied further service. ISPs involved with
spamming have been sued by ISPs who are their targets (Himelstein, 1995). Finally, in response to the threat of government regulations, ISPs have begun to
bond together to regulate themselves. Most major ISPs prohibit spamming and
many offer to filter inbound mail to recipients.

By creating e-mail addresses such as "abuse@" ISPs are making it easier for
victims to identify spammers. Compuserve and America Online have won court
support for their policies preventing spammers from sending mail to their subscribers (Richards, 1997). While strongly unified action could raise anti-trust issues (Carroll, 1996), these efforts have put pressure on spammers.

Trade Organizations

Leading trade organizations favor self-regulation over government intervention
and have released spam policies to guide members. The Direct Marketing Association, the leading organization of direct marketers, has issued guidelines suggesting that members post commercial messages "only when consistent with the forum's
stated policies" (Direct Marketing Association, 1997). The DMA's position on
unsolicited e-mail is less stringent, suggesting clearly identifying the messages as
solicitations, disclosing the marketer's identity, and a mechanism for requesting
removal from the list, preferably via e-mail. Some consumer advocates are resist-
ing this because they feel it could destigmatize spam.

The Internet Service Providers Consortium argues that ISPs should forbid
unsolicited commercial e-mail from their users and networks buying connectivity
from them. They believe that "opt-out" schemes are not sufficient because the
recipient firms still bear an unreasonable proportion of the cost. Opt-in programs,
in contrast, would be considered "solicited" and therefore not subject to the policy.
The North American Internet Service Providers organization takes an even stronger stance, terminating memberships of ISPs that allow unsolicited commercial e-
mail on their systems.

Public Policy Makers

The culture of the Internet is still quite strong, and has helped keep major
marketers from spamming. Given the economics, however, smaller players can

generate just as much communication as even the largest firms. Existing laws address some of the problems with spam. In particular, many spams are fraudulent and are prosecutable under existing statutes.

Many analysts have equated problems with spam with the tragedy of the commons (Hardin, 1968), since the marginal cost of spam is near zero. The Federal Trade Commission and the House and Senate, spurred by consumer and ISP complaints, are considering legal and regulatory remedies for the problem (Murphy, 1997). Some individuals and groups are strongly in favor of this approach (Bray, 1997). Others, however, object to legislation on the grounds that it would violate freedom of speech rights (Broder, 1997), or simply because it would not work (Sandberg, 1997).

Government regulation would not be unprecedented. Junk faxes were outlawed by the Telephone Consumer Protection Act of 1991 in part because the cost was paid by the recipient and because the line could be tied up by unwanted transmissions. The government's right to impose limits on commercial speech if "real harm" can be demonstrated, and the regulation is narrowly drawn and the regulation addresses the harm is well established.

There is a growing trend toward offshore Internet businesses, including casinos and alleged money laundering operations (Selvin, 1997). These operations are far harder to regulate and control given the open structure of the Internet and the ability of unscrupulous firms to mask their identity.

Hagel and Rayport (1997) argue much of the consumer resistance labeled privacy concerns are actually a reflection of the lack of value in forfeiting privacy. One widely offered solution for spam is to force spammers to pay the full cost of their messages through some form of "e-postage" (Metcalfe, 1997). Part of the postage could be collected by the recipient upon reading the message through a micropayments scheme, but this would still require a substantial change in the infrastructure and culture of the Internet. It would also make abuse of e-mail servers more attractive and raise the financial costs for targeted firms.

While the current load on the network from spam is a nuisance, it is not yet crippling. As video and audio clips are routinely added to spam, the bandwidth used, and therefore the costs to recipients and the network, will increase, while the cost to the sender will remain relatively stable.

CONCLUSION

Individuals and many firms are struggling to manage spam. As the technology becomes more widely diffused, we may reasonably expect the trend to grow worse. The proposed remedies will differ in their effectiveness depending on the type of undesirable Internet communication, as illustrated in Appendix 1.

Spam will always be susceptible to different definitions, because at least part of what makes a message spam involves how it is interpreted by the recipient. Table 1 classified undesirable messages and reflected the role of individual differences in the relationship and values congruence categories. This suggests that

Appendix 1: Remedies for Spam

Remedy	Responsible Party/Parties	Limitations
Ignore	All	No longer viable due to volume of spam Does not alleviate bandwidth usage Does not reduce volume of spam for recipients
Norms	All	Not sufficiently enforceable Does not alleviate bandwidth usage
Phony/multiple accounts	I	Inconvenient Does not alleviate bandwidth usage
Filtering	I, F, ISP	Time consuming Needs constant updating May screen out desirable communication Does not alleviate bandwidth usage
Filing Complaints/ Abuse@	I, F, ISP	Time-consuming Unlikely to change spammers' behavior May not reduce volume of spam for recipients
Vigilantism	I, F	Ethically questionable Sometimes illegal Invites retaliation May not reduce volume of spam for recipients
Enforce Valid Return Address	F, TO, PPM	Does not alleviate bandwidth usage May not reduce volume of spam for recipients
Banning/Access Restrictions	F, ISP, TO, PPM	May screen out desirable communication
Moderated Groups	UDG	Time-consuming May introduce moderator bias Delays reader access to posts
Labeling	UDG, TO, PPM	Does not alleviate bandwidth usage May not reduce volume of spam for recipients
Opt Out	TO, PPM	Only works after spam is sent
Opt In	TO, PPM	Expensive Eliminates potentially desirable communication
E-Postage	ALL	Complex to implement Creates transactions costs Violates norm of "free" access

Key:
I = Individual
F = Recipient Firm
UDG = USENET Discussion Group
ISP = Internet Service Provider
TO = Trade Organization
PPM = Public Policy Makers

whatever policy measures are taken, there will still be the need for individualized screening and software.

Future research might include assessing the relative incidence and offensiveness of the different types of undesirable Internet communications. Further empirical analysis of the costs of spam to all stakeholders would also be useful.

REFERENCES

Bovee, C. L., Thill, J. V., Dovel, G. P. et al. (1995). *Advertising Excellence*. New York, NY: McGraw-Hill.

Bray, H. (1997). Antispam Persuasions. *Boston Globe* (June 12) C1.

Broder, J. (1997). Ban Spam? Not So Fast, Salon On-Line Magazine. June 11: http://www.salonmagazine.com/june97/news/news2.html.

Canter, L. and Siegel, M. (1994). *How to Make a Fortune on the Information Superhighway: Everyone's Guerrilla Guide to Marketing on the Internet and Other On-Line Service*. New York: HarperCollins.

Carroll, M. W. (1996). Garbage In: Emerging Media and Regulation of Unsolicited Commercial Solicitations. *Berkeley Technology Law Journal* 11(2): http://server.Berkeley.EDU/BTLJ/articles/11-2/carroll.html.

Direct Marketing Association (1997). DMA's Marketing Online Privacy Principles and Guidance, http://www.the-dma.org/busasst6/busasst-onmarkprivpr6a7.shtml.

Evans, J. R. and Berman, B. (1997). *Marketing*. Upper Saddle River, NJ: Prentice Hall.

Garfinkel, S. (1996). Spam King! Your Source for Spams Netwide! *Wired* 4(2): 84-92.

Gimon, C. A. (1997). The Parameters of Spam, http://www.info-nation.com/spam.html.

Godin, S. (1996). When Stamps Are Free: Using E-Mail and the Internet for Direct Response. *Direct Marketing* (December): 46-49.

Hagel, J. and Rayport, J. F. (1997). The Coming Battle for Consumer Information. *Harvard Business Review* (January-February): 53-65.

Hardin, G. (1968). The Tragedy of the Commons. *Science* 162: 1243-1248.

Himelstein, L. (1995). Law and Order in Cyberspace? *Business Week*: 44.

Hoffman, D. L. and Novak, T. P. (1995). Marketing in Hypermedia Computer-Mediated Environments: Conceptual Foundations, Project 2000: Research Program on Marketing In Computer-Mediated Environments (http://www2000.ogsm.vanderbilt.edu/).

Hoffman, P. E. (1997). *Internet Mail Consortium Public Comments*. Public Workshop on Consumer Information Privacy, Federal Trade Commission.

Jacobellis v. Ohio (1964).

Lewis, C. (1997). Current Spam Thresholds and Guidelines, posted weekly to news.admin.net-abuse.usenet.

Metcalfe, R. M. (1997). E-Postage Would Not Only Help Fund the System, But it Could Stop Spammers. *InfoWorld* 19(3): 44.

Morris, M. and Ogan, C. (1996). The Internet as Mass Medium. *Journal of Communciation* 46(1): 39-50.

Murphy, K. (1997). Lots of Fretting Over Spam, But No Easy Solutions. *Web Week*(June 16): 4.

Nass, S. (1997). *PANIX/Public Access Networks Corporation Public Comments*. Public Workshop on Consumer Information Privacy, Federal Trade Commission.

Peterson, R. A., Sridhar Balasubramanian and Bart J. Bronnenberg (1997). Exploring the Implications of the Internet for Consumer Marketing. *Journal of the Academy of Marketing Science* 25(4): 329-346.

Raymond, E. (1996). The Jargon Dictionary. July, http://www.netmeg.net/jargon/terms/s.html#spam.

Richards, J. (1997). Legal Potholes on the Information Superhighway. *Journal of Public Policy & Marketing* 16(2): 319-326.

Sandberg, J. (1997). Recipe For Halting Spread of 'Spam' Is Proving Elusive. *Wall Street Journal* (June 13) B1.

Selvin, P. S. (1997). International: New decisions on jurisdiction and the Internet. *Internation Commercial Litigation*(25): 47-48.

Sterling, B. (1993). A Short History of the Internet. *The Magazine of Fantasy and Science Fiction* 5(February).

Wilen, J. (1996). Tale of Possible Spamming and Bombing. *Philadelphia Business Journal* 15(4): 1.

Chapter 18

Application of Information Management with Meeting Automation Tool

Andrey Naumenko and Alain Wegmann.
ICA, Swiss Federal Institute of Technology
Lausanne, Switzerland

INTRODUCTION

Presented work describes technologically supported solution that helps people in a workgroup to deal with information related to their common projects. The solution supports different scenarios of group organizations including the case of geographically distributed workgroups. It positions workgroup meetings as a key concept within a project framework. The paper will explain its foundations and show the positive value that it brings to everyday group work.

Diagrams 2-7 use UML (Object Management Group, 1997).

ORIGINS

We present current results of "Meeting Automation Tool" (M.A.T.) research project that was initiated by Swisscom, the biggest Internet provider in Switzerland. They needed a solution to improve their regular project meetings automating standard processes such as production of meeting minutes document.

According to the client requirements, several constraints were established from the outset of the project. In particular:
- To use the tool, each of the meeting participants should have a PC or a laptop;
- The tool should support local and remote participations;

Previously Published in *Challenges of Information Technology Management in the 21st Century*, edited by Mehdi Khosrow-Pour, Copyright © 2000, Idea Group Publishing.

- M.A.T. should be easily used in combination with popular office software products;
- The tool should be designed to provide different levels of access to project-related information (see later in the Section 3.1). It was planned as a WWW based solution allowing functional integration with Personal Desktop Assistant (PDA) systems.

SOLUTION

M.A.T. provides a computer-supported framework for the meeting process that concentrates on capturing the content of meetings and its future use. We implemented strong points that were found in other solutions and proposed functionalities that we didn't find in existing products. For example, Ventana Groupsystems concentrates on meeting process and has nice utilities to support it, but it doesn't consider the evolution of the meeting-related information from one meeting to another. We can view meetings as milestones within projects, and the information discussed during a meeting can very well represent the current state of the project. So the evolution of this information has a value since it gives a continuous representation of the project. In our solution we have tried to provide a means to work with meeting-related information not only during a meeting but also before and after.

Information Management foundations of the tool

Model shown in Figure 1 was built to demonstrate theoretical foundations of the tool; it represents the domain of Information Management from the perspective of activities that can be performed in it.

The model shows a cycle of activities that are performed by collaborators in information-driven workgroups. Information itself is a central point of the model. People in everyday life are surrounded by numerous factors and events that offer an *Access* to information related to their ideas and activities. Every event, as soon as it can be considered relevant with regard to particular interests of a person or group, carries certain informational potential, that is to be consumed. Once a relevant piece of information has been obtained it needs to be combined with other pieces that are coherent with each other. *Gathering* of pieces combines together their informational potentials. It continues until the overall potential becomes significant enough to be realized by the person or group, in other words, for the idea that was behind the informational poten-

Figure 1: Information Management

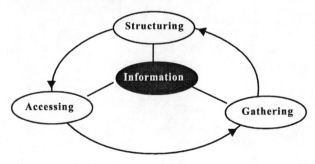

tial to be understood. Here, a physical analogy with Ohm's law may be very well applied: the bigger the resistance of a person or group against the realization of information, the bigger the informational potential is needed to generate the realization. As soon as an understanding of an idea is triggered, it needs to be saved for future applications. The *Structuring* of understanding (understanding being *the way* concepts are understood) can help in the storing the experience that is being accumulated. Structuring is just a convenient way to memorize what once was realized. The accumulated experience is then available for future access.

This model presents our vision of work with information in everyday life. The ideas highlighted for the Gathering part are exploration on experiential learning (Dewey, 1938; Novak, 1998). We designed our tool in correlation with the presented model. The core function of M.A.T. is to provide the means for the Gathering of information, more concretely, for collecting workgroup-related information through the evolution of a project. It is applied in workgroup meetings that are considered as milestones in a project timeline. The tool implements interfaces for Structuring and Accessing parts of the Information Management model. For Structuring it is linked with Group Information Base, which is designed to help people conceptualize information by means of Concept Maps (Novak, 1998). It's shared within the group, and all information collected with M.A.T. goes there. For Accessing, the tool supports different levels of information access: Individual, Group and Community levels mapped to PDA, Intranet and Internet.

Process and activities

Figure 2 introduces a state diagram that represents a process supported by M.A.T. We can distinguish two parts: one of them is related to the project evolution, another to the meeting itself. The state diagram shows consecutive steps, which are performed in project, together with their stereotypes. The stereotypes represent sequence Information – Conceptualization – Action – Reflection, which is repeated iteratively in the process of project development. This sequence was taken from findings of Xavier

Figure 2: M.A.T. State Diagram

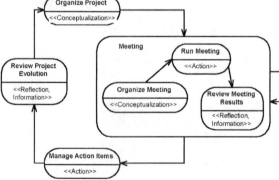

Gilbert and to be published by Irwin Publishers: X. Gilbert, "Competing with Information". A similar paradigm was expressed earlier by Jean Piaget (Piaget, 1970).

The state *Organize Project* represents part of the tool where a user can either organize a new project, including its name, description, participants and initial agenda, or change the organization of existing one. This state can be mapped to the *Conceptualization* part of the process. Projects can be considered as concepts, within a workgroup, that are either created or modified according to their previous evolution.

After conceptualization was performed, we can start acting on the concept that was developed. Here we move to project meetings that can be considered as a significant part of these actions. While being an action within a project, a meeting itself is a concept, and is separated in states within our tool. *Organize Meeting, Run Meeting,* and *Review Meeting Results* – are the states that correspond to time phases: before, during and after a meeting. Meeting organization includes scheduling of meeting and its resources, creation of agenda, and sending invitations to participants. The running of a meeting implements collecting of the participants' contributions during a meeting and assigning action items within a project to corresponding responsible people. To review meeting results, users can read meeting minutes documents that are generated automatically after meetings, and review actions assigned during meetings. The last activity goes beyond the scope of the meeting concept. Manipulation with action items also contributes to a project lifecycle. An action is a concept by itself. It can be carried forward from one meeting to another; can have different statuses: not begun, completed, due, overdue; its statement can be modified over time. So in the tool we implemented a separate part, *Manage Action Items*, that supports all these aspects.

According to the described sequence of stereotypes, after making these different activities for a project, users pass to the *Reflection* and *Information* phases, which correspond to the *Review Project Evolution* state. Here the tool provides users with different views of project development over time. Dynamics of changes in a project's agenda, traces of project actions, and a timeline of key decisions may help to under-

Figure 3: M.A.T. Use Case Diagram

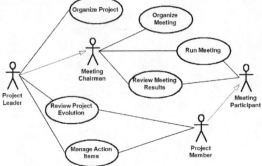

Figure 4: Implemented meeting-related Use Cases

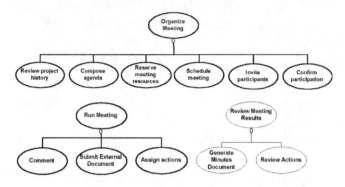

stand a current project's results and to make appropriate conclusions on its future development. The Group Information Base, which is complementary to the tool, should be also employed on this step, making use of the concepts that were contributed to it through a projects' evolution.

The tool implements Use Cases corresponding to the described states; they are shown on the Use Case diagram at Figure 3. Actors involved in the process are: *Project Leader*, *Project Member*, *Meeting Chairman* and *Meeting Participant*. Their relationships and actions with respect to the use cases are also shown on Figure 3.

Figure 4 presents meeting-related Use Cases from Figure 3 that consist of different activities that are performed before, during and after a meeting.

Structure and Functionality

Figure 5 presents conceptual model implemented by M.A.T. Each *Project* has *Project Participants* and a set of *Meetings*. A meeting of a project has its *Participants*, who are at the same time participants of the project, and an *Agenda* that is

Figure 5: M.A.T. conceptual model

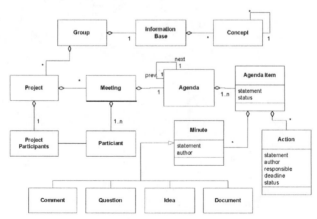

Figure 6: M.A.T. architecture

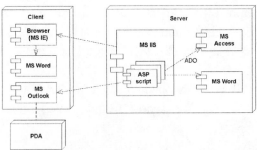

Figure 7: Scenario of organizing new meeting

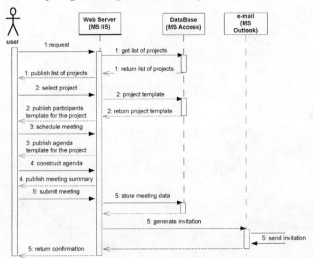

produced taking into account the agenda, which is previous to it in the project. *Agenda Items* contribute to the meeting's agenda and consist of the *Minutes* and *Actions* that are entered during the meeting. The minutes themselves can be of different kinds, such as *Comment, Question, Idea* or *Document*.

Meeting participants use all the concepts that compose the concept of meeting. They can participate with their comments and decide to assign an action. All contributions during a meeting are authored by their corresponding contributors. An action has its responsible person, status, and, optionally, deadline.

Architecture and Implementation

Keeping in mind the described use cases, the conceptual model and the technological constraints set from the client requirements, we built solution for the system architecture that is presented on Figure 6.

The client part of the tool assumes that users have a WWW browser, installed on their PCs. By means of a browser via HTTP, clients access the main application based on a server that runs MS IIS as a WWW service.

The application consists of set of HTML pages with ASP scripts residing on them. These scripts are responsible for all use cases from Figure 3. Most of the scripts perform interface between users that interact with HTML pages and database that structures and stores meeting-related data. This interface is implemented with ADO; the database is done in MS Access. The automatic generation of meeting minutes, invitations and tasks messages are other applications of ASP scripts in our system. Integration of the tool with MS Word and MS Outlook was implemented here.

As an example Figure 7 shows sequence diagram for procedures that are performed when new meeting is organized.

CONTRIBUTION

M.A.T. solves problems of information gathering during workgroup meetings and offers a means for future management of captured information within the scope of the process that was described in Section 3.2. It also gives means to include project-related information in the Group Information Base for further conceptualization for exploration of given information as it was described in Section 3.1.

Architecture of the system allows integration of popular e-office software components and presents it on the WWW. It supports not only a web based (Internet) level of information access but also personal (mobile) access with the aid of PDA systems.

The system implements an interesting approach, presenting meetings that happen in everyday group work as milestones in the timeline of the projects that they contribute to. All data associated with these milestones contribute to the Group Information Base, represent evolution, informational concepts, and know-how of the project, and once collected can be applied as shared experiences in everyday group work.

The presented tool supports the process of a project's evolution in workgroups and contributes to Information Management for the project's content. The present version of M.A.T. is used for research and educational projects at EPFL-ICA and promoted for everyday use in research laboratory of Swisscom.

REFERENCES

Dewey, J. (1938). Experience and Education, Simon & Schuster, First Touchstone Edition.

Novak, J. (1998). Learning, Creating and Using Knowledge: Concept Maps as facilitative Tools in Schools and Corporations, Lawrence Erlbaum Associates Publishers.

Object Management Group (1997). UML Specification, http://www.omg.org/ hprocess/meetings/schedule/Technology_Adoptions.html#tbl_UML_Specification.

Piaget, J. (1970). L'Epistémologie Génétique Presses Universitaires de France, Que sais-je? collection, no. 1399.

Chapter 19

A Distributed Cognition Analysis of Mobile CSCW

Mikael Wiberg and Åke Grönlund
Umeå University, Sweden

We use a distributed cognition perspective to analyse mobile CSCW (computer supported co-operative work) among service technicians at a telecom operator. We focus on three aspects, the physical conditions for the interaction, the knowledge necessary for the management of the interaction, and the technology (cognitive tools) that can support the interaction.

INTRODUCTION

Mobile work is not equivalent with telework, but the two share some characteristics. Our definition of mobile CSCW (Computer Supported Co-operative Work) includes (1) Individual workers move among several locations, as required by the objects of activity being to at least some part located outside of the computer; (2) People working together may be physically separated. Let us at some length explain this definition. While telework means working at a distance from colleagues and/or customers, the mobile worker is

"one whose 'place of work' isn't fixed at all, and who needs to be effective in a range of different work settings [....] for example, field service engineers" (Dix & Beale, 1996).

This does not imply total independence of any place. In fact, mobility is often required by the fact that certain places have to be visited - it is hard to repair a telephone pole if you are not on the particular site.

Another thing differentiating mobile work from telework is that in telework, the main activities typically take place "inside the computer," e.g., working on a spreadsheet or supervising a computer from a distance, whereas in mobile work, impor-

Previously Published in *Challenges of Information Technology Management in the 21st Century*, edited by Mehdi Khosrow-Pour, Copyright © 2000, Idea Group Publishing.

tant parts of the work takes place "outside" the computer. Thus travelling becomes a necessary part of the work.

So far, most studies of mobile work concern the technology itself, such as mobile networks, RPC (Remote Procedure Call), ATM, satellite systems etc, or usability and reliability aspects of PDAs and other handholds (Kristoffersen et al, 1998; Varshney, 1998). Little is done on charting the social and psychological territory of the mobile worker such as the work situation and the ability of the technical tools to support people in completing tasks alone and in co-operation with others. This study is part of an attempt to do this.

METHOD

We used ethnographic techniques to collect data, the objective being to "present a portrayal of life as seen and understood by those who live and work within the domain concern" (Hughes et al. 1993). We made participant observation of mobile service workers for approximately 40 hours and five qualitative interviews (Mason, 1989) with staff and their manager (each lasting 60 - 90 minutes).

Distributed cognition (DC), focusing on the distributed nature of cognitive phenomena across individuals, artefacts, and internal and external representations (Hutchins, 1995), was used as a theoretical framework.

THE 'ARENA' OF WORK PRACTICE: A DISTRIBUTED COGNITION INFORMED TOOL FOR CHANGE ANALYSIS

The framework of distributed cognition gives an opportunity to conceptualise services as the dynamic outcome of the interaction and communication of different intelligent agents, organisational settings, and cognitive and physical artefacts. For the analysis we used the following categories:

The physical conditions for interaction form the *arena* for the actors involved in the interactions. Since mobile work takes place at several locations with very different physical conditions this means studying conditions at individual work places such as cars and customers' sites, but also travel patterns.

The knowledge that is necessary for the management of the interaction concerns where knowledge is allocated - "in the heads" of the workers, in machines, in some central administration body, or other, and how it is represented. This influences how interaction episodes are initiated, maintained and managed.

The technologies (cognitive artefacts) that can support the interaction refers to the issue of how the ICT is used for getting work done, and what role the technology has on how the cognition is distributed.

MOBILE WORK AT TELIA NÄRA

Telia Nära is part of the Swedish government owned telephone operator Telia. Telia Nära is divided into 40 market companies each containing three divisions; (1), *Service,* including service technicians serving the telephone network (2), *Support,* including a call centre and task dispatching unit called "The Station", and (3) *The Store,* where products pertaining to use of Telia's communication system are sold; telephones, faxes, modems, computers, subscriptions, etc.

A recent reorganisation provided the technicians with advanced computer and telephony technology for the purpose of making them more self-contained. The ICT consists of three distinct but fully integrated systems:

(1) *Car systems* with terminals at all times connected to the Station over a radio LAN. The cars have systems to support scheduling of activities, putting work on waiting lists, searching the telephone network for errors, getting in contact with the other cars, redirecting missions to free technicians if something unexpected occurs, etc.

(2) *Cellular phones,* receiving SMS messages (short message service) from the Station, telling of new tasks. An SMS message contains the customer's telephone number (address indicator) and information about what kind of problem there is from the description given by the customer. The SMS-system is connected to the mobile car system, so the task can be further investigated by consulting the car system.

(3) *Station systems,* necessary to receive calls from phone customers needing help, scheduling of tasks, and resource allocation, i.e. where to send which car.

The new technology has increased the possibilities to work from anywhere so as to reduce the travelling and make the technicians more free to decide how, where, and when to carry out their work. They can check the work assignments from home in the morning and plan the route for the day, or schedule a whole week. They also receive new assignments, additional information, and changes continuously during the day.

A distributed cognition analysis of the mobile CSCW at Telia Nära

Summarising the results from our study under the three categories of physical conditions, knowledge, and supporting technologies, we saw the following changes:

Physical conditions

- Much *information has been geographically distributed.* Information like task descriptions and diagnoses, customer addresses, and schedules is now available both at the Station and at the mobile workplaces in the cars.

- A "natural" (i.e., existing because of the nature and location of the professional activities) *social forum* - the Station - disappeared but was re-created on a social basis only - the staff required it.
- Similarly, a natural *forum for exchange of professional knowledge* disappeared but reappeared as a consequence of recreating the social forum.
- A physical *forum for negotiation* of task distribution and schedules disappeared. It was partially replaced by telephones, but support for more complex negotiations, such as involving more than two parties, is now lacking.

Knowledge

- *New knowledge was distributed to technicians,* including stock management, scheduling, transfer of responsibilities, and general IT knowledge.
- The staff at the *Station maintains the same knowledge* as before so as to be able to make a qualified assessment when a customer reports a problem and to participate in error fixing when possible.
- *Some knowledge dissemination to customers.* The incentive system rewards avoiding travelling, so technicians try to make customers fix simple problems themselves by telling them how to do over the phone.

Supporting technologies

- The technicians have been assigned new technology for technical parts of the work: error searching, error fixing from a distance, scheduling, stock management, and communication.
- Technical support is lacking for some activities that the new organization made necessary:
  - *negotiations* including more than two parties, e.g. more complicated scheduling of tasks and transfer of assignments
  - *representation of ongoing activities*, e.g. where a specific technician is at a specific time, where he is going, estimated time of arrival etc. This, in combination with the fact that the same knowledge and tools are available both at the Station and to individual technicians sometimes led to conflicts; it happened that the Station staff fixed a problem while a technician was on his way to the customer's site. This meant not only annoyance, but also wasted - not reportable - time on part of the technician.
  - *professional discourse* involving more than two people.
  - *social intercourse*.
  - *representation of causality* in the report system, e.g. why a task took longer than the assigned time.

In short, some decentralisation of tasks, knowledge, and responsibilities occurred. Generally, knowledge was decentralised:

- stock control (from the Station to technicians)
- scheduling, partially (from the Station to technicians)
- route planing (from the Station to technicians)
- transfer of tasks (from the Station to technicians)
- Knowledge about error fixing:
  a) from the Station to the technicians, because the ICT makes error fixing from a distance possible.
  b) from the technicians to customers, because technicians try to avoid travelling by trying to explain to customers over the phone how to fix simple things.

  This general decentralisation is moderated by two important factors:
  - A stricter control system; work time and stock are now accounted for in more detail.
  - The reward system directs day planning by rewarding minimising travel.

CONCLUSIONS & FURTHER RESEARCH

Our case study has indicated that there are social issues pertaining to the quality of the work done as well as to the work situation of the technicians that were not adequately catered for the way work and ICT use was arranged.

Forums for professional and social intercourse were closed in the new organisation, and there was no technology substitute for this. The staff made up for this by arranging their schedules in a way that made it possible to maintain such forums, thus reducing the envisioned effects in terms of reduced travelling and time saved. This was done despite of the control system, which punished such behaviour.

There are two issues worth further research:

(1) Can technology be used as a substitute in any way? Would the effect have been different if there had been tools for communication? Would it have made a difference if the staff had been younger and more used to socialising using ICT tools?

(2) Would the effects have been different if the group of technicians had been different? The people studied saw themselves as a group having been dispersed by management decision, which they rejected. What if the organisation had started without that history? Maybe, because we saw considerable change over time. First, people were very upset by the change, but after some time of getting used to the system - and adjusting it - unrest settled and people felt quite comfortable in the new organisation.

Taking social issues into account is important for understanding the "ecology" of the mobile workplace. Such understanding is necessary for organising mobile work properly and for designing proper CSCW systems for use in mobile environments.

REFERENCES

Dix, A. & Beale, R. (Eds.) (1996*). Remote cooperation: CSCW issues for mobile and teleworkers.* London: Springer-Verlag.

Hughes, J., Randall, D. and Shapiro, D. (1993). From ethnographic record to system design. Some experiences from the field, *Computer Supported Cooperative Work,* 1(3).

Hutchins, E. (1995). *Cognition in the Wild*, Cambridge, MA: The MIT Press.

Kleinrock, L. (1996). Nomadic Computing: Information Network and Data Communication, IFIP/ ICCC International Conference on Information Network and Data Communication, Trondheim, Norway, pp. 223-233.

Kleinrock, L. (1998). Nomadicity: Anytime, anywhere in a disconnected world, Invited paper, *Mobile Networks and Applications*, 1(4), pp 351-357.

Kristoffersen, S., Herstad, J., Ljungberg, F., Løbersli, F., Sandbakken, J. R., and Thoresen, K. (1998). Developing scenarios for Mobile CSCW, In *Proceedings of the First Workshop on Human Computer Interaction with Mobile Devices*, pp. 34-47.

Mason, R.O. (1989). MIS experiments: A pragmatic perspective, in I. Benbasat (ed.), *The Information Systems Research Challenge: Experimental Research Methods*, 2, pp. 3-20, Boston: Harvard Business School Press.

Varshney, U. (1999). Networking support for mobile computing, *Communications of the Association for Information System*, 1(1).

About the Editor

Mehdi Khosrow-Pour, BBA, MBA, MS, DBA, CSP
Executive Director, Information Resources Management Association (IRMA)

Dr. Khosrow-Pour received his Bachelor of Business Administration (BBA) and Master of Science (MS) in Computer Information Systems from the University of Miami (Fla.), a Master of Business Administration (MBA) from the Florida Institute of Technology, and a Doctorate in Business Administration (DBA) from the Nova Southeastern University. He is also a Certified Systems Professional (CSP). Dr. Khosrow-Pour has taught undergraduate and graduate information system courses at the Pennsylvania State University for 20 years where he was the chair of the information Systems Department for 14 years. He has also lectured at the Florida International University, American University, University of Lyon (France), University of West Indies (Jamaica), Kuwait University, University Carlos III - De Madrid, and Tehran University (Iran). He is currently the Executive Director of the Information Resources Management Association (IRMA) and Senior Editor for Idea Group, Inc.

He is also the Editor-In-Charge of the *Information Resources Management Journal (IRMJ)*, the *Annals of Cases on Information Technology (ACIT)*, the *Information Management (IM)*, and consulting editor of the *Information Technology Newsletter (ITN)*. He also serves on the editorial review board of seven other international academic information systems journals. He is the former Editor-In-Charge of the *Journal of End User Computing* and the *Journal of Database Management*.

During the past 20 years, Dr. Khosrow-Pour has served as a consultant to many organizations such as: United Nations, Mutual of New York, Pennsylvania Department of Commerce, and Foodynamics Inc. He is the founder and currently Executive Director of the Information Resources Management Association (IRMA), a professional association with over thousand members throughout the U.S., Canada, and 52 other countries. He has served as the Program Chair and Proceedings Editor of IRMA International Conferences for the past 14 years.

Dr. Khosrow-Pour is the author/editor of more than 20+ books on various topics of information technology utilization and management in organizations, and more than 50+ articles published in various conference proceedings and journals such as *Journal of Information Systems Management*, *Journal of Applied Business Research*, *Journal of Systems Management*, *Journal of Education Technology Systems*, *Computing Review*, and *Review of Accounting Information Systems*. He is a frequent speaker at many international meetings and organizations such as: the Association of Federal IRM, Contract Management Association, Financial Women Association, National Association of States IRM Executives, IBM, and the Pennsylvania Auditor General Department.

Index

NEW from Idea Group Publishing

- **Data Mining: A Heuristic Approach,** Hussein Aly Abbass, Ruhul Amin Sarker & Charles S. Newton
  ISBN: 1-930708-25-4 / eISBN: 1-59140-011-2 / 310 pages / US$89.95 / © 2002
- **Managing Information Technology in Small Business: Challenges and Solutions,** Stephen Burgess
  ISBN: 1-930708-35-1 / eISBN: 1-59140-012-0 / 367 pages / US$74.95 / © 2002
- **Managing Web Usage in the Workplace: A Social, Ethical and Legal Perspective,** Murugan Anandarajan
  & Claire A. Simmers
  ISBN: 1-930708-18-1 / eISBN: 1-59140-003-1 / 386 pages / US$74.95 / © 2002
- **Challenges of Information Technology Education in the 21st Century,** Eli Cohen
  ISBN: 1-930708-34-3 / eISBN: 1-59140-023-6 / 290 pages / US$74.95 / © 2002
- **Social Responsibility in the Information Age: Issues and Controversies,** Gurpreet Dhillon
  ISBN: 1-930708-11-4 / eISBN: 1-59140-008-2 / 282 pages / US$74.95 / © 2002
- **Database Integrity: Challenges and Solutions**, Jorge H. Doorn and Laura Rivero
  ISBN: 1-930708-38-6 / eISBN: 1-59140-024-4 / 300 pages / US$74.95 / © 2002
- **Managing Virtual Web Organizations in the 21st Century: Issues and Challenges,** Ulrich Franke
  ISBN: 1-930708-24-6 / eISBN: 1-59140-016-3 / 368 pages / US$74.95 / © 2002
- **Managing Business with Electronic Commerce: Issues and Trends,** Aryya Gangopadhyay
  ISBN: 1-930708-12-2 / eISBN: 1-59140-007-4 / 272 pages / US$74.95 / © 2002
- **Electronic Government: Design, Applications and Management,** Åke Grönlund
  ISBN: 1-930708-19-X / eISBN: 1-59140-002-3 / 388 pages / US$74.95 / © 2002
- **Knowledge Media in Health Care: Opportunities and Challenges**, Rolf Grutter
  ISBN: 1-930708-13-0 / eISBN: 1-59140-006-6 / 296 pages / US$74.95 / © 2002
- **Internet Management Issues: A Global Perspective,** John D. Haynes
  ISBN: 1-930708-21-1 / eISBN: 1-59140-015-5 / 352 pages / US$74.95 / © 2002
- **Enterprise Resource Planning: Global Opportunities and Challenges,** Liaquat Hossain, Jon David
  Patrick & M. A. Rashid
  ISBN: 1-930708-36-X / eISBN: 1-59140-025-2 / 300 pages / US$89.95 / © 2002
- **The Design and Management of Effective Distance Learning Programs,** Richard Discenza, Caroline
  Howard, & Karen Schenk
  ISBN: 1-930708-20-3 / eISBN: 1-59140-001-5 / 312 pages / US$74.95 / © 2002
- **Multirate Systems: Design and Applications,** Gordana Jovanovic-Dolecek
  ISBN: 1-930708-30-0 / eISBN: 1-59140-019-8 / 322 pages / US$74.95 / © 2002
- **Managing IT/Community Partnerships in the 21st Century,** Jonathan Lazar
  ISBN: 1-930708-33-5 / eISBN: 1-59140-022-8 / 295 pages / US$89.95 / © 2002
- **Multimedia Networking: Technology, Management and Applications,** Syed Mahbubur Rahman
  ISBN: 1-930708-14-9 / eISBN: 1-59140-005-8 / 498 pages / US$89.95 / © 2002
- **Cases on Worldwide E-Commerce: Theory in Action,** Mahesh Raisinghani
  ISBN: 1-930708-27-0 / eISBN: 1-59140-013-9 / 276 pages / US$74.95 / © 2002
- **Designing Instruction for Technology-Enhanced Learning,** Patricia L. Rogers
  ISBN: 1-930708-28-9 / eISBN: 1-59140-014-7 / 286 pages / US$74.95 / © 2002
- **Heuristic and Optimization for Knowledge Discovery,** Ruhul Amin Sarker, Hussein Aly Abbass &
  Charles Newton
  ISBN: 1-930708-26-2 / eISBN: 1-59140-017-1 / 296 pages / US$89.95 / © 2002
- **Distributed Multimedia Databases: Techniques and Applications,** Timothy K. Shih
  ISBN: 1-930708-29-7 / eISBN: 1-59140-018-X / 384 pages / US$74.95 / © 2002
- **Neural Networks in Business: Techniques and Applications,** Kate Smith and Jatinder Gupta
  ISBN: 1-930708-31-9 / eISBN: 1-59140-020-1 / 272 pages / US$89.95 / © 2002
- **Managing the Human Side of Information Technology: Challenges and Solutions,** Edward Szewczak
  & Coral Snodgrass
  ISBN: 1-930708-32-7 / eISBN: 1-59140-021-X / 364 pages / US$89.95 / © 2002
- **Cases on Global IT Applications and Management: Successes and Pitfalls,** Felix B. Tan
  ISBN: 1-930708-16-5 / eISBN: 1-59140-000-7 / 300 pages / US$74.95 / © 2002
- **Enterprise Networking: Multilayer Switching and Applications,** Vasilis Theoharakis &
  Dimitrios Serpanos
  ISBN: 1-930708-17-3 / eISBN: 1-59140-004-X / 282 pages / US$89.95 / © 2002
- **Measuring the Value of Information Technology,** Han T. M. van der Zee
  ISBN: 1-930708-08-4 / eISBN: 1-59140-010-4 / 224 pages / US$74.95 / © 2002
- **Business to Business Electronic Commerce: Challenges and Solutions,** Merrill Warkentin
  ISBN: 1-930708-09-2 / eISBN: 1-59140-009-0 / 308 pages / US$89.95 / © 2002

Excellent additions to your institution's library! Recommend these titles to your Librarian!

*To receive a copy of the Idea Group Publishing catalog, please contact (toll free) 1/800-345-4332,
fax 1/717-533-8661,or visit the IGP Online Bookstore at: [http://www.idea-group.com]!
Note: All IGP books are also available as ebooks on netlibrary.com as well as other ebook
sources. Contact Ms. Carrie Stull at [cstull@idea-group.com] to receive a complete list of sources
where you can obtain ebook information or IGP titles.*